I0793258

IMAGES
of Rail

NEW YORK, SUSQUEHANNA & WESTERN RAILROAD IN NEW JERSEY

On the Cover: NYS&W RS-1 No. 252 leads three sister RS-1s and one S-2 with an eastbound Hainesburg Extra freight train past North Hawthorne Station and the former NYS&W shops in this scene captured on September 14, 1960. Today the station is long gone and only a few pieces of the shop complex exist. (Photograph by Donald P. Wallworth; courtesy of Patrick J. Reynolds and the Maywood Station Museum Collection.)

IMAGES
of Rail

New York, Susquehanna & Western Railroad in New Jersey

Edward S. Kaminski

ARCADIA
PUBLISHING

ISBN 978-0-7385-7367-0

Published by Arcadia Publishing
Charleston, South Carolina

Printed in the United States of America

Library of Congress Control Number: 2010925346

For all general information, please contact Arcadia Publishing:
Telephone 843-853-2070
Fax 843-853-0044
E-mail sales@arcadiapublishing.com
For customer service and orders:
Toll-Free 1-888-313-2665

Visit us on the Internet at www.arcadiapublishing.com

This book is dedicated to the past and present employees and their families of the New York, Susquehanna & Western Railroad

Contents

Acknowledgments

The New York, Susquehanna & Western Railroad is a fabled northeastern U.S. rail carrier that emerged from 40 years of Erie Railroad control; survived several bankruptcies, reorganizations, abandonments, and retrenchments through innovative passenger and freight service offerings; and transformed into today's regional rail carrier with a size far greater than ever imagined.

The objective of this book is to provide a photographic history of the original route of the NYS&W in New Jersey, with emphasis on the commuter district between Jersey City, New Jersey, and Butler, New Jersey. Since both passenger and freight operations were conducted in this corridor, a greater amount of photographic coverage could be offered. Another objective is to showcase the diversity of the NYS&W locomotive, passenger, and freight equipment that was employed by the line. In writing this book, I was fortunate that a great many images and information about the New York, Susquehanna & Western Railroad had been preserved by numerous individuals who were more than willing to share their memories and collections of material.

I would like to thank the photographers and sources of photographs, postcards, illustrations, and information on the subject matter: George Berisso; Thomas J. Callan; Vincent DeSantis; Nathan R. Fenno; Mary Gardner; Jim Howarth; Joseph M. Katzenstein; Robert Kurdock; Johnson Public Library, New Jersey; Maywood Station Historical Committee; Maywood Station Museum; Timothy Moses; Dave Mustaine; New York Susquehanna & Western Railway; New York, Susquehanna & Western Technical & Historical Society; Arthur E. Owen; Robert P. Pisani; Edwin D. Quinn; Kevin Quinn; Railroad Avenue Enterprises; Sy Reich; Barbara Logue Reynolds; Patrick J. Reynolds; Cynthia A. Sansone; James C. Schmitt; Robert L. Steele; John L. Treen; Emil Walerko; Donald P. Wallworth; Walter E. Zullig Jr.; and John Zuidema.

I would like to also thank the staff at Arcadia Publishing who greeted the project with encouragement and enthusiasm, in particular, Erin Rocha, Lynn Beahm, Lisa Vear, Hunter Byrd, and Beth McKenna. As always, a big thank you and all my love to my wife, Rosemarie, and our three daughters, Kristen, Kaitlyn, and Kayleigh, for their patience and support during the process of gathering and writing this book.

INTRODUCTION

In 1826, an engineer named John L. Sullivan made a survey for a proposed railroad from the Hudson River to the Pennsylvania coalfields. The route he chose became the one used by the New Jersey Midland Railway, a predecessor of the New York, Susquehanna & Western Railroad. A group of businessmen (including Jacob M. Ryerson, Samuel Fowler, Thomas C. Ryerson, James Stoll, William Dickey, John Bell, Daniel M. Broadhead, Joseph E. Edsall, William Heyberger, John Haggerty, John Moore, and James M. Porter) took action on Sullivan's survey, and on March 8, 1832, the State of New Jersey legislature granted their petition to charter the New Jersey, Hudson & Delaware Railroad. All of these men were closely associated with iron mining and manufacturing concerns in Sussex, Morris, and Passaic counties in New Jersey. The charter authorized construction of a railroad commencing at any point or place on the Delaware River between the New York State line and where the Paulinskill River empties into the Delaware River, along with the authority to construct a bridge or bridges across the Delaware River by and with the consent of the State of Pennsylvania. From that point of crossing the Delaware, the line would extend east through Snufftown, New Jersey, (now Stockholm in Hardyston Township in Sussex County) to the Hudson River opposite New York City or join any other railroad chartered or proposed to be chartered that would lead to a terminus on the Hudson River. The group of men planned to raise the necessary capital through stock offerings, but the plan ran into problems due to the financial panic of 1837. The proposed railroad then lay dormant until 1853, when the charter was transferred to the Pennsylvania Coal Company. However, the financial panic of 1857 caused the building of the railroad to be put off once again.

In 1867, some of the original owners of the charter purchased it back from the Pennsylvania Coal Company. Plans to finance the new railroad once again encountered problems since it would be constructed near the general area of the successful Morris Canal, which was built years earlier. However, due to ever increasing per-ton prices for coal delivered by the canal, there was an added incentive to have the railroad built, which would allow coal to be transported more cheaply and efficiently to the major manufacturing centers in northern New Jersey. Work on the new railroad was finally started on January 31, 1867, with grading taking place in Bloomingdale, New Jersey. As work progressed slowly, a multitude of rechartering occurred, and as a result, the New Jersey Midland Railway (NJM) was formed, combining four existing railroad lines. Cornelius Wortendyke became the first president of the NJM. Wortendyke had controlled the New Jersey Western Railroad, a line that was being built west from Hawthorne, New Jersey, to Bloomingdale, New Jersey, which was one of the four lines combined into the NJM.

In 1871, the New York & Oswego Midland Railroad began eyeing the NJM as part of a through route from the Great Lakes to New York Harbor, eventually assuming control of the NJM. The NY&OM planned to connect with the NJM in Middletown, New York. On March 11, 1872, the NJM opened between Hackensack, New Jersey, and New Foundland, New Jersey. However, the financial panic of 1873 greatly affected the NY&OM, and it was placed into receivership, losing its control of the NJM. The NY&OM emerged in 1880 as the New York, Ontario & Western and gained access to New York Harbor through another route at Kingston, New York, on the West Shore Railroad (New York Central), no longer needing the NJM. In 1875, the NJM also entered receivership and emerged in 1880 as the Midland Railroad Company of New Jersey, with Garrett A. Hobart serving as its receiver. Hobart would later go on to become vice president of the United States under Pres. William McKinley.

In June 1881, after several reorganizations, the line became known as the New York, Susquehanna & Western Railroad and, by the early 1890s, consisted of about 230 miles of track from Jersey City, New Jersey, to the coalfields near Scranton, Pennsylvania, with a branch to Hanford, New York. In 1882, the NYS&W reached Stroudsburg, Pennsylvania, in an effort to tap the anthracite coal–rich Pocono region in the northeast section of the state. To access the coalfields, a new subsidiary was formed named the Wilkes-Barre & Eastern Railroad, which built a connecting line from Stroudsburg to Kingston, Pennsylvania, near Wilkes-Barre. This line was opened in 1894 and commenced shipping coal to a new terminal that was built on the Hudson River in Edgewater, New Jersey.

In 1898, the NYS&W came under Erie Railroad control and was run as a division. During Erie control, the physical plant was modernized with new locomotives and equipment, while bridges were rebuilt and the track upgraded. In 1937, the NYS&W fell into bankruptcy, was reorganized under trustees Walter Kidde and Henry K. Norton, and gained independence from Erie. Gradual retrenchments of trackage occurred on the NYS&W west of Butler. In 1939, the WB&E was abandoned and the western terminus of the railroad became Stroudsburg, Pennsylvania. In 1940, all trackage west of Hainesburg Junction was abandoned. In the 1940s, the NYS&W became an innovator in the use of self-propelled rail diesel cars in commuter service. While the service was successful into the 1950s, losses from commuter operations began to mount at an accelerated rate. In 1962, all trackage west of Sparta Junction was abandoned due to the closure of the Lehigh & New England Railway connection at Hainesburg and not enough local business to support keeping the 25 miles of track in operation. In 1968, the Lehigh & Hudson River Railway connection at Sparta Junction was severed due to a questionable bridge, and the line was cut back to Oak Ridge. In 1971, a washout occurred near Kinnelon, New Jersey, and the western terminus of the railroad was cut back to Butler. The NYS&W fought for freight traffic while slowly reducing its passenger train frequency, eventually ceasing all passenger operations on June 30, 1966. In 1976, the NYS&W once again fell into bankruptcy after years of retrenching into what eventually became a 38-mile terminal operation from Jersey City, New Jersey, to Butler, New Jersey.

In 1980, the railroad was purchased by Delaware Otsego Corporation. With a forward-looking management team led by the late Walter G. Rich, the NYS&W reactivated dormant track; acquired additional lines cast off by Conrail in New Jersey, New York State, and Pennsylvania; and arranged trackage rights to connect its lines, which now consisted of about 400 miles from Jersey City, New Jersey, to Syracuse, New York. In 1985, the NYS&W acquired from Conrail a portion of the L&HR between Warwick, New York, and Sparta, and the NYS&W began rebuilding the out-of-service track between Butler and Sparta. In 1986, the trackage was reopened with a connection to the original L&HR at Sparta, and transcontinental container trains began using the route. The NYS&W had come full circle and offered intermodal shipping options originating and terminating out its Little Ferry, New Jersey, facility. Today the NYS&W continues as a progressive freight railroad serving the Northeast with a stock interest held by mega-railroad's CSX Transportation and Norfolk Southern Corporation.

One

Jersey City to North Bergen

The railroad begins in Jersey City, New Jersey, and its original entry came by way of a connection with the Pennsylvania Railroad at a section called Marion. The NYS&W utilized the Pennsylvania Railroad's terminal in Jersey City until 1911 when there was a changeover in operations due to Erie Railroad ownership, which occurred in June 1898, thus moving all passenger trains into the Erie's own Pavonia terminal in Jersey City. The NYS&W continued to use Pavonia terminal until 1961, well after the 1937 date when it had become independent of the Erie. Heading from Jersey City, the NYS&W line runs in a northerly direction. A section of North Bergen, originally known as Homestead, was once the site of a depot, team track, coal trestle, and online industries. New Durham was another section in North Bergen located about a mile north of Homestead. The Erie-controlled Northern Railroad of New Jersey's tracks parallel the NYS&W to Jersey City at this location, and the New York Central's West Shore Railroad was nearby to the east, heading into Weehawken, New Jersey, via their West Shore tunnel under Tonnelle Avenue. The NYS&W continues north from New Durham for roughly another mile before reaching another section of North Bergen that was known as Babbitt, named after the nearby Soap Works, which was served by an extensive array of sidings. The Erie tracks diverge and cross under the New York Central (West Shore) tracks just north of the Babbitt depot. Granton Junction tower controlled the interlocking between the Erie and NYS&W and was located just east of Babbitt station. Under Erie control, the NYS&W and parallel Northern Railroad of New Jersey were jointly operated from Granton Junction to Jersey City as a four-track railroad.

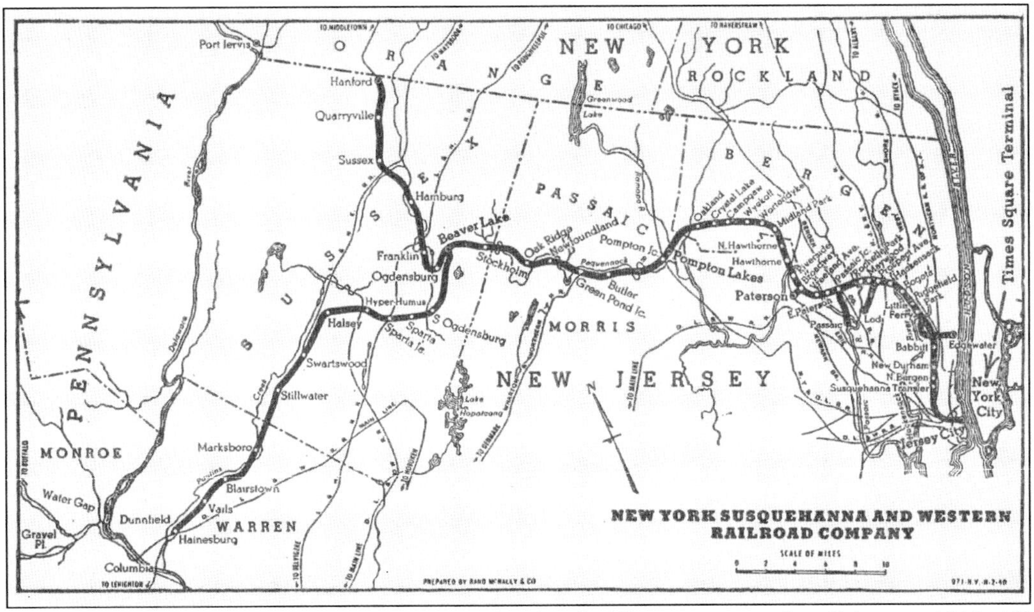

This map shows the NYS&W system (highlighted in bold) as it appeared in February 1940. All NYS&W lines were within the borders of the state of New Jersey, and the Wilkes-Barre & Eastern subsidiary trackage into Pennsylvania had been recently abandoned. The lines shown on the map from Jersey City to Hainesburg and Hanford form the basis of this book. (Courtesy of the Maywood Station Museum Collection.)

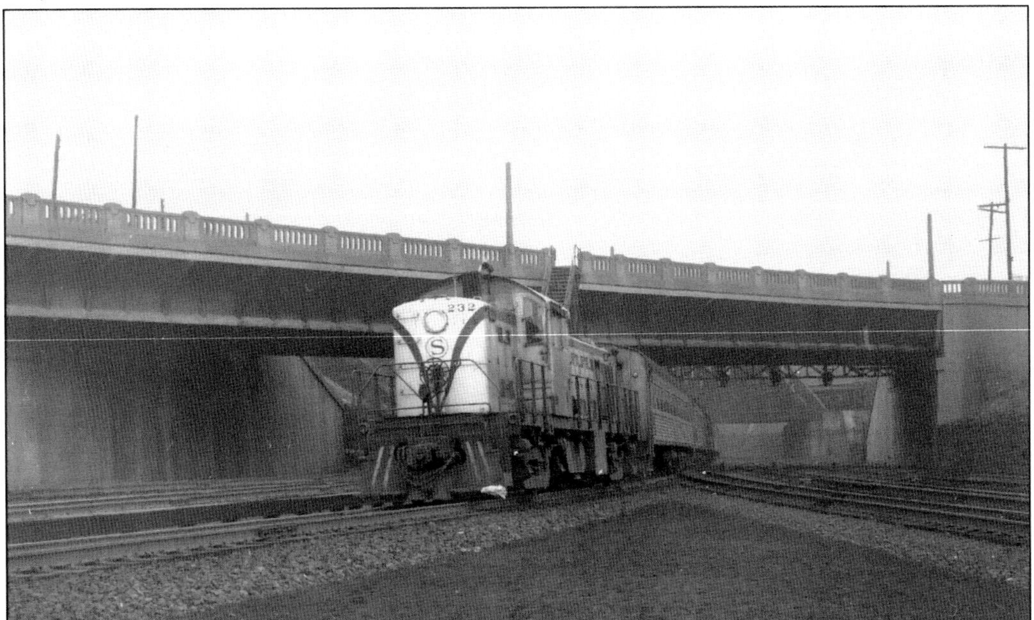

NYS&W RS-1 No. 232 works its way west with a four-car passenger train in this view taken at West End in Jersey City in April 1955. From 1911 through 1961, the NYS&W used Erie Railroad's Pavonia terminal in Jersey City for passengers using the ferry to commute to and from New York City. (Courtesy of Railroad Avenue Enterprises; author's collection.)

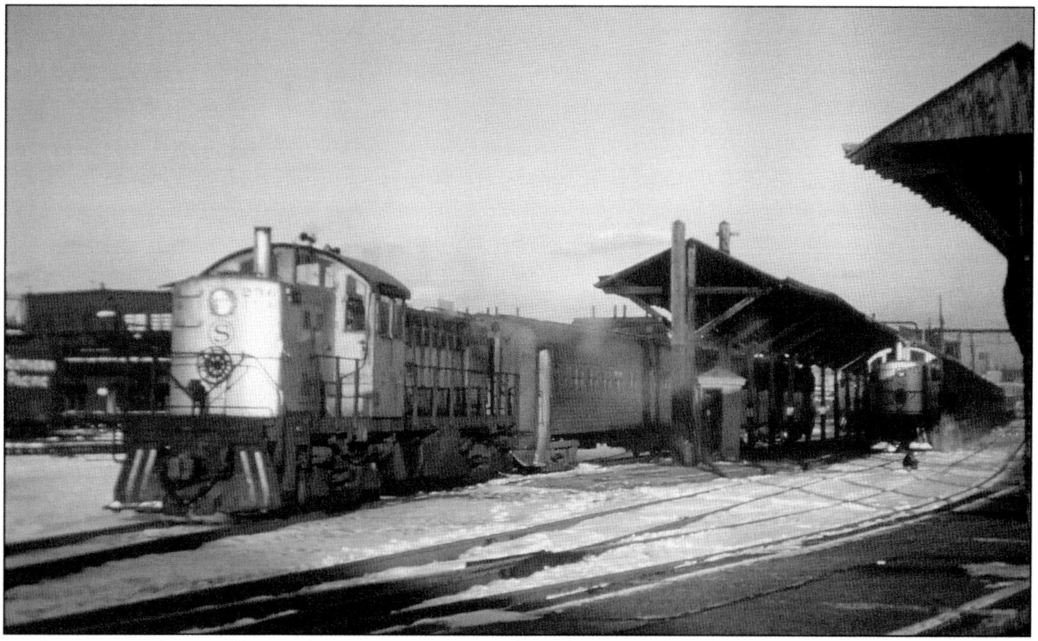

In this view taken in December 1960 at Erie Railroad's Pavonia terminal in Jersey City, NYS&W RS-1 No. 236 begins to pull away with its two passenger cars, heading west as NYS&W RS-1 No. 231 waits on an adjacent track to go west with its five-car passenger train. (Author's collection.)

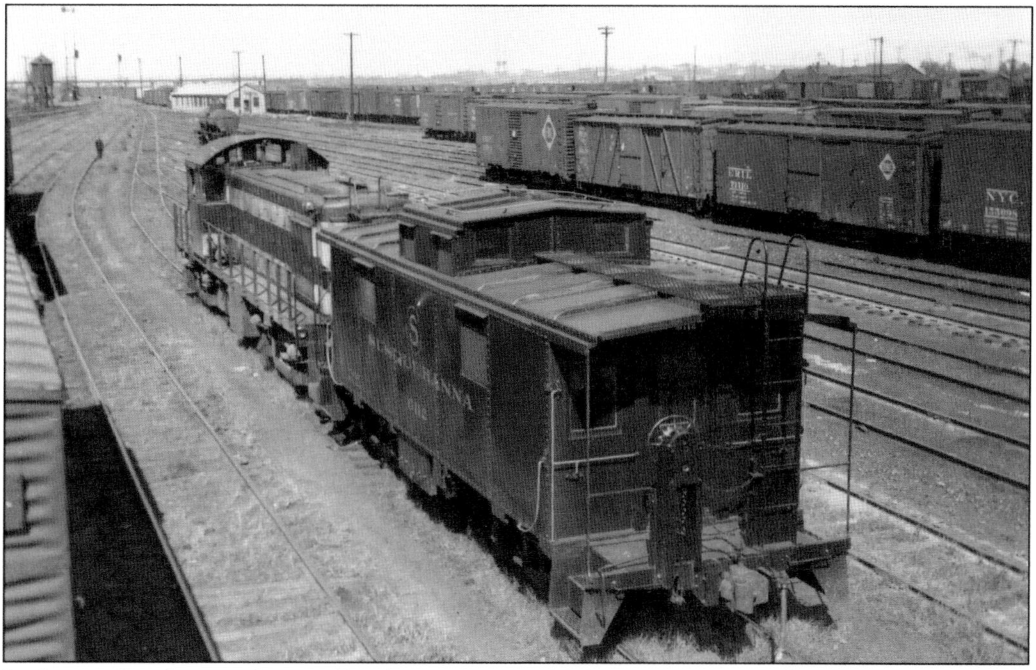

In this overhead view taken on October 4, 1948, NYS&W RS-1 No. 230 is shown in Erie Railroad's Croxton yard in Secaucus picking up brand-new NYS&W caboose No. 0112 from interchange. The caboose was built for the NYS&W by the International Car Company in Kenton, Ohio, and was part of a 10-car order delivered to the railroad that fall. (Photograph by John L. Treen; courtesy of Thomas J. Callan and the Maywood Station Museum Collection.)

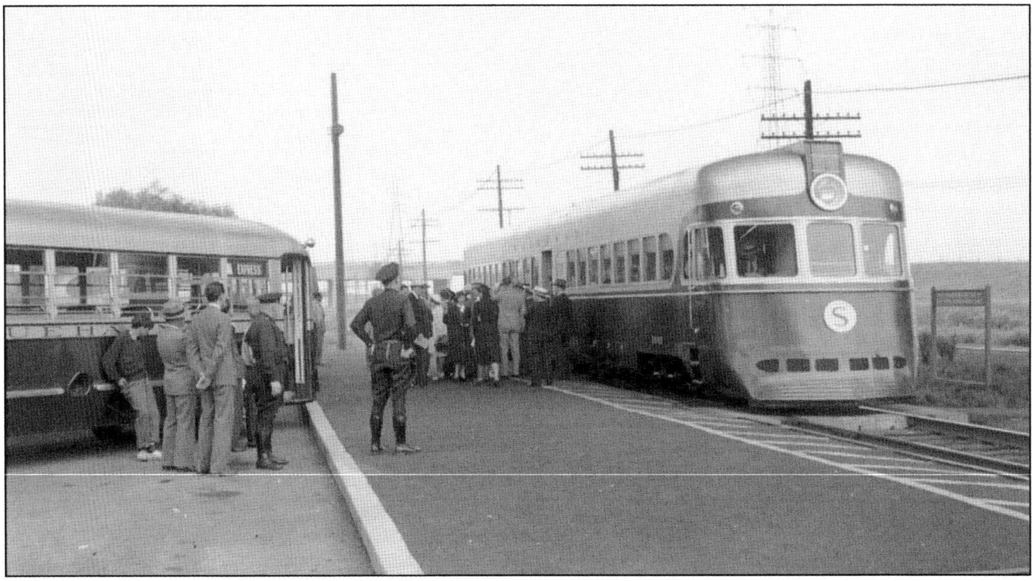

Freshly delivered, NYS&W American Car & Foundry–built Motorailer No. 1001 is surrounded by dignitaries and the press before one of its inaugural runs in early 1940 in North Bergen. The NYS&W made a station stop at this location named Susquehanna Transfer near Route 3 as a means to commute to and from New York City via bus connections versus the longer route via trains to Jersey City and the ferry. Note also the NYS&W bus. (Courtesy of Robert Kurdock and the Maywood Station Museum Collection.)

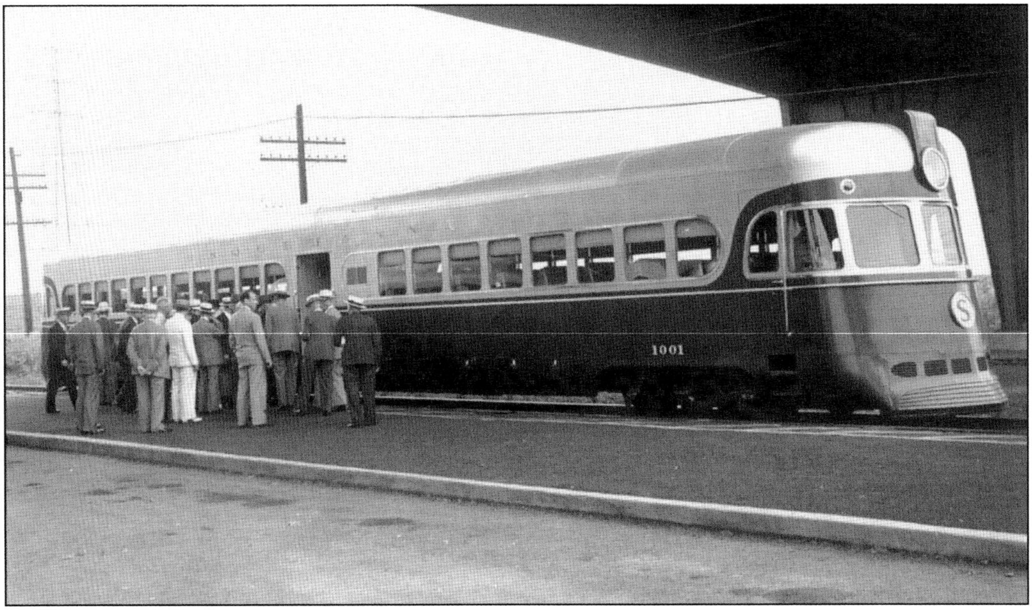

Dignitaries and the press are shown boarding one of the inaugural runs of NYS&W No. 1001, an American Car & Foundry–built Motorailer, at Susquehanna Transfer in North Bergen in this early 1940 scene. The 85-seat, air-conditioned, self-propelled Motorailer was an initial hit for the railroad, as commuter ridership totals increased. The NYS&W eventually rostered a fleet of six Motorailer's numbered 1001 to 1006. (Courtesy of Robert Kurdock and the Maywood Station Museum Collection.)

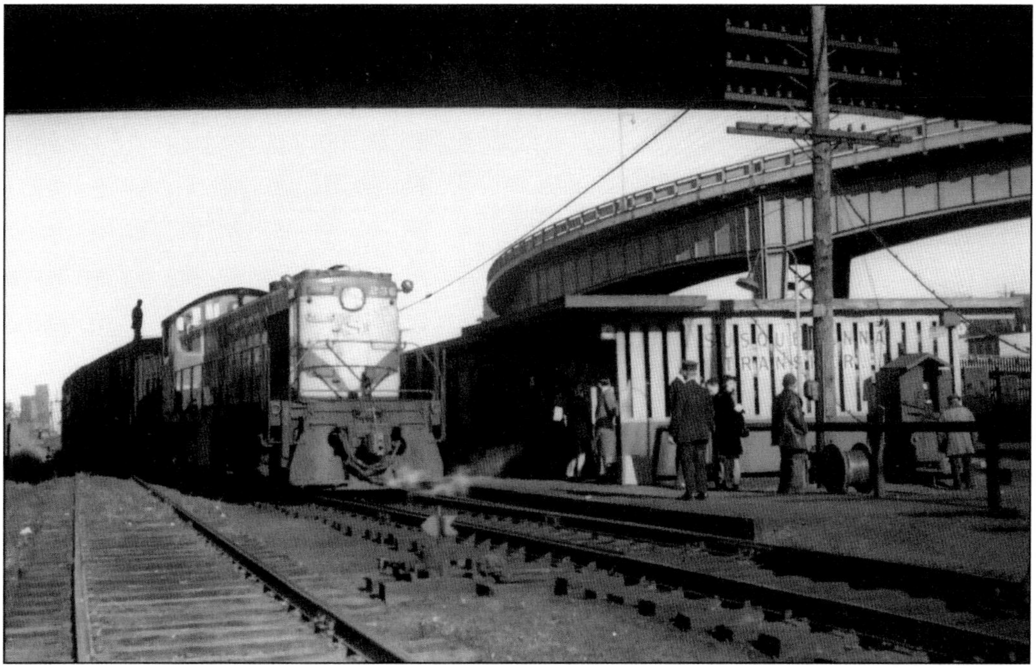

In this view taken on December 31, 1946, a brakeman rides atop the first car in this local freight led by NYS&W RS-1 No. 236 as it crosses tracks at Susquehanna Transfer in North Bergen. The train is about to go under the approach leading to the Lincoln Tunnel. (Photograph by John L. Treen; courtesy of Thomas J. Callan and the Maywood Station Museum Collection.)

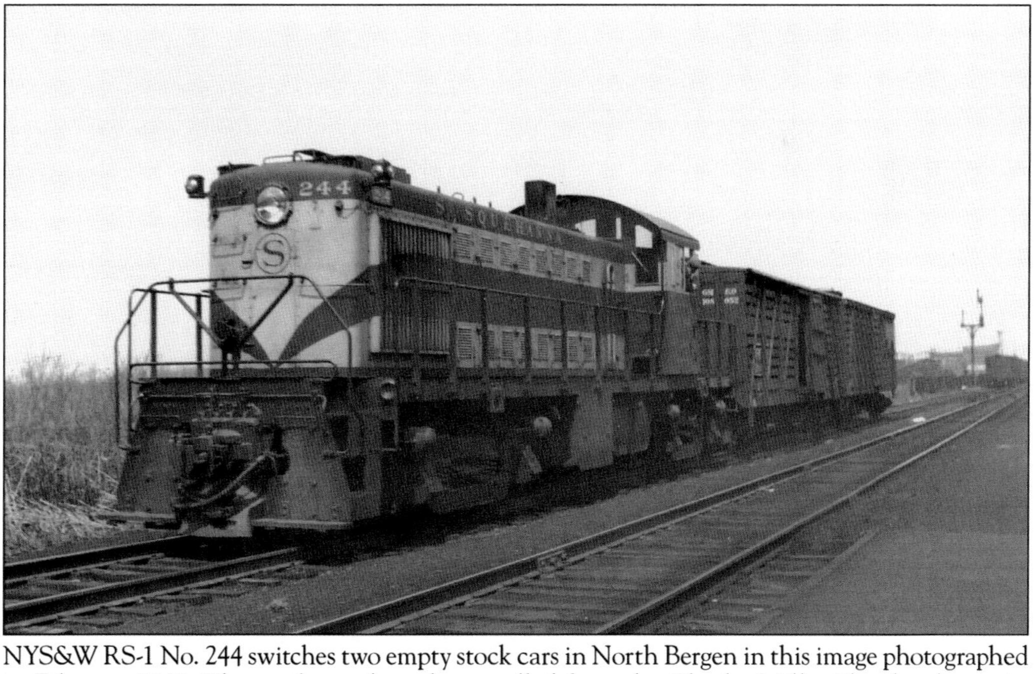

NYS&W RS-1 No. 244 switches two empty stock cars in North Bergen in this image photographed in February 1948. The stock cars have been pulled from the Charles Miller Slaughterhouse in North Bergen, which was an active shipper on the railroad for many years through the 1960s. (Photograph by John L. Treen; author's collection.)

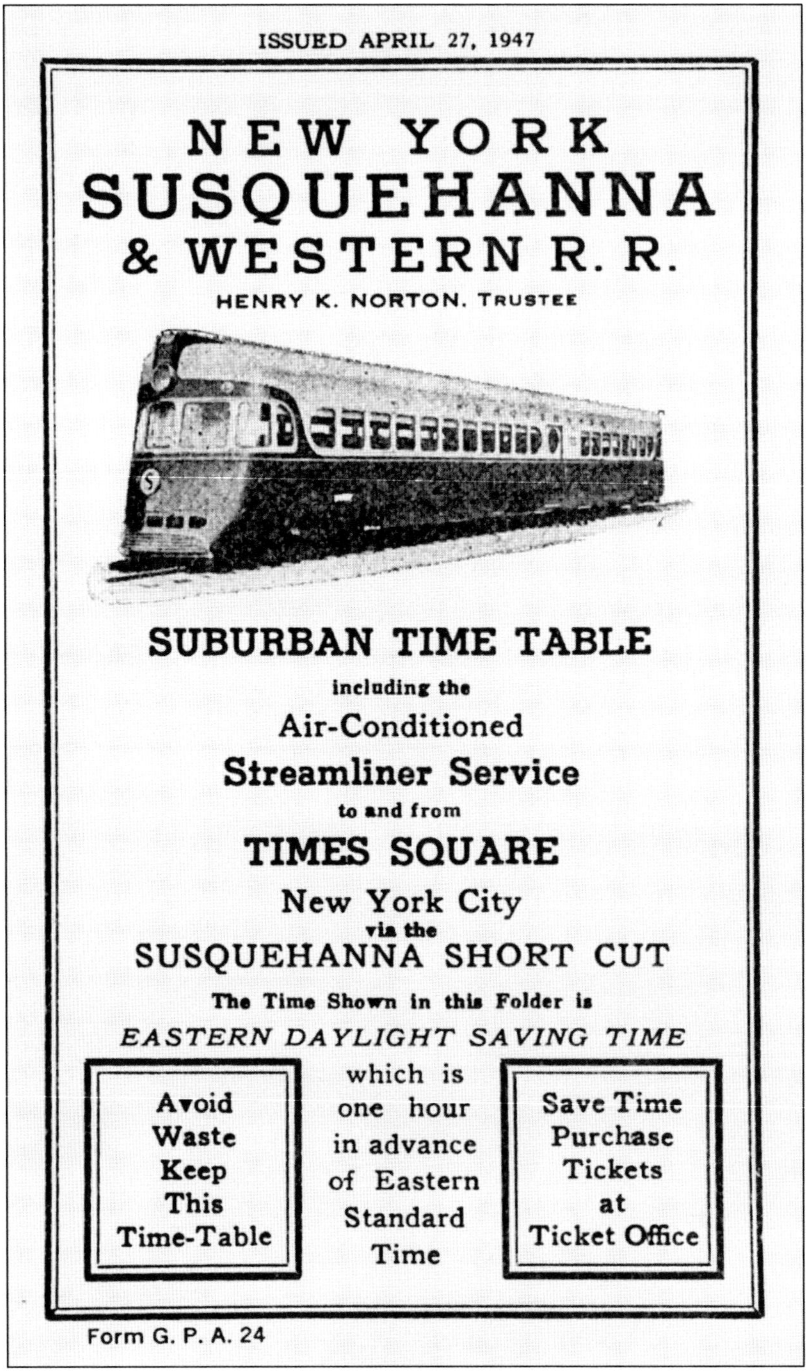

ISSUED APRIL 27, 1947

NEW YORK
SUSQUEHANNA
& WESTERN R. R.

HENRY K. NORTON, TRUSTEE

SUBURBAN TIME TABLE
including the
Air-Conditioned
Streamliner Service
to and from
TIMES SQUARE
New York City
via the
SUSQUEHANNA SHORT CUT

The Time Shown in this Folder is
EASTERN DAYLIGHT SAVING TIME
which is one hour in advance of Eastern Standard Time

Avoid Waste Keep This Time-Table

Save Time Purchase Tickets at Ticket Office

Form G. P. A. 24

This cover of an April 27, 1947, timetable features an NYS&W American Car & Foundry–built Motorailer advertising "Air-Conditioned Streamliner Service" to and from Times Square in New York City via the Susquehanna Short Cut. The Susquehanna Short Cut in North Bergen was also called the Susquehanna Transfer, where commuters transferred to buses to and from New York City instead of via a ferry connection in Jersey City. The NYS&W promoted the Susquehanna Short Cut as a way commuters could save 15 minutes of travel time. (Author's collection.)

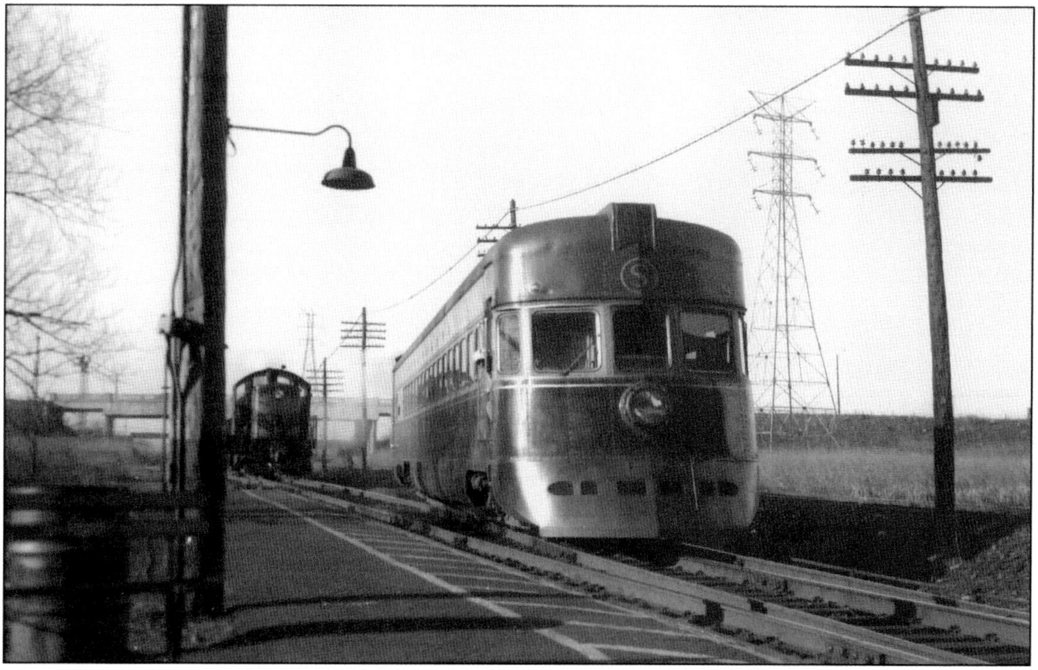

NYS&W No. 1005, an American Car & Foundry–built Motorailer, is shown in this scene departing Susquehanna Transfer and switching tracks to go westbound with train No. 809 on March 9, 1949, as an NYS&W RS-1 waits to proceed east in the background. (Photograph by John L. Treen; courtesy of Thomas J. Callan and the Maywood Station Museum Collection.)

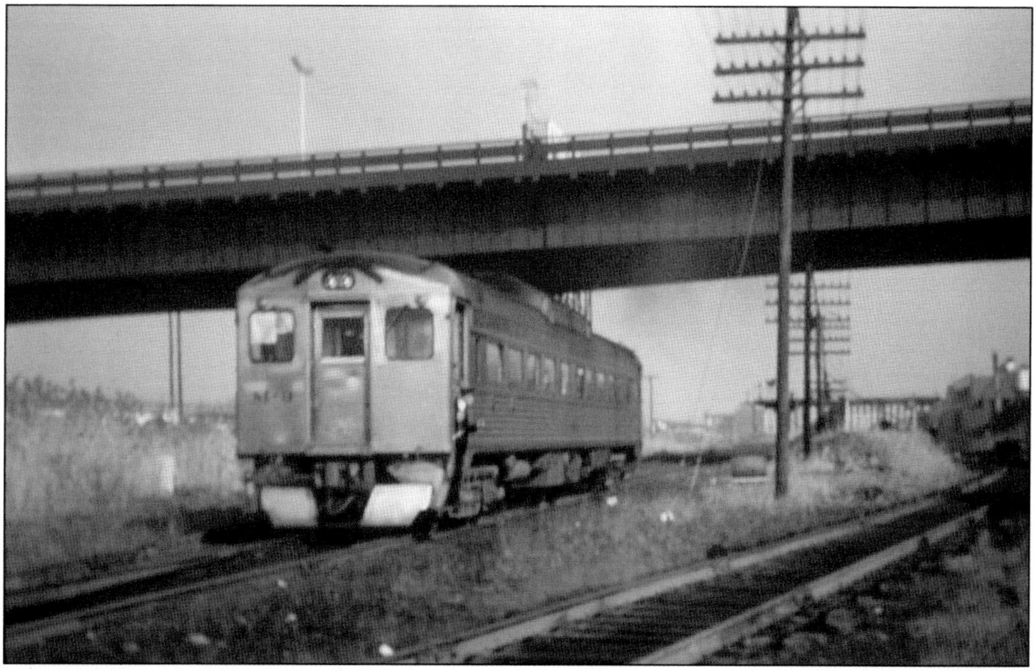

NYS&W Budd-built Rail Diesel Car M-3 is shown in this scene arriving at Susquehanna Transfer in North Bergen in March 1957. The approach to the Lincoln Tunnel dominates the scene above M-3. (Author's collection.)

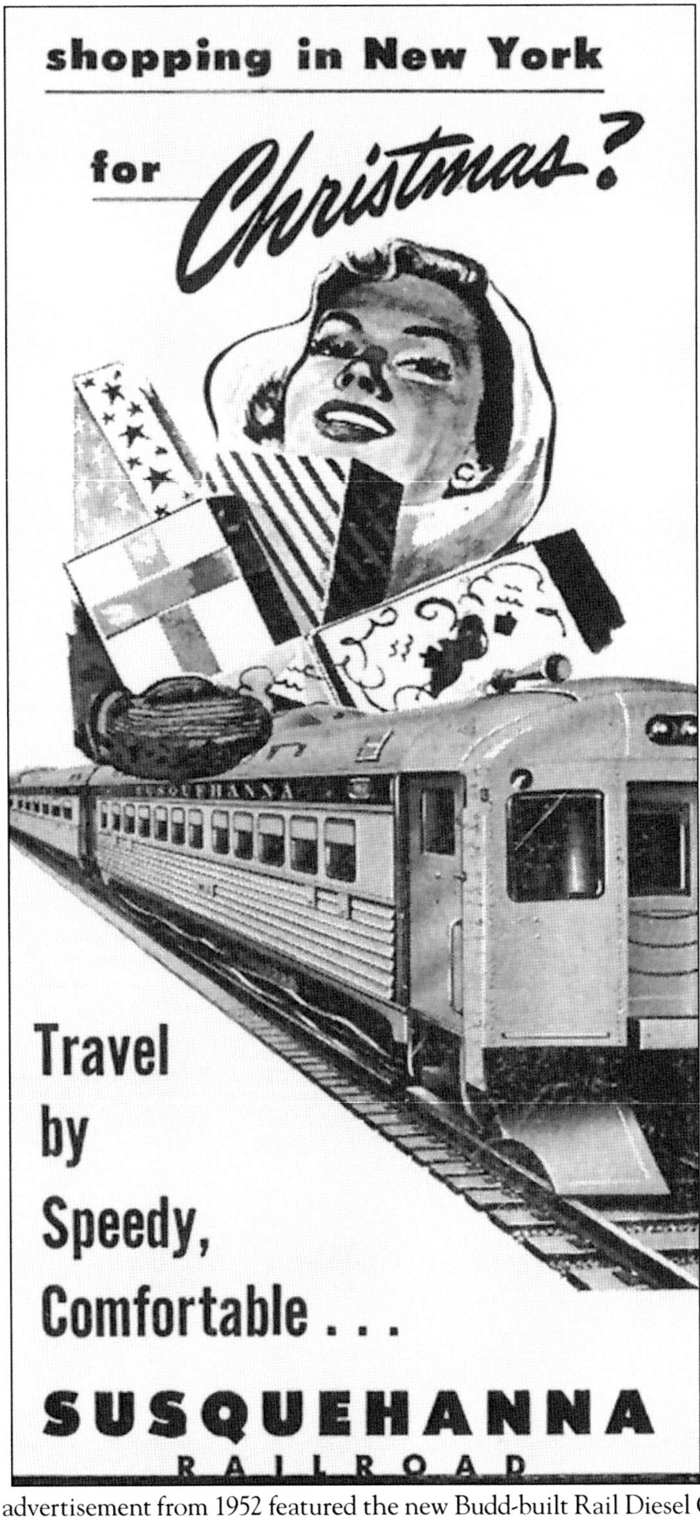

This NYS&W advertisement from 1952 featured the new Budd-built Rail Diesel Cars to promote using the railroad to and from New York City for Christmas shopping. (Author's collection.)

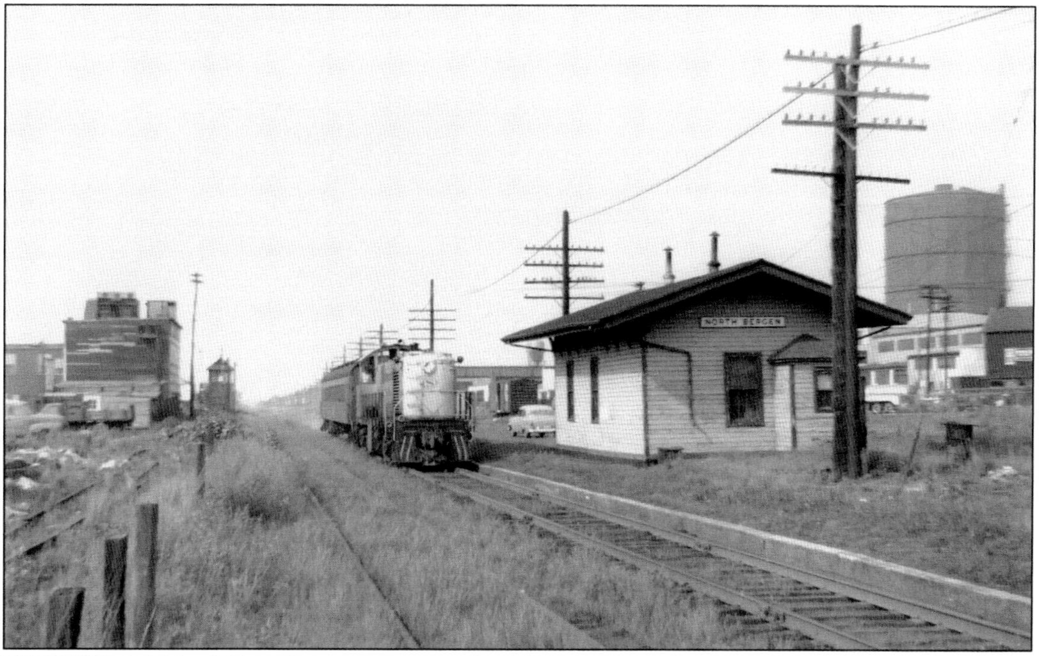

NYS&W RS-1 No. 234 is about to arrive with its one-car passenger train at North Bergen station in this scene photographed on June 5, 1961. The station was formerly known as Homestead on the railroad and was located near Paterson Plank Road. (Courtesy of Railroad Avenue Enterprises; author's collection.)

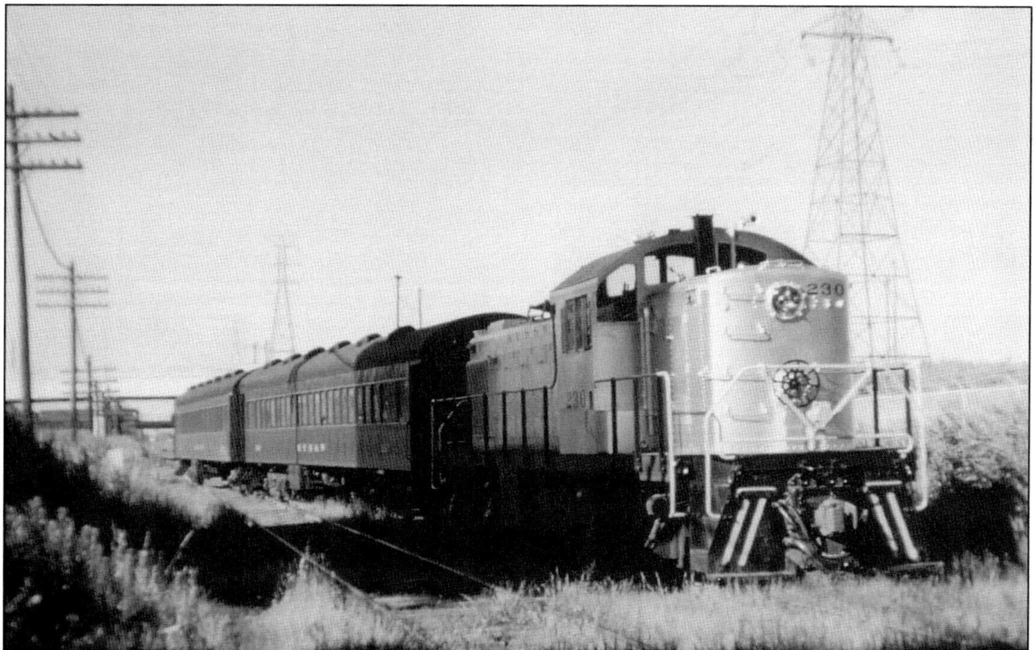

NYS&W RS-1 No. 230 is shown here with two passenger cars arriving at Susquehanna Transfer in North Bergen in October 1964. This location was in the New Jersey Meadowlands, and the terrain was very marshy and prone to flooding. (Author's collection.)

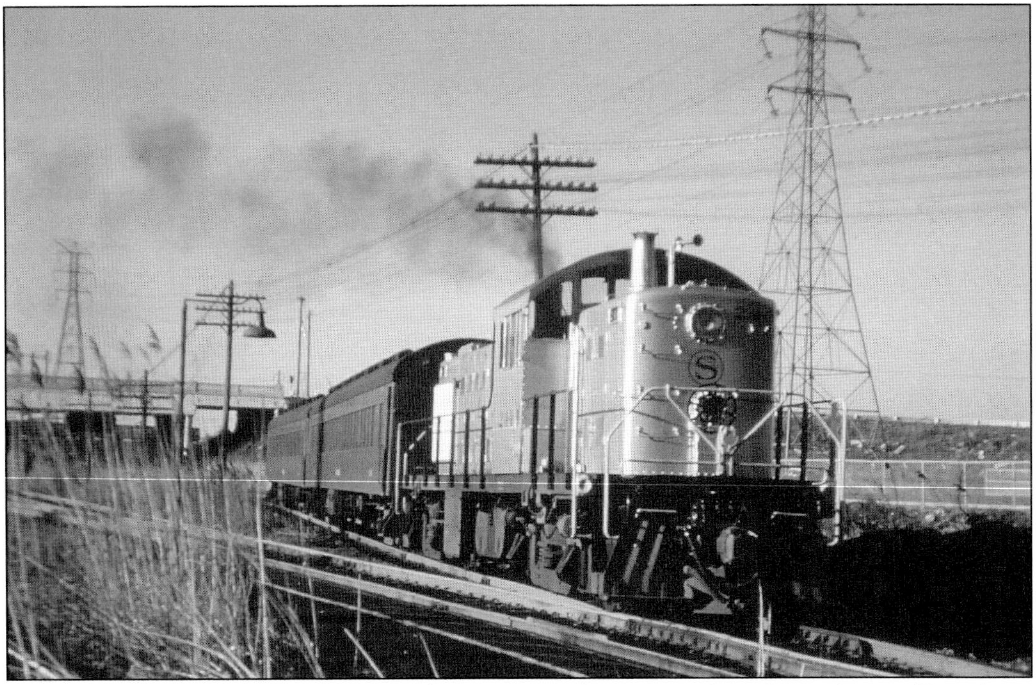

Freshly painted NYS&W RS-1 No. 244 begins to accelerate away from Susquehanna Transfer in North Bergen and through the marshes with its two-car passenger train in this December 1964 image. (Author's collection.)

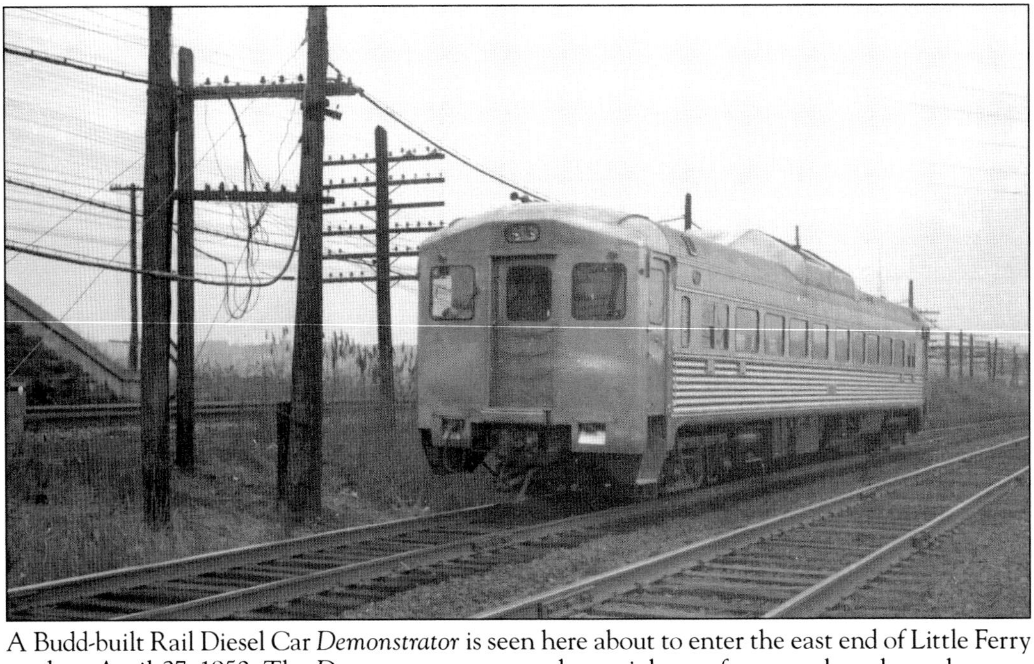

A Budd-built Rail Diesel Car *Demonstrator* is seen here about to enter the east end of Little Ferry yard on April 27, 1950. The *Demonstrator* was used on trial runs for several weeks and was so successful that the NYS&W ordered four units, which replaced the American Car & Foundry–built Motorailers in the fall of 1950. (Photograph by John L. Treen; courtesy of Thomas J. Callan and the Maywood Station Museum Collection.)

Two

Little Ferry to Hackensack

The railroad enters Bergen County at a location known as Little Ferry, which was the hub of the NYS&W, where a major yard, roundhouse, and locomotive maintenance facility were once found. At this location, the New York Central (West Shore) ran north-south parallel to the yard and an interchange was maintained. The Edgewater branch also began at the south end of the yard and proceeded in an eastern direction. The NYS&W performed their locomotive maintenance and car repairs at Little Ferry until the mid-1980s when Sealand (CSX) acquired the land for development of an intermodal yard. The NYS&W then moved their locomotive servicing tracks just north to Ridgefield Park, near New Jersey State Route 46, and additional yard tracks were added north of there between Mount Vernon Street in Ridgefield Park and Cross Street in Bogota to replace the trackage that was displaced in Little Ferry yard. At one time, Ridgefield Park was such a busy location for both the NYS&W and New York Central (West Shore) that a union station was built in 1927 to serve both roads' passengers. A sizeable amount of industry was also found in Ridgefield Park, with most of it served by the NYS&W. The borough of Bogota is located on the eastern shore of the Hackensack River, with the NYS&W running north and parallel to the river. The western end of Bogota, just before the Hackensack River bridge, once had a large asphalt plant served by the NYS&W on a vast array of sidings. Heading west from Bogota, the NYS&W crosses the Hackensack River into the city of Hackensack on a steel girder bridge and essentially bisects Hackensack in a westerly direction by running through the central business district, where a station was once located on Main Street. This station was originally built of wood but was replaced in the early 1900s with a brick structure. Several sidings for shippers and a team track were also located there. In the 1950s, the station was replaced by a smaller station on River Street.

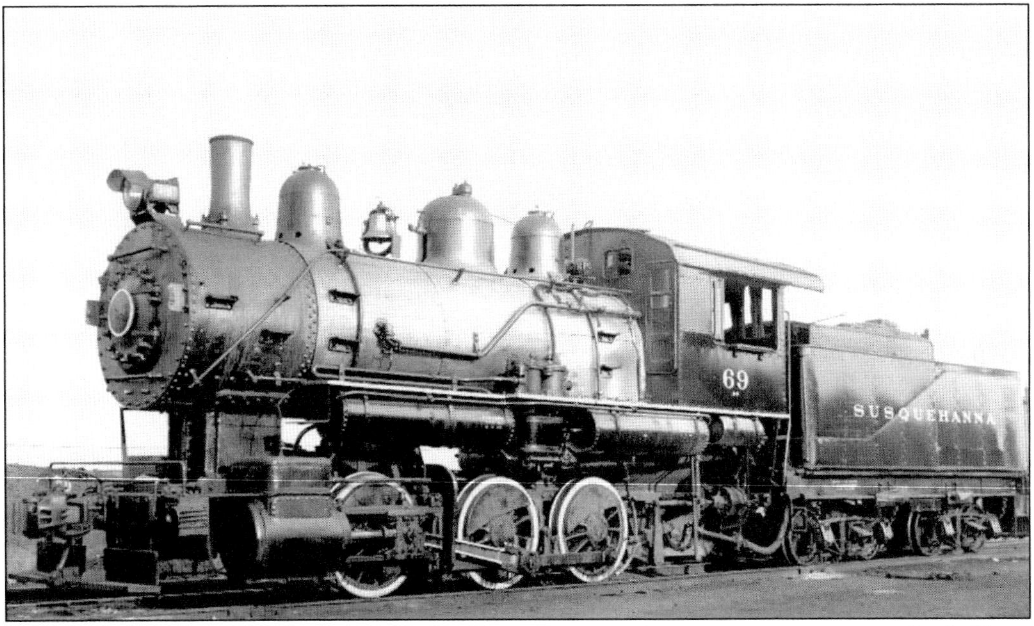

NYS&W 0-6-0 No. 69 is shown in this photograph resting between assignments in Little Ferry yard on October 12, 1940. Little Ferry yard went through many changes over the years, the most radical occurring in the 1940s when construction of the New Jersey Turnpike caused a major redesign, including elimination of one of the two hump yards. (Author's collection.)

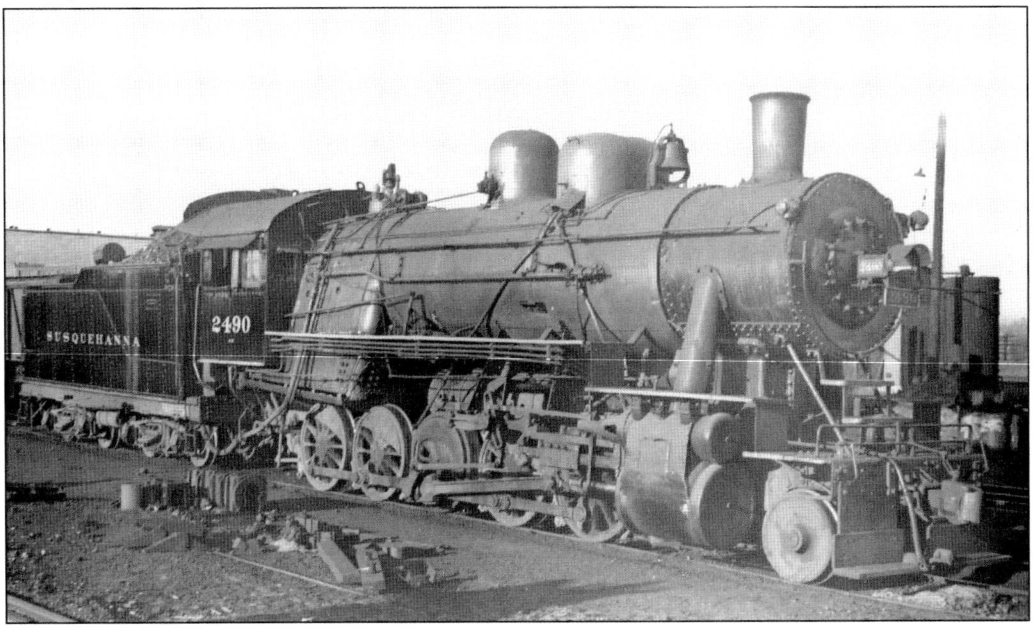

NYS&W 2-10-0 Russian Decapod No. 2490 sits in the sun in Little Ferry yard in this view taken in February 1941. The NYS&W bought and leased a group of these steam engines from Erie Railroad, which originally bought them in 1918 when the Bolshevik Revolution occurred in Russia in 1917 and they were not delivered. The Decapods were retrofitted from 60-inch Russian track gauge to 56.5-inch standard gauge, as used in North America. (Photograph by Vincent DeSantis; author's collection.)

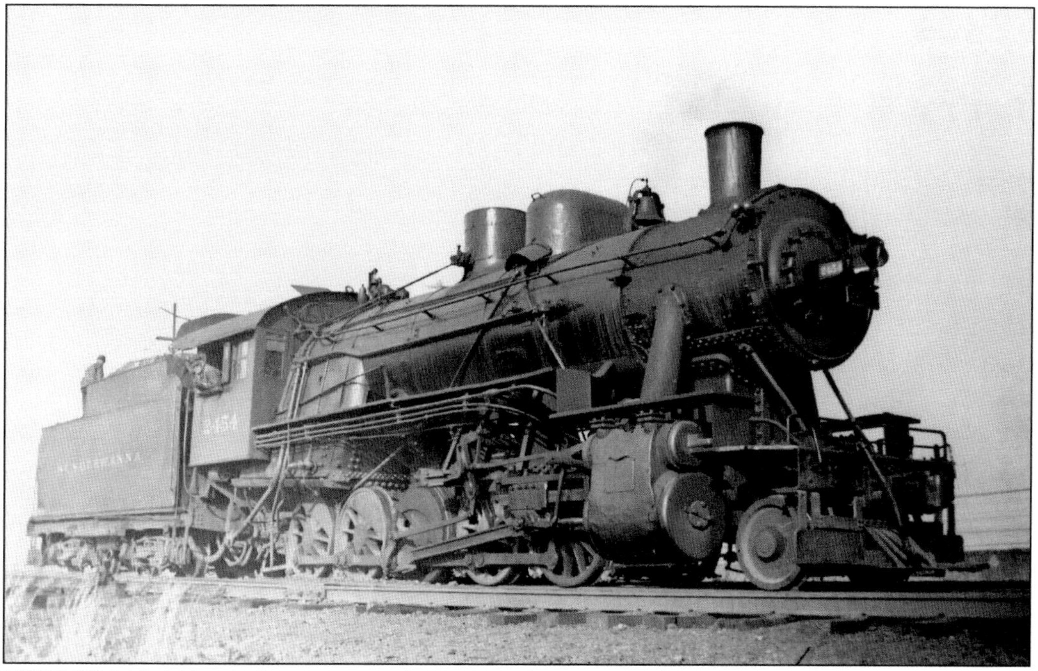

NYS&W 2-10-0 No. 2454 is seen working in Little Ferry yard in March 1941 in this view. From the 1920s through early 1940s, the 2-10-0s formed the backbone of the road freight power on the NYS&W. Their smaller driving wheels were particularly suited for the NYS&W's track profile. (Photograph by Vincent DeSantis; author's collection.)

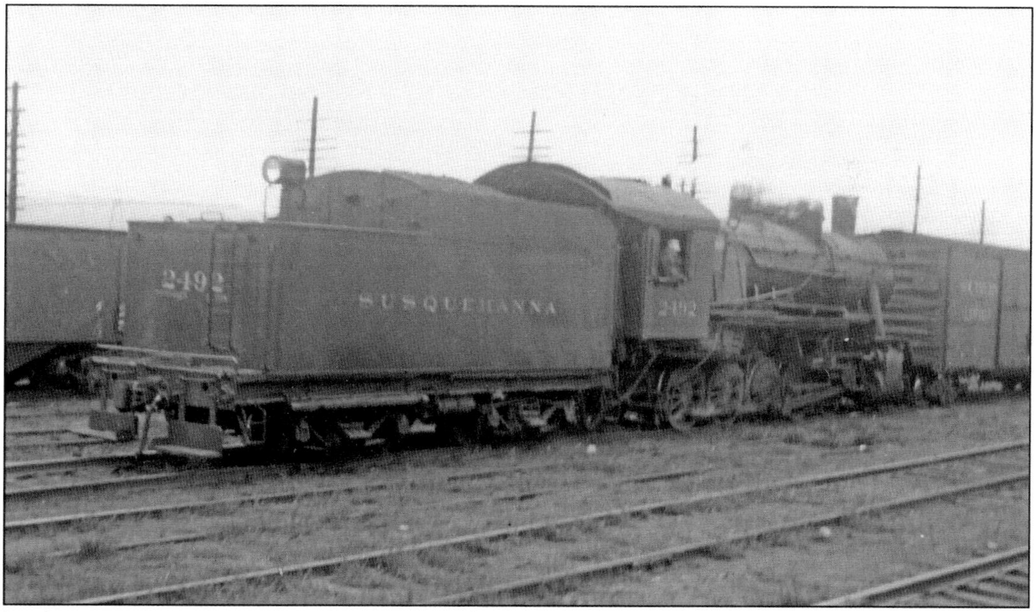

In this view, NYS&W 2-10-0 No. 2492 is shown working in Little Ferry yard on September 6, 1946. With the arrival of the diesel S-2s and RS-1s and their utilization in main line freight duty, some of the 2-10-0s were bumped to yard service before their eventual retirement. The NYS&W completely dieselized by late 1947. (Photograph by John L. Treen; courtesy of Thomas J. Callan and the Maywood Station Museum Collection.)

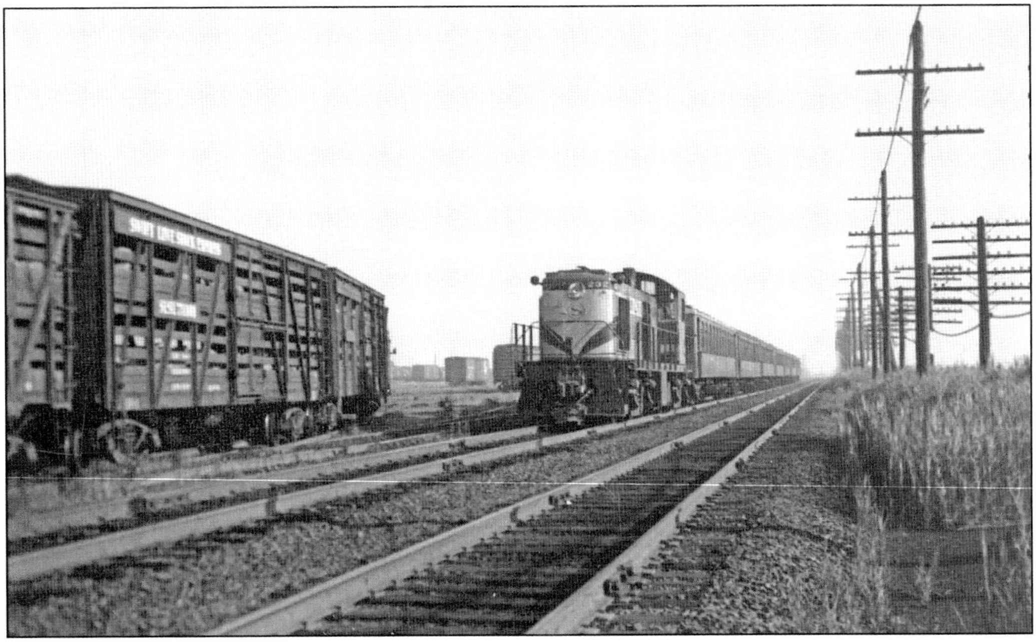

NYS&W RS-1 No. 232 proceeds east through Little Ferry yard with Train No. 910's seven-car Stillwater passenger train in this scene taken during the morning of July 16, 1948. The Swift Line Stock Express stock cars to the left are loaded with livestock destined for the Charles Miller Slaughterhouse in North Bergen. (Photograph by John L. Treen; courtesy of Thomas J. Callan and the Maywood Station Museum Collection.)

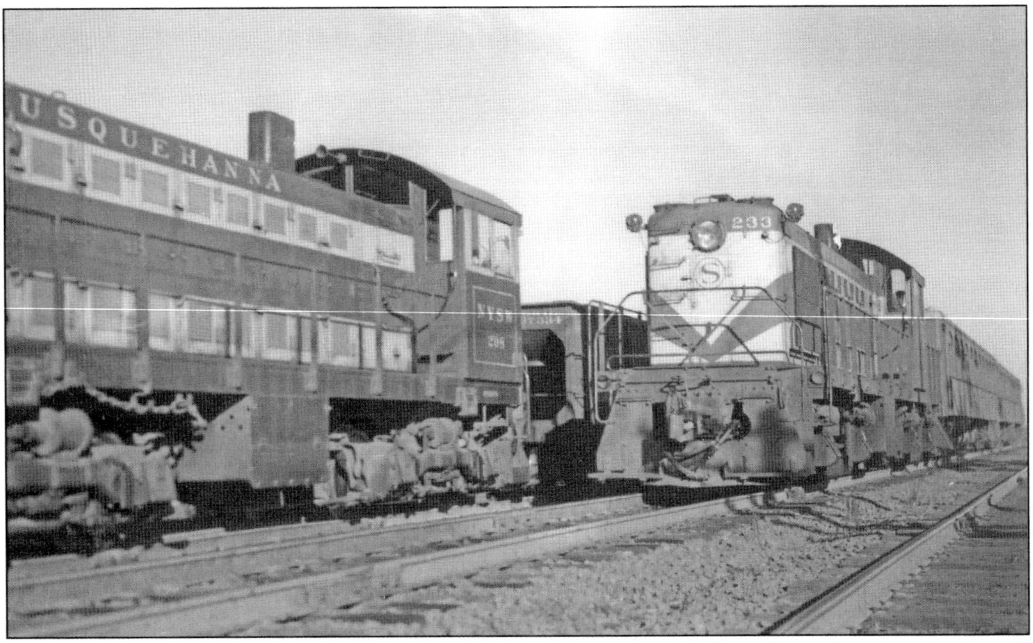

NYS&W RS-1 No. 233 is on the main line heading eastbound through Little Ferry yard with Train No. 810 and two former Erie Railroad Stillwell coaches as they pass NYS&W S-2 No. 208 with its train working in the yard. This image was taken on November 3, 1949. (Photograph by John L. Treen; courtesy of Thomas J. Callan and the Maywood Station Museum Collection.)

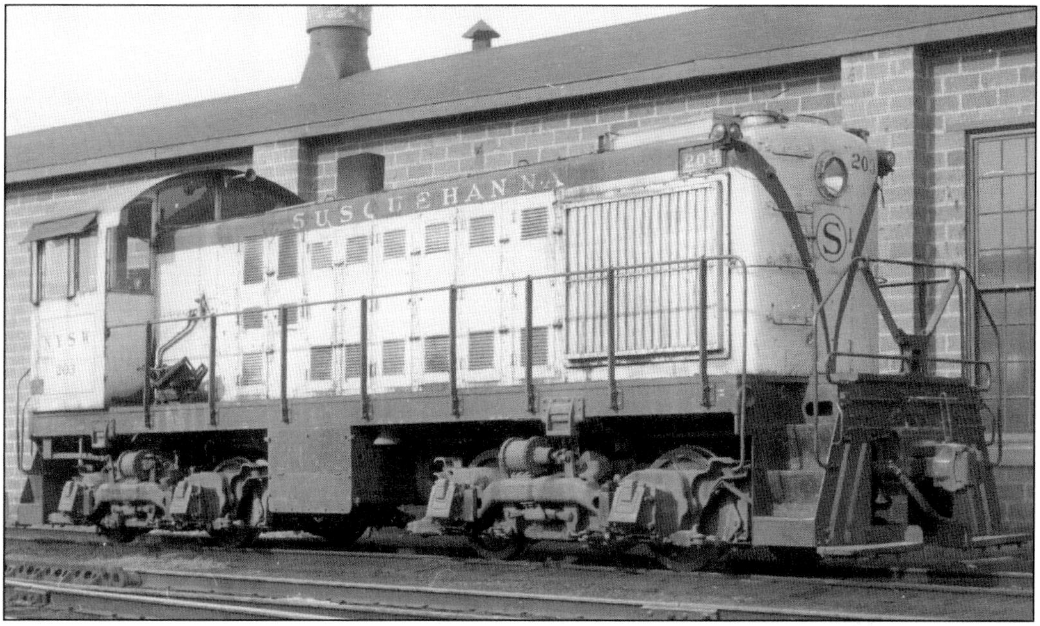

NYS&W S-2 No. 203 is shown resting next to the Little Ferry yard engine house in June 1960. The 1,000-horsepower locomotive was built in 1942 by the American Locomotive Company in Schenectady, New York. The unit wears the second diesel locomotive paint scheme adopted by the NYS&W, featuring a silver body and maroon stripes with a black underframe and trucks. (Photograph by Donald P. Wallworth; courtesy of Patrick J. Reynolds and the Maywood Station Museum Collection.)

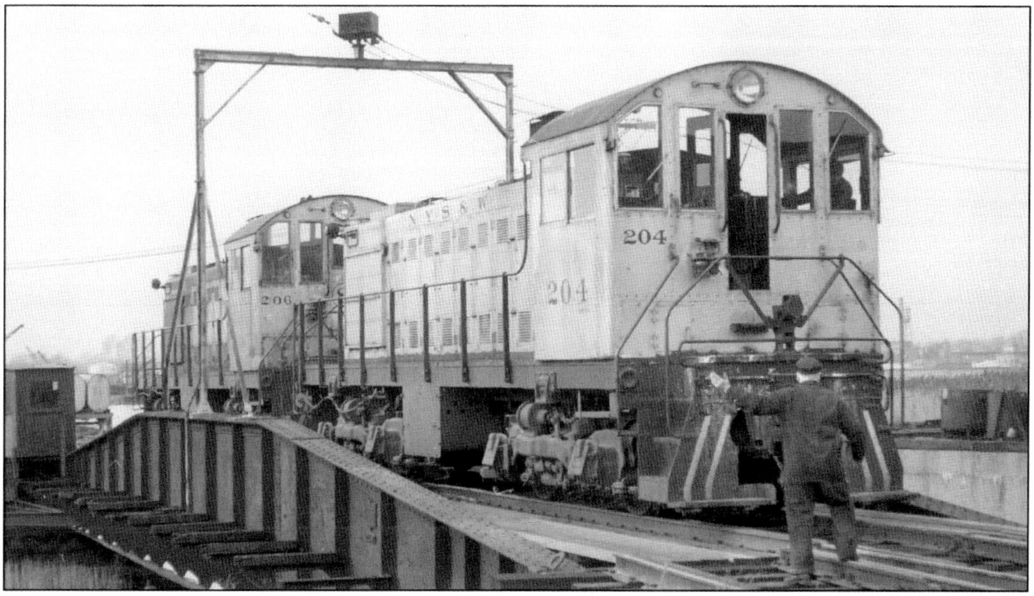

NYS&W S-2 Nos. 204 and 206 take a ride on the turntable in this December 1960 view of Little Ferry yard. Today this turntable still exists, but very little remains of the original Little Ferry yard. In the early 1990s, much of the yard was torn up and the trackage reconfigured to build a CSX intermodal yard. (Photograph by Donald P. Wallworth; courtesy of Patrick J. Reynolds and the Maywood Station Museum Collection.)

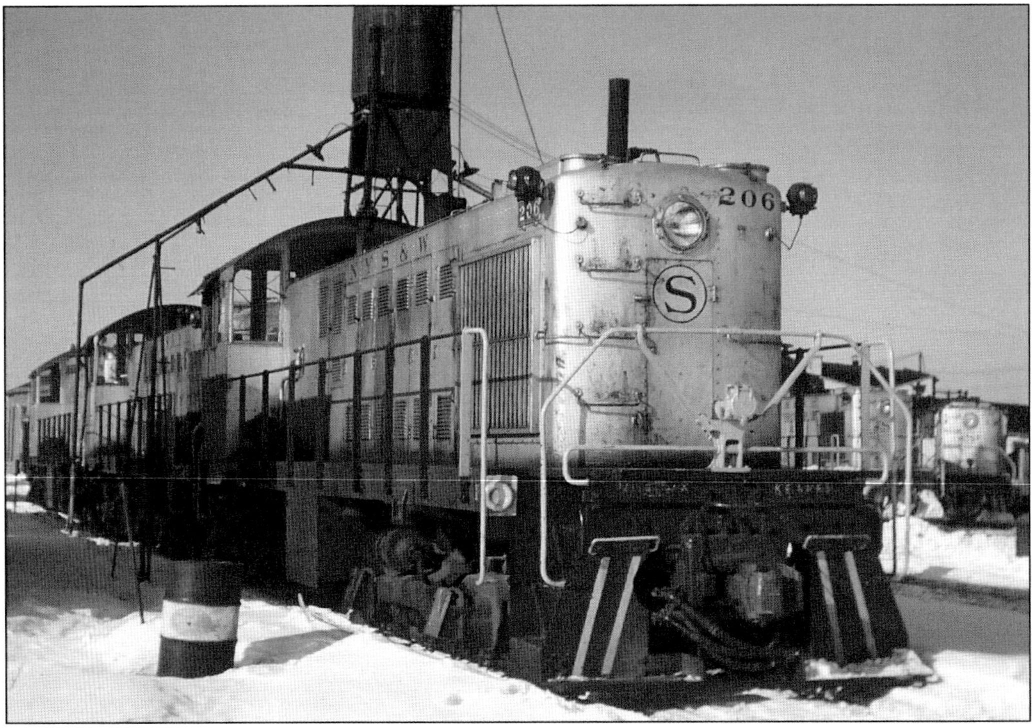

NYS&W S-2 No. 206 is in the foreground on the ready track, awaiting its next assignment in this January 1961 look at the Little Ferry engine terminal. ALCO S-2 and RS-1 diesel locomotives dominate the scene. (Photograph by Donald P. Wallworth; courtesy of Patrick J. Reynolds and the Maywood Station Museum Collection.)

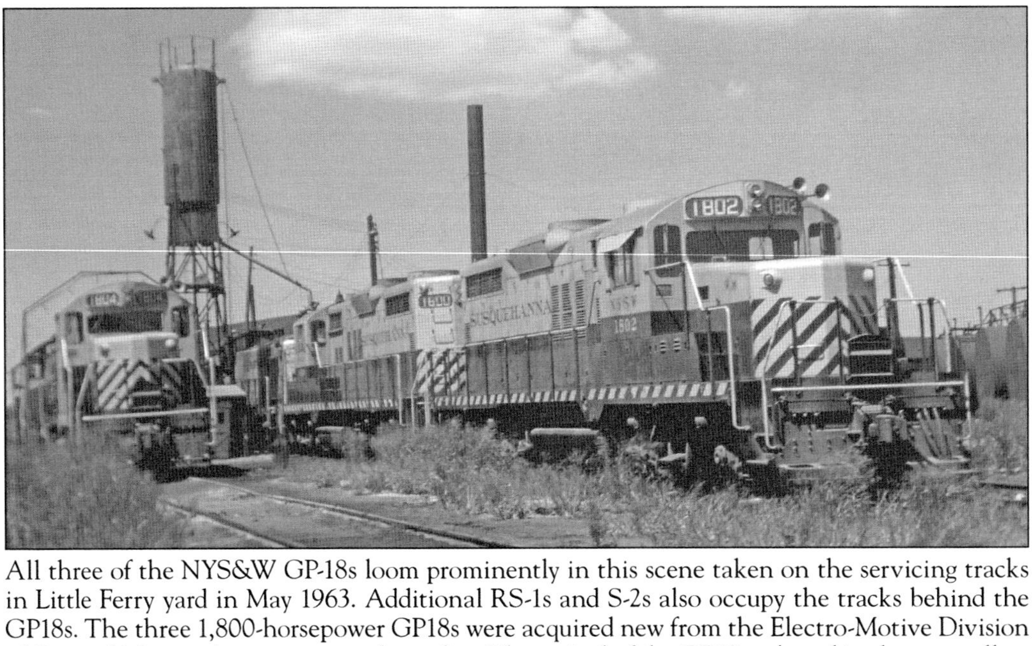

All three of the NYS&W GP-18s loom prominently in this scene taken on the servicing tracks in Little Ferry yard in May 1963. Additional RS-1s and S-2s also occupy the tracks behind the GP18s. The three 1,800-horsepower GP18s were acquired new from the Electro-Motive Division of General Motors about nine months earlier. The arrival of the GP18s ushered in the new yellow and black paint scheme. (Author's collection.)

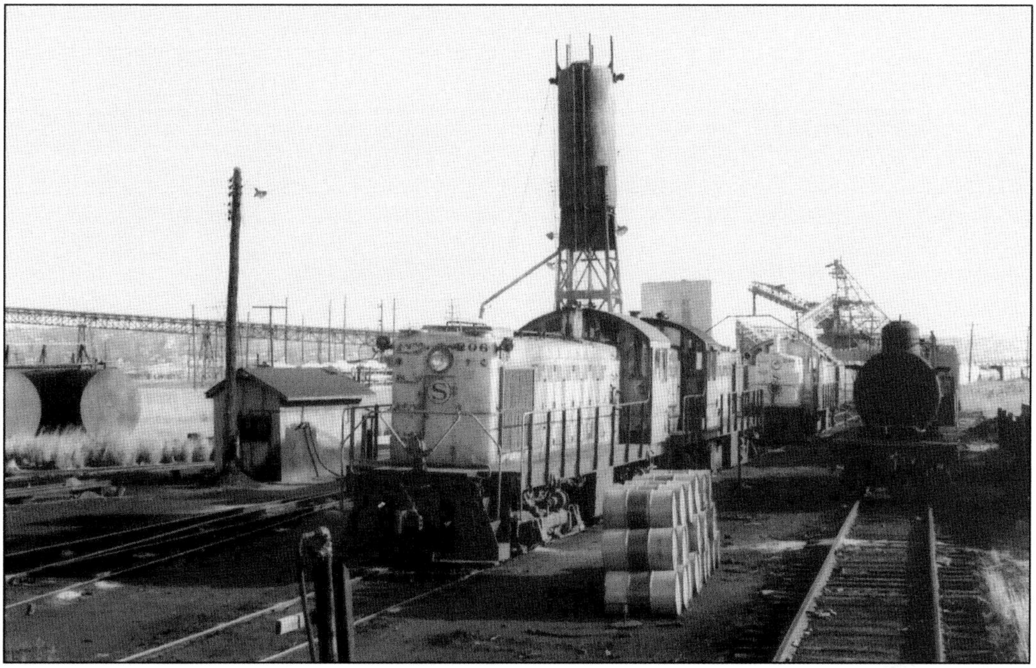

In this image taken April 1965, NYS&W S-2 No. 206 rests by the sand tower in the company of several other locomotives at the engine facility in Little Ferry yard. Note the old riveted tank car on a wooden underframe in the right of the photograph. This car was used for storing fuel at the facility. (Photograph by George Berisso; courtesy of Thomas J. Callan and the Maywood Station Museum Collection.)

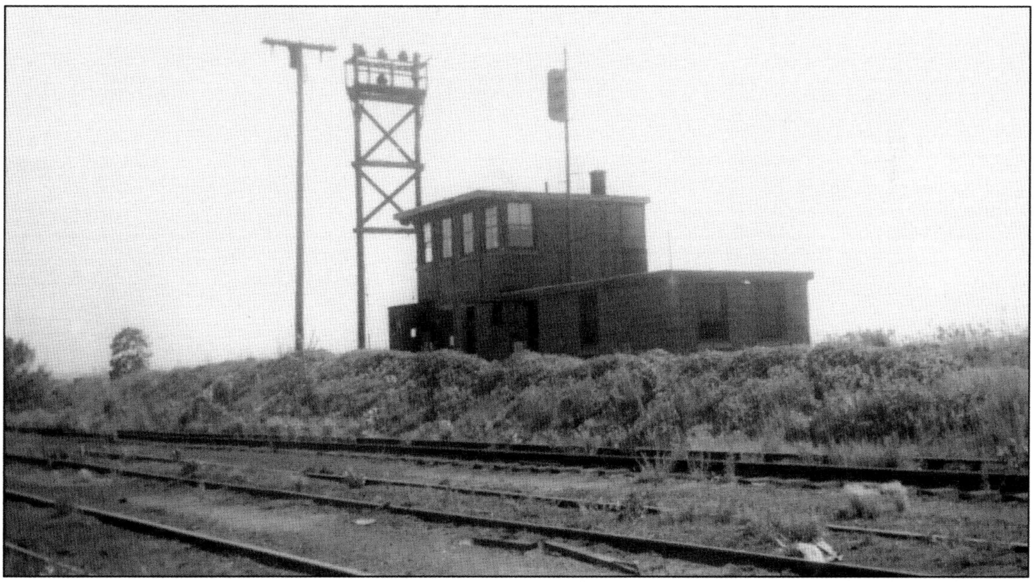

The Little Ferry yard office and tower are shown in this view taken in July 1969. Little Ferry yard featured an automated hump yard that was controlled by the tower. The use of an automated hump yard was quite sophisticated for a railroad the size of the NYS&W. Although the hump yard was lesser used in later years, it remained in operation into the 1980s. (Courtesy of Railroad Avenue Enterprises; author's collection.)

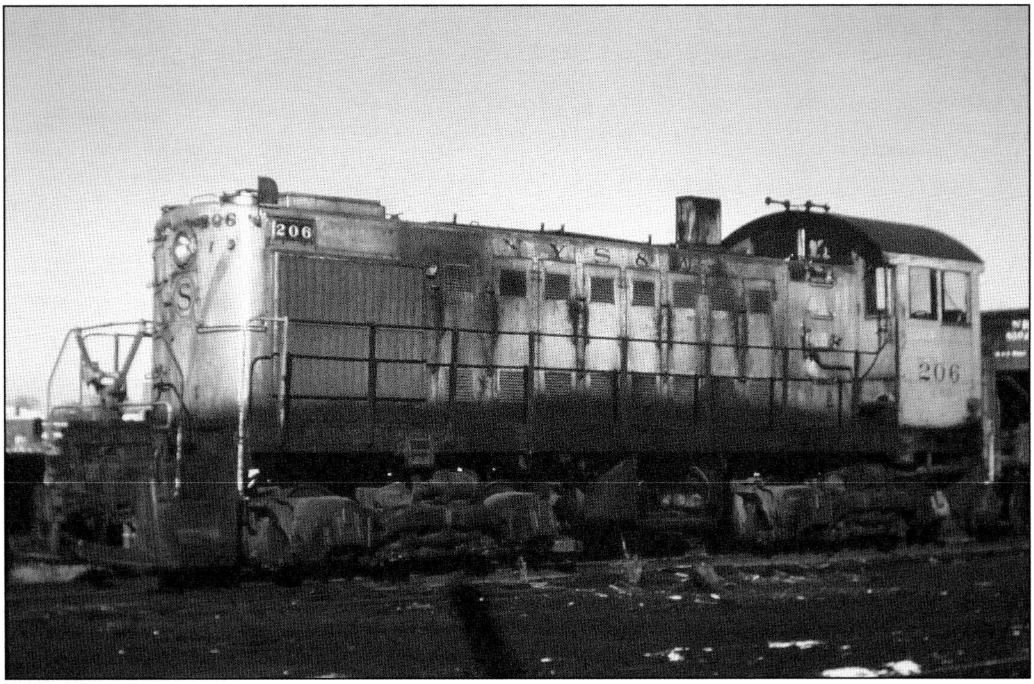

NYS&W S-2 No. 206 is looking a lot worse for wear in this November 1970 view taken in Little Ferry yard. Beneath all of the road grime, traces of its 1950s paint scheme that featured maroon stripes can be seen on the locomotive's front nose. (Courtesy of Patrick J. Reynolds collection.)

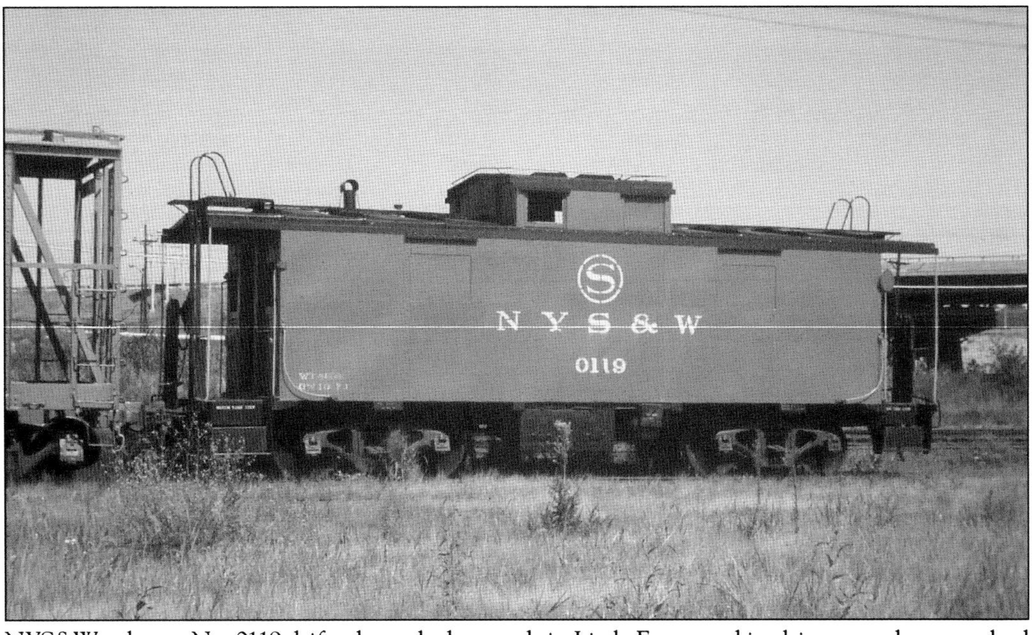

NYS&W caboose No. 0119 drifts through the weeds in Little Ferry yard in this scene photographed in September 1974. Originally built by International Car Company of Kenton, Ohio, in 1948, the caboose has soldiered on in service for the NYS&W for 27 years. It was repainted and had its windows boarded up a year prior to when this photograph was taken. (Photograph by Edwin D. Quinn.)

NYS&W GP18 No. 1804 and S-2 No. 206 sit beneath the sanding tower in Little Ferry yard in this view taken on September 17, 1974. After the NYS&W vacated Little Ferry yard in the early 1990s, this sand tower was moved to their new engine facility near Route 46 in Ridgefield Park and is still in use today. (Photograph by Donald P. Wallworth; courtesy of Patrick J. Reynolds and the Maywood Station Museum Collection.)

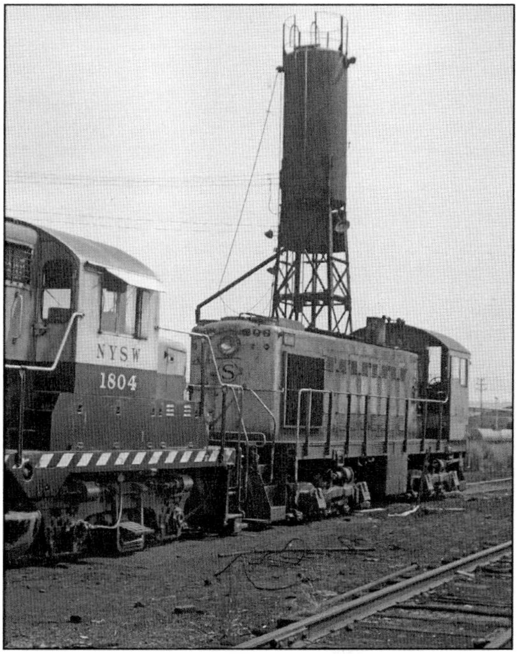

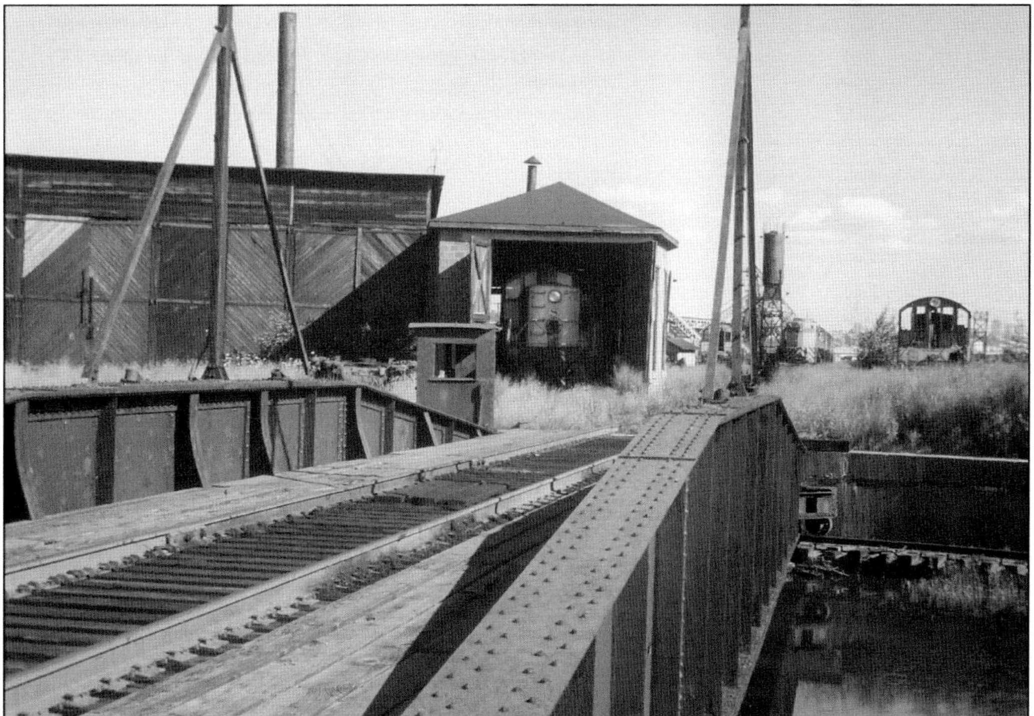

This September 1974 image gives a glimpse of the turntable, roundhouse and, in the right background, a portion of the locomotive servicing facility in Little Ferry yard. NYS&W RS-1 No. 240 is poking its nose out of the old cinder block streamliner shed that was added to the wood roundhouse in 1940 to provide cover and a work space for the then new American Car & Foundry–built Motorailers. (Photograph by Edwin D. Quinn.)

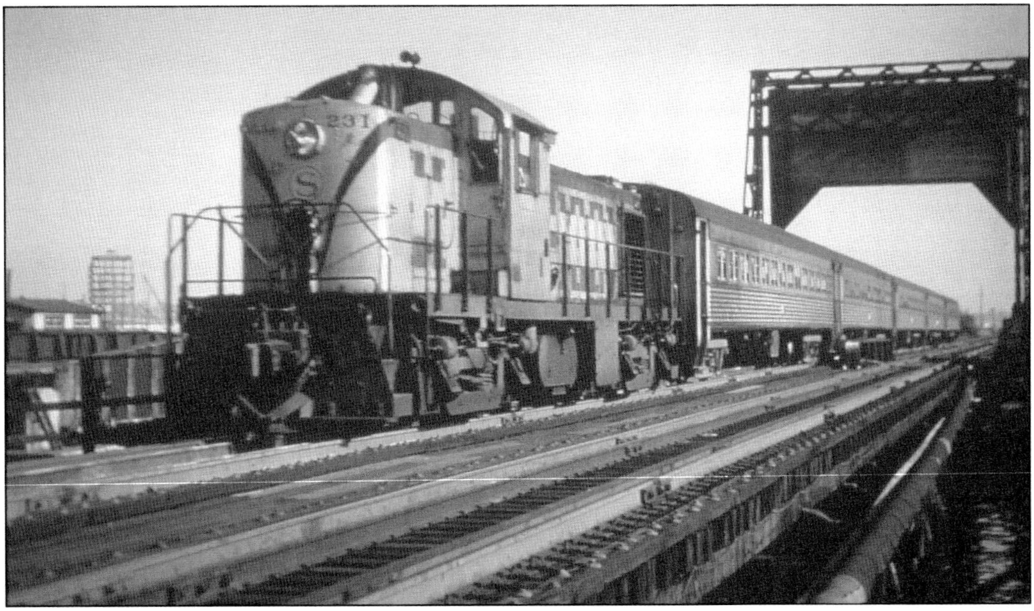

Passenger business must be good on this day in June 1955 as NYS&W RS-1 No. 231, working westbound, crosses the Overpeck Creek drawbridge in Ridgefield Park in this scene. Five of the Budd-built 85-seat passenger cars are in tow behind No. 231. Trains crossed this double track counter-weighted bridge that was built in 1913, which replaced an older two-track wooden bridge. The parallel two-track swing bridge of the New York Central's West Shore Division can be seen just to the left of the front of No. 231. (Author's collection.)

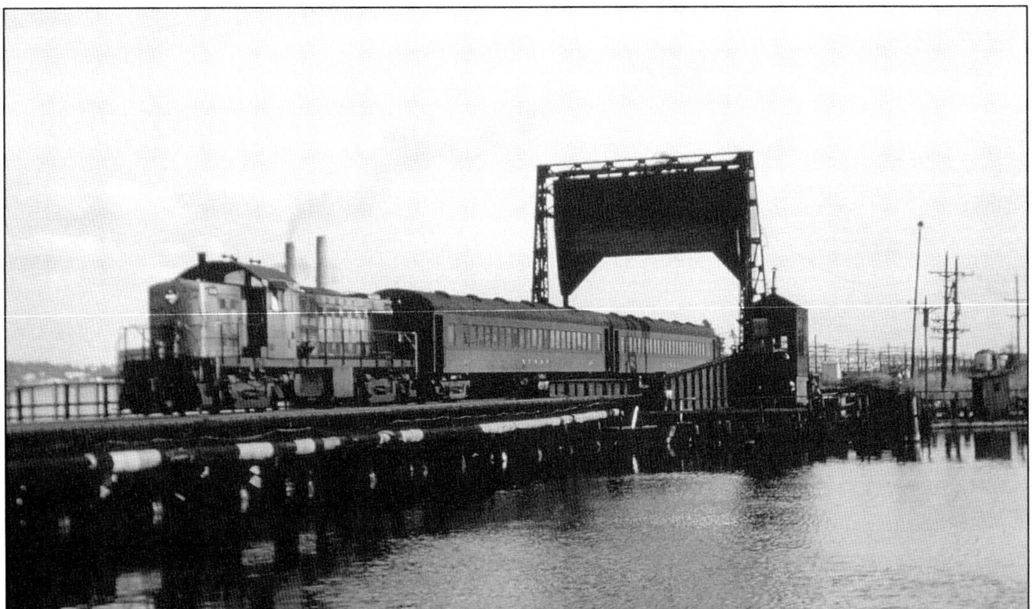

NYS&W RS-1 No. 236 hurries a two-car passenger train west as it crosses the Overpeck Creek drawbridge in Ridgefield Park in May 1964. The two smokestacks above No. 236 are in the background at the Public Service generating plant across the creek. An RS-1 is also visible in the far right of this photograph, sitting in Little Ferry yard. (Author's collection.)

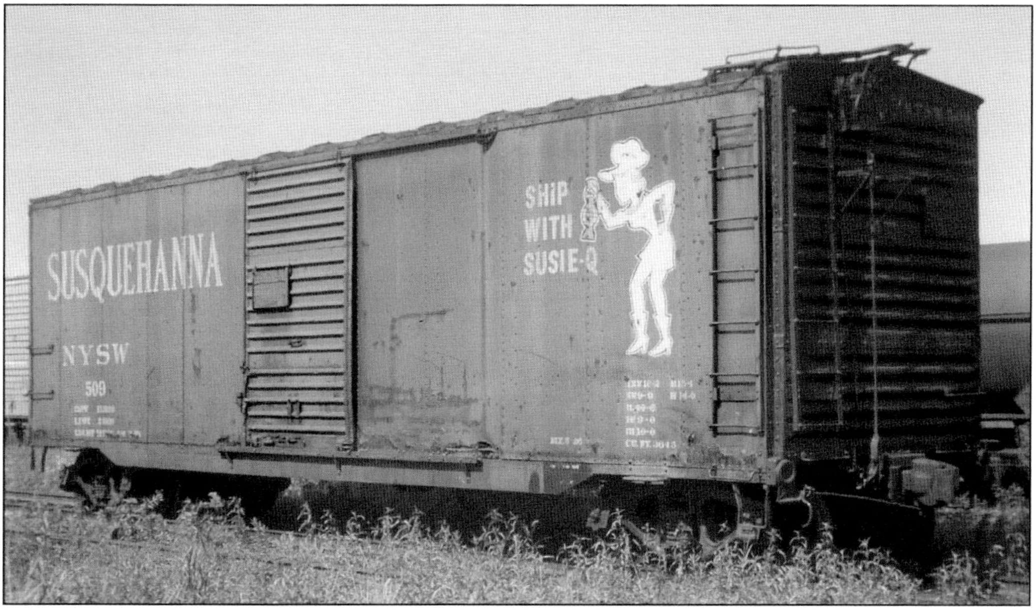

The NYS&W never had a very large fleet of freight equipment, although it did have a few notable variations. One of which is shown here in this photograph taken in September 1974 at Little Ferry yard. This 40-foot boxcar, built in May 1926, was in the 501–525 series and was purchased secondhand from the Lehigh Valley Railroad. It wears the Susie-Q herald that appeared in the mid-1960s and was featured on this group of cars. (Photograph by Edwin D. Quinn.)

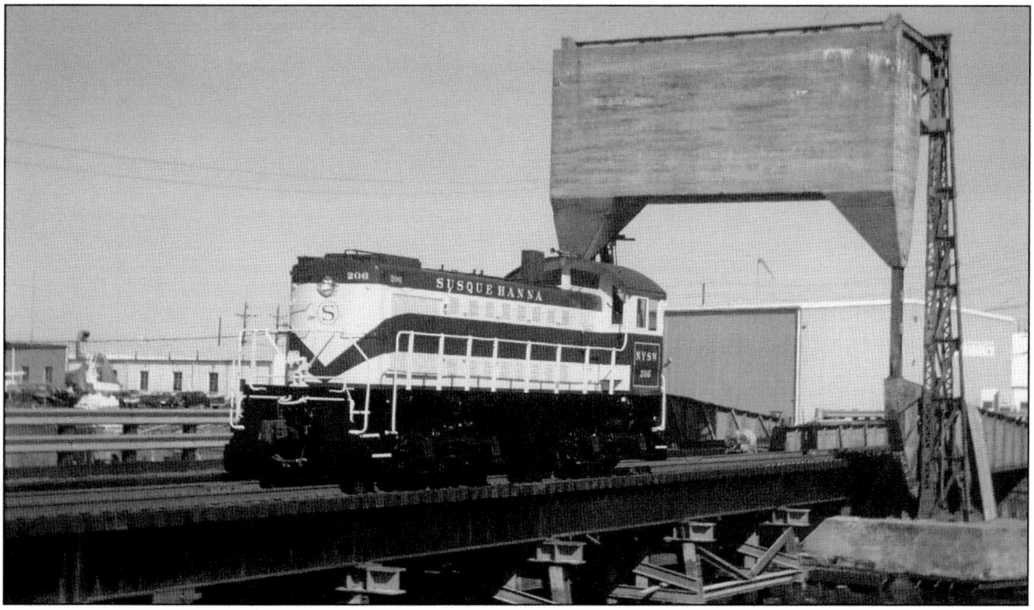

NYS&W S-2 No. 206 is shown in this March 1985 view on the Overpeck Creek drawbridge in Ridgefield Park. The locomotive was just released from the Little Ferry shop after being rebuilt and repainted into its as-delivered 1942 maroon and gray paint scheme. Today NYS&W S-2 No. 206 has been cosmetically restored by the Maywood Station Historical Committee at the Maywood Station Museum in Maywood. (Photograph by George Berisso; courtesy of Thomas J. Callan and the Maywood Station Museum Collection.)

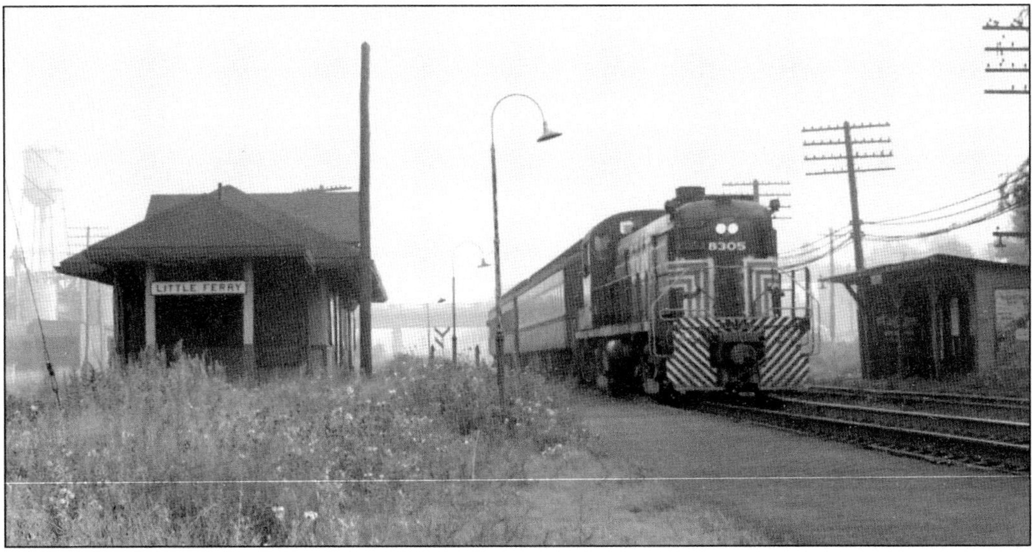

New York Central RS-3 No. 8305 is shown arriving in Little Ferry in July 1959 with an eastbound commuter train destined for its terminal in Weehawken, New Jersey. The New York Central and NYS&W paralleled each other in this area for about 3 miles. The NYC's passenger waiting shelter is on the right, and the NYS&W's station is on the left. The actual location here is Ridgefield Park, but the NYC and NYS&W called their stations at the Bergen Turnpike "Little Ferry." (Photograph by Donald P. Wallworth; author's collection.)

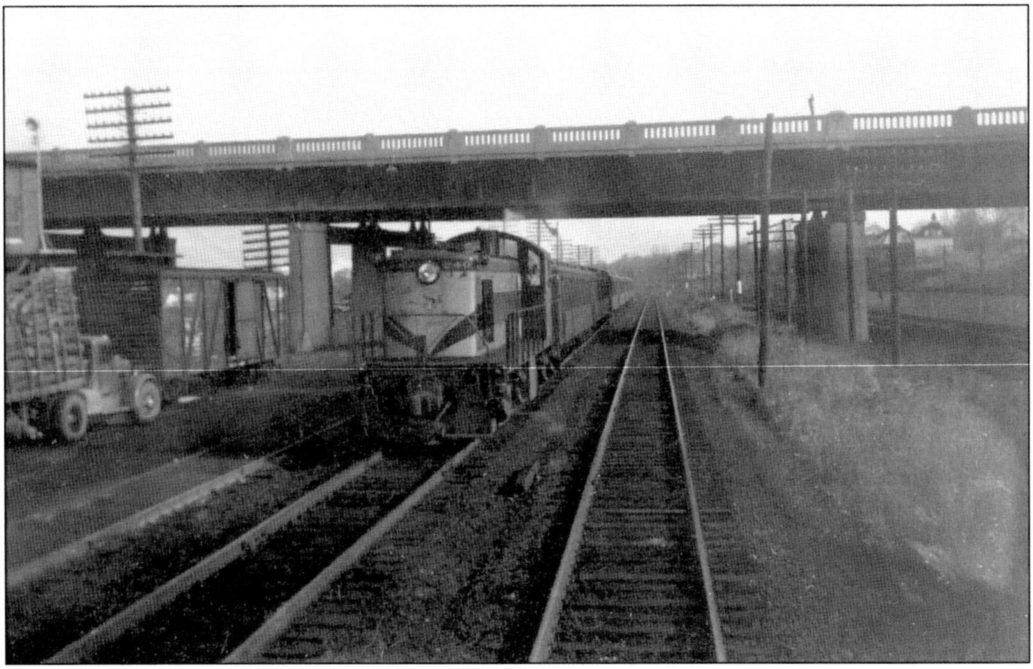

NYS&W RS-1 No. 240 leads eastbound passenger train No. 910 with seven cars through Ridgefield Park in this scene taken on April 7, 1949. The Route 46 overpass is directly above the train, and the parallel New York Central's West Shore Division track is visible to the right. Today the NYS&W has a locomotive-servicing facility at this location. (Photograph by John L. Treen; courtesy of Thomas J. Callan and the Maywood Station Museum Collection.)

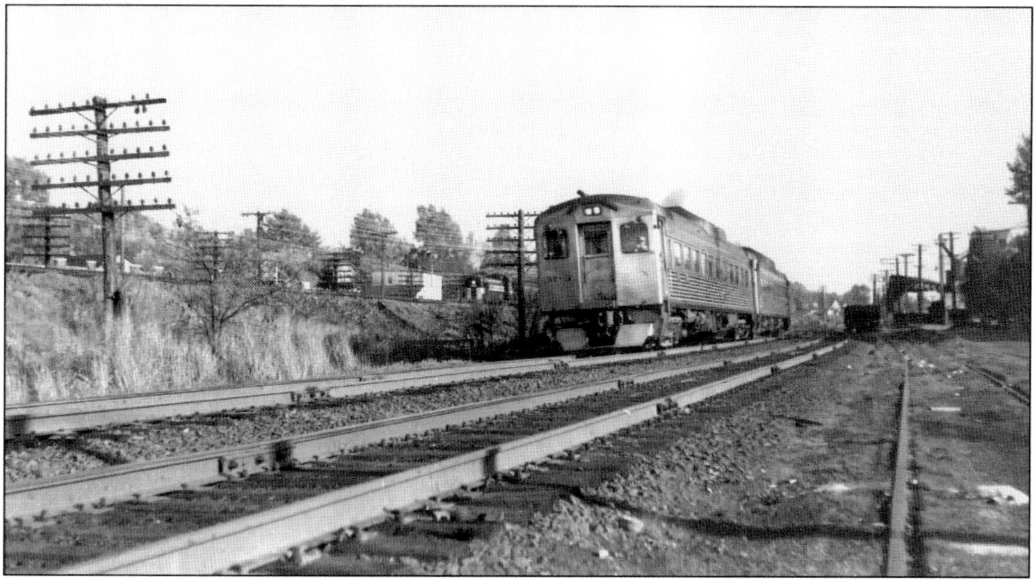

NYS&W Budd-built Rail Diesel Cars M-3 and M-4 speed westbound through Ridgefield Park with train No. 833 in this scene photographed on May 7, 1957. Barely visible to the left of the front of M-3 is a New York Central RS-3 heading up a westbound passenger train on its West Shore Division, which paralleled the NYS&W through Ridgefield Park. (Photograph by John L. Treen; author's collection.)

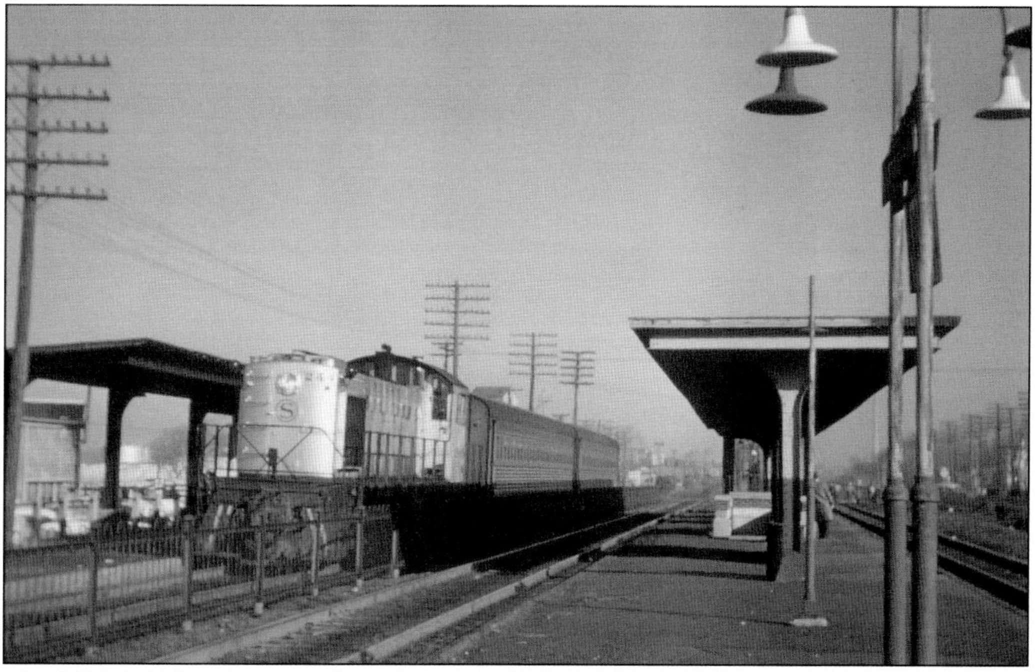

NYS&W RS-1 No. 244 arrives from the west at Ridgefield Park with a two-car passenger train in this view taken in November 1959. The NYS&W had their own station at this location until 1927, when a union station was built by the New York Central to serve both railroads. The NYS&W station was subsequently demolished, and waiting sheds were erected in its place. Commuters could cross the tracks via a tunnel to the union station. (Author's collection.)

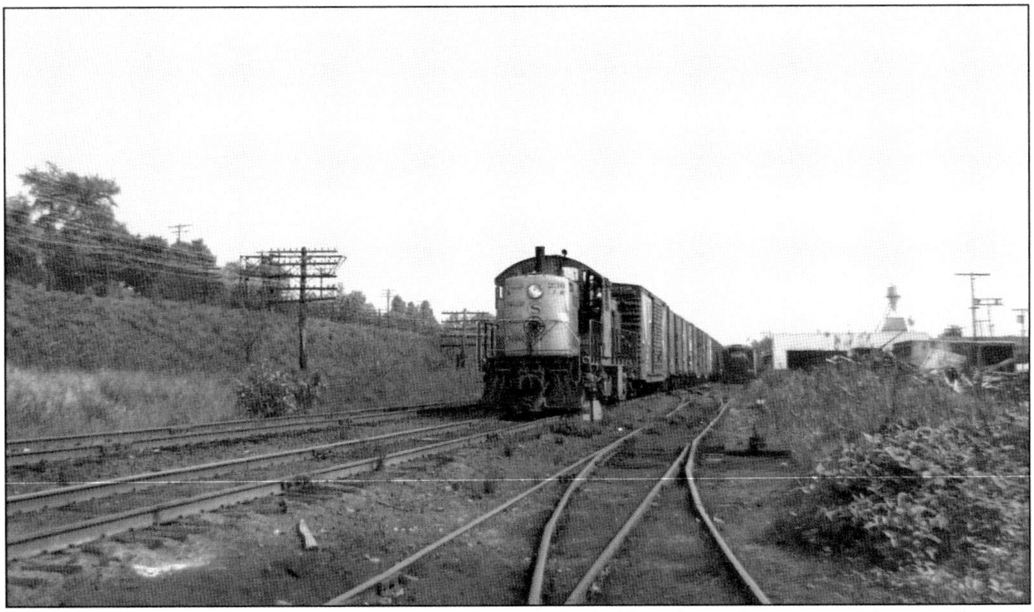

NYS&W RS-1 No. 236 switches freight cars in Ridgefield Park in this scene taken on June 7, 1961. The embankment on the left is the New York Central's West Shore Division. This view is looking east, and the photographer is standing close to where Interstate Route 80 overpass is today. (Courtesy of Railroad Avenue Enterprises; author's collection.)

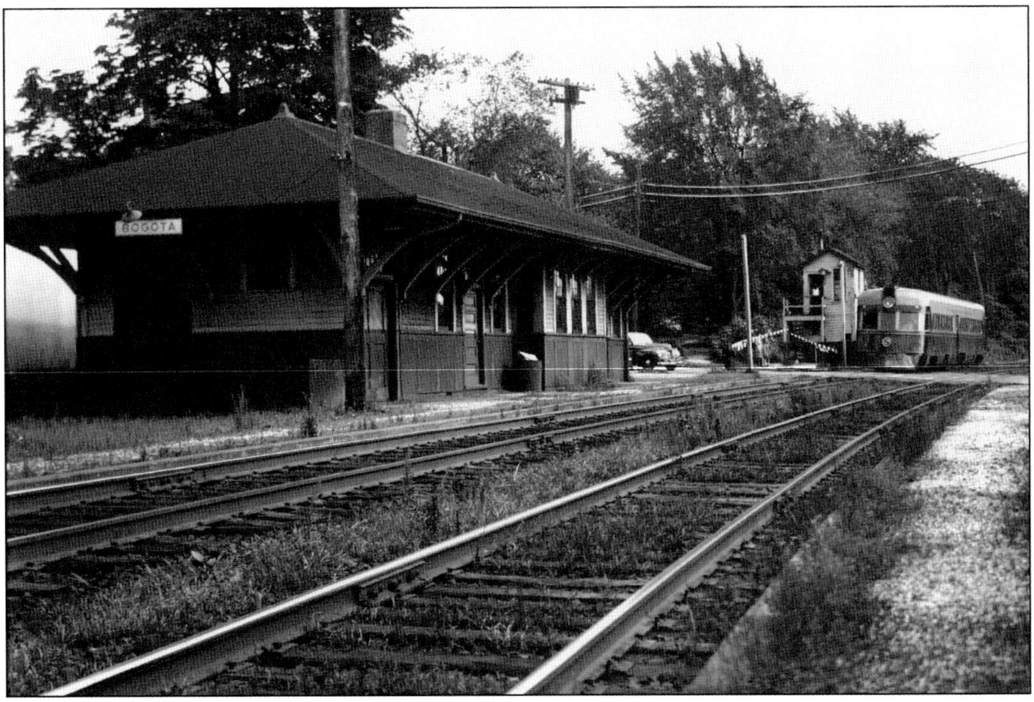

American Car & Foundry–built Motorailer NYS&W No. 1002 glides toward Bogota station, working westbound, in this view taken in July 1945. The Motorailer's sleek exterior design and interior comfort created quite a splash among the NYS&W's regular commuters and helped bring new riders to the railroad. (Courtesy of Railroad Avenue Enterprises; author's collection.)

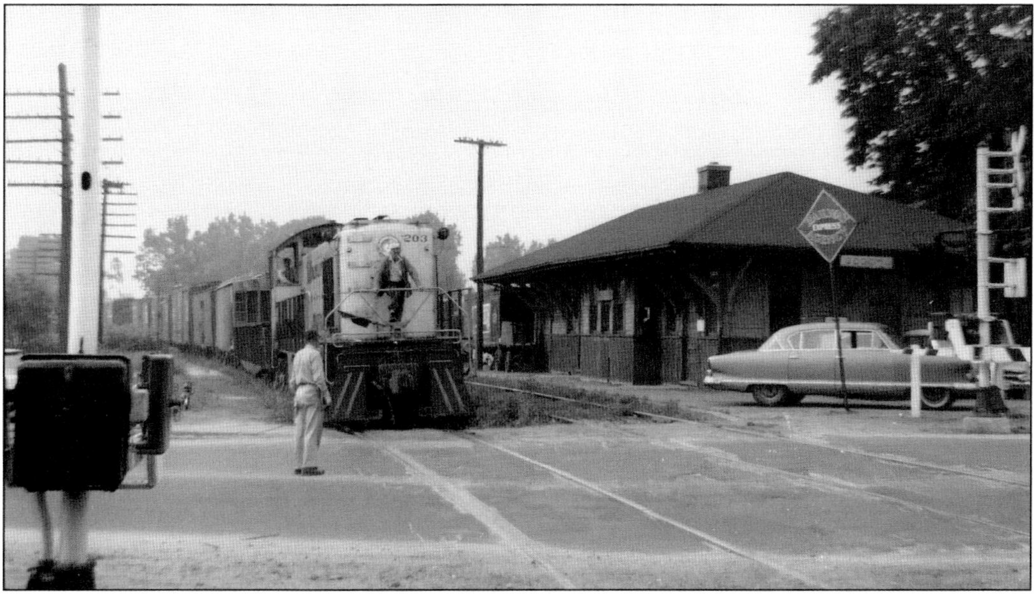

NYS&W S-2 No. 203 is shown working east with a local freight as it is about to cross Fort Lee Road at Bogota station on June 8, 1961 in this view. At this date, Railway Express Agency shipments to and from the station were handled on a daily basis. Today, the station still exists and is privately owned but has been greatly altered from the appearance in this photograph. (Courtesy of Railroad Avenue Enterprises; author's collection.)

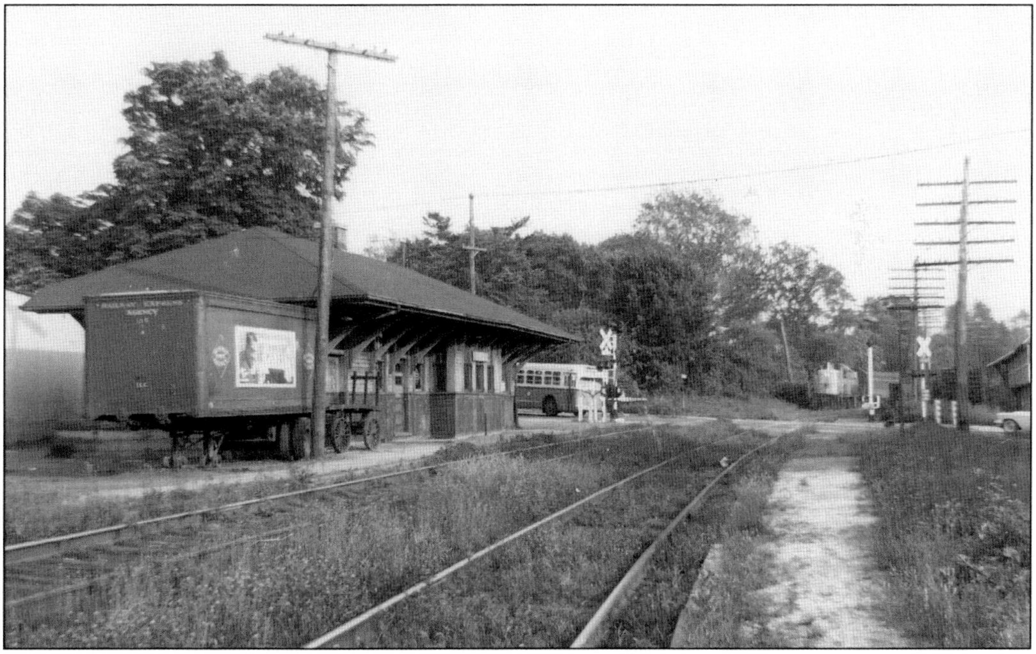

Bogota station is the subject of this image taken in July 1961 as a westbound NYS&W passenger train is about to cross Fort Lee Road. Many historic details are in this photograph: the Public Service bus stopped at the crossing; the Railway Express Agency trailer and baggage cart at the station; and the telephone/former telegraph pole that is prominent at the rear of the station. (Courtesy of Railroad Avenue Enterprises; author's collection.)

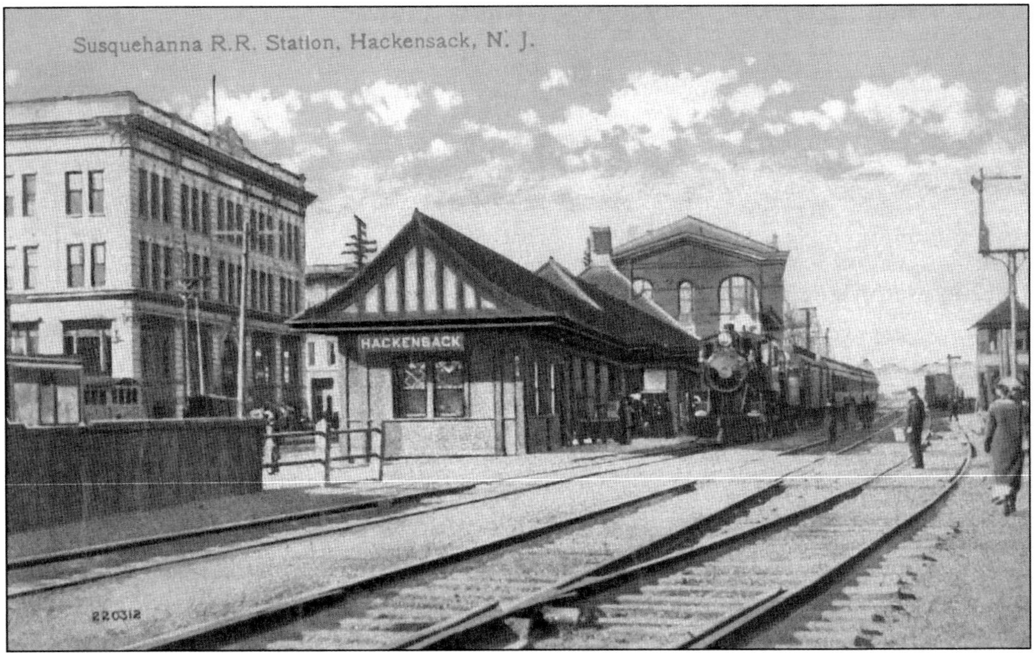

The brick Main Street Hackensack station replaced an earlier wood-built station at this location and was the subject of several postcards from the early 1900s to 1920s. This postcard view dates from 1920 and shows an eastbound five-car passenger train arriving at the station with a baggage/mail car behind one of the NYS&W 4-6-0 camelback-type steam locomotives. (Author's collection.)

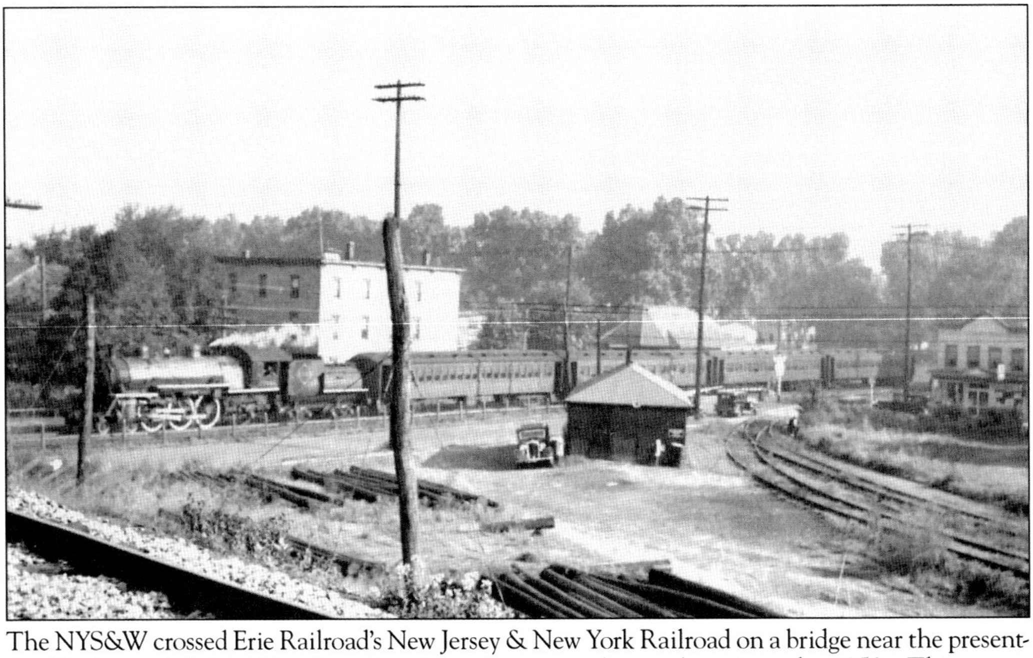

The NYS&W crossed Erie Railroad's New Jersey & New York Railroad on a bridge near the present-day Hackensack High School, and an interchange track was there into the 1950s. This scene, taken on August 3, 1938, from the NYS&W embankment, shows Erie 4-6-2 No. 2554 heading east to Jersey City with a passenger train about to cross underneath the NYS&W tracks. The interchange track is seen to the right. (Courtesy of the Maywood Station Museum Collection.)

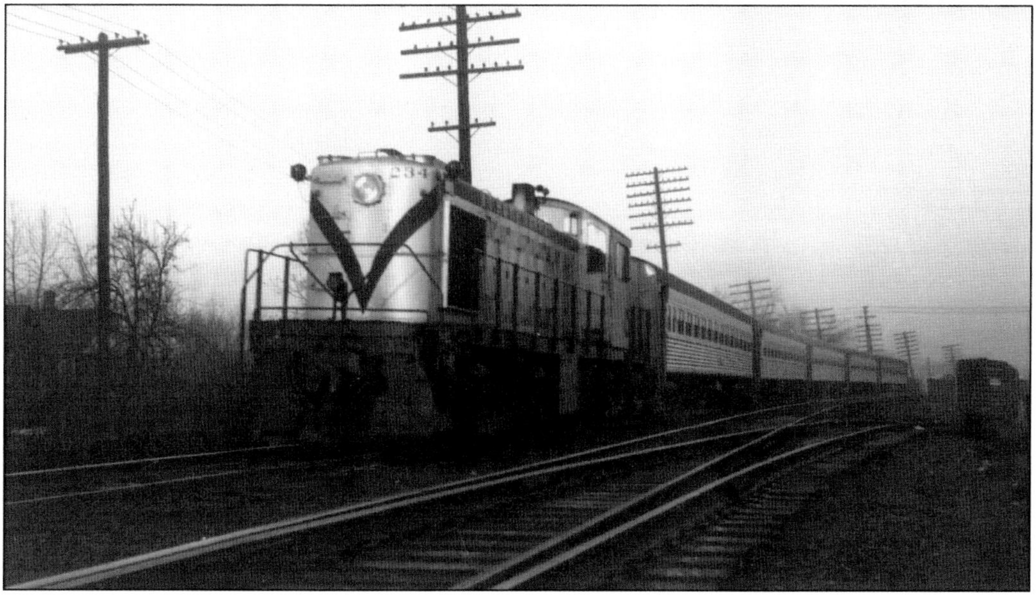

NYS&W RS-1 No. 234 rolls east through Hackensack with train No. 910 consisting of five Budd-built, 85-seat, stainless steel passenger cars in this scene taken on December 29, 1952. Note the unusual wide width and curvature of the nose striping and lack of the S-ball logo on the freshly painted No. 234. The boxcar on the right is on the interchange track with the Erie Railroad's New Jersey & New York Railroad near Union Street. (Photograph by John L. Treen; courtesy of Thomas J. Callan and the Maywood Station Museum Collection.)

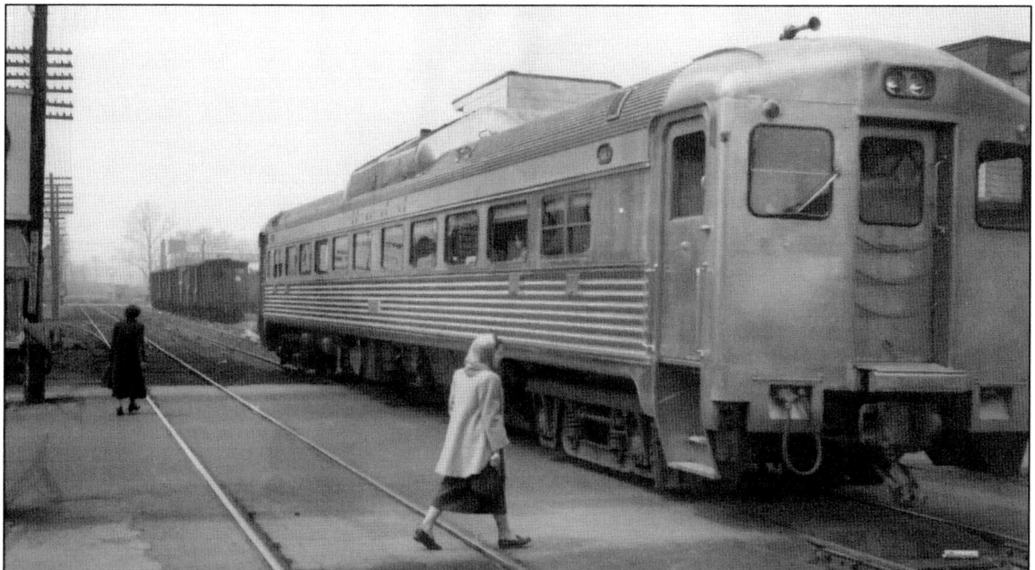

A Budd-built Rail Diesel Car (RDC) *Demonstrator* unit has just departed the Main Street station in Hackensack as a woman crosses the tracks in this view taken on April 27, 1950. The Budd-built RDCs were an immediate success, and the NYS&W placed an order for four shortly after the *Demonstrator* trial runs were concluded. (Photograph by John L. Treen; courtesy of Thomas J. Callan and the Maywood Station Museum Collection.)

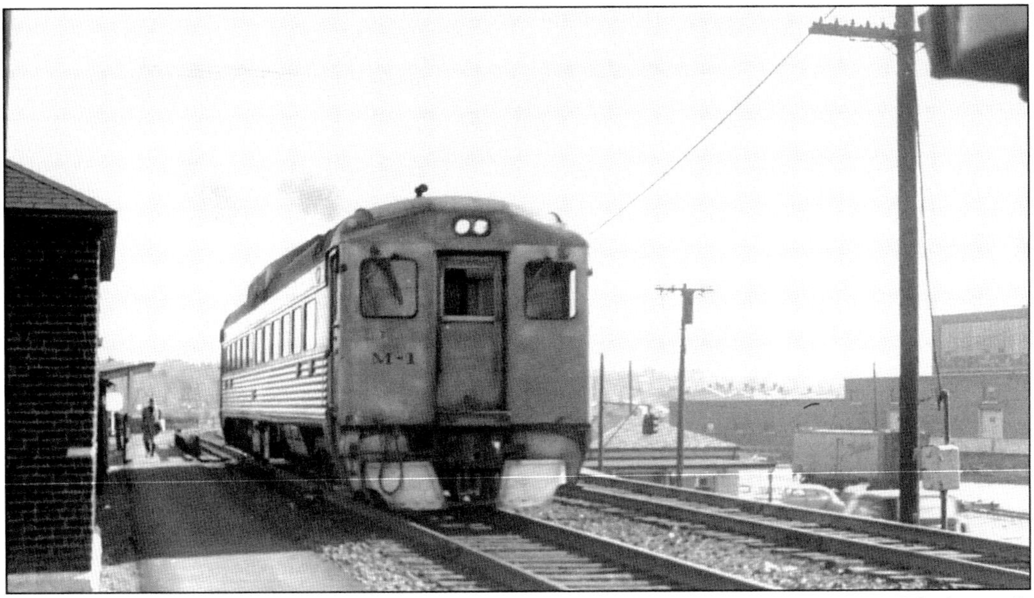

NYS&W Budd-built Rail Diesel Car M-1 has just arrived at the River Street station in Hackensack in this view taken in December 1957. While Hackensack never had a major industrial base that shipped by rail, the Bergen Evening Record newspaper plant built in the 1950s was a large receiver of paper products by rail for many years. A portion of the plant can be seen in the right distance. (Author's collection.)

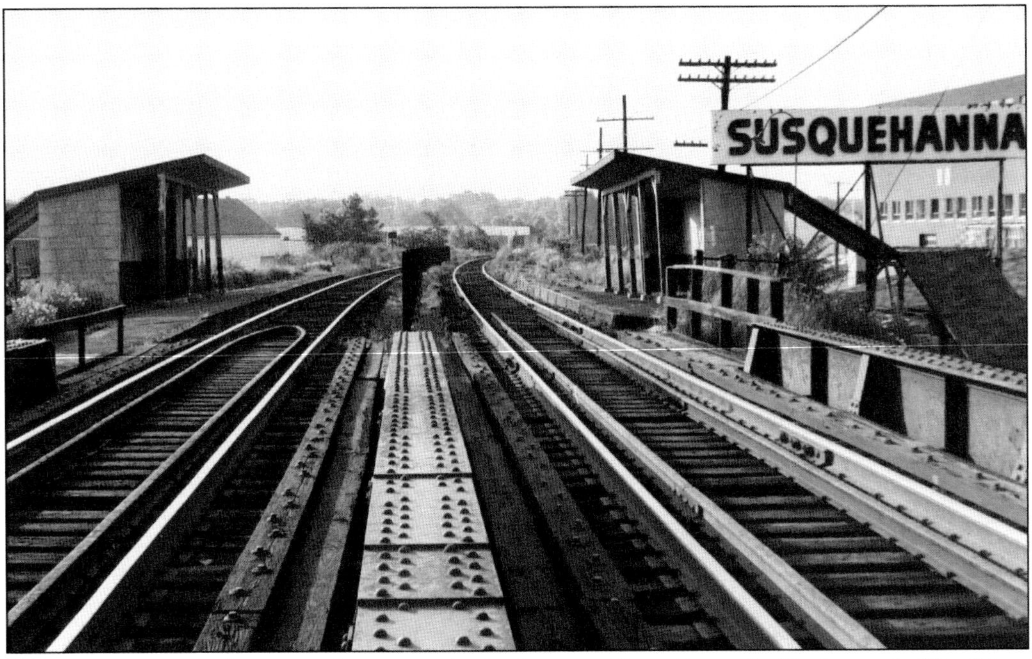

This neat view is looking east from atop the bridge over River Street in Hackensack. The River Street station was at street level, and stairs brought commuters up to track level, where waiting shelters were found on each side of the tracks. The large "Susquehanna" neon sign on the right was illuminated at night. A portion of the Bergen Evening Record plant is visible in the distance behind the sign. (Courtesy of Railroad Avenue Enterprises; author's collection.)

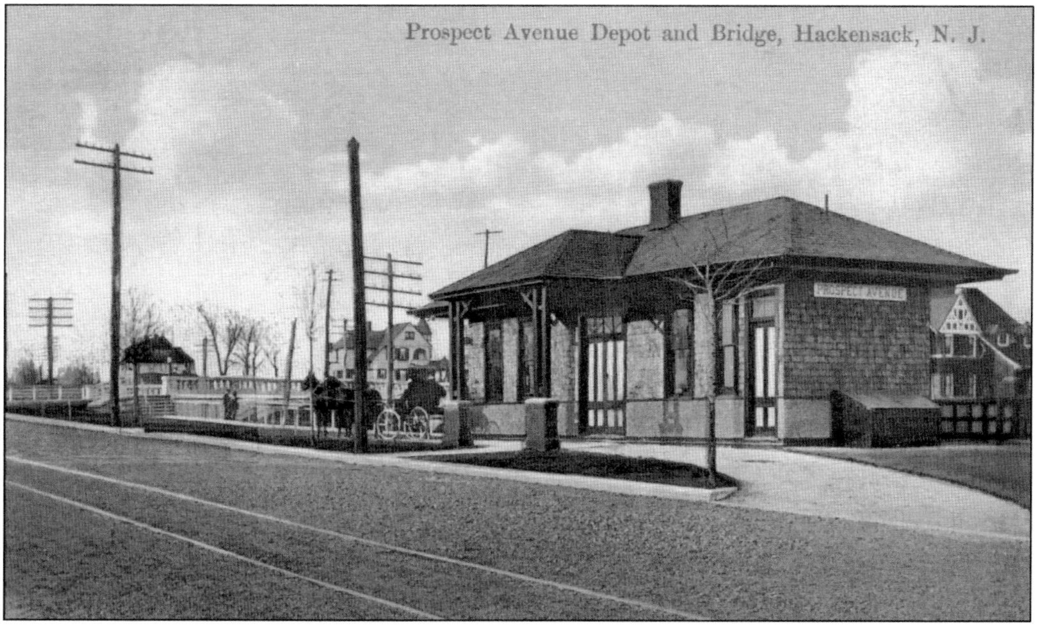

The Prospect Avenue station in Hackensack was very unique on the NYS&W. The station was built on street level with stairs leading down to track level, which was built through the Red Hill Cut. This postcard view dates from 1910. The tracks in the foreground belonged to the New Jersey & Hudson River Railway & Ferry Company, which operated a trolley line that paralleled the NYS&W through part of Hackensack until 1938 when it was abandoned. (Author's collection.)

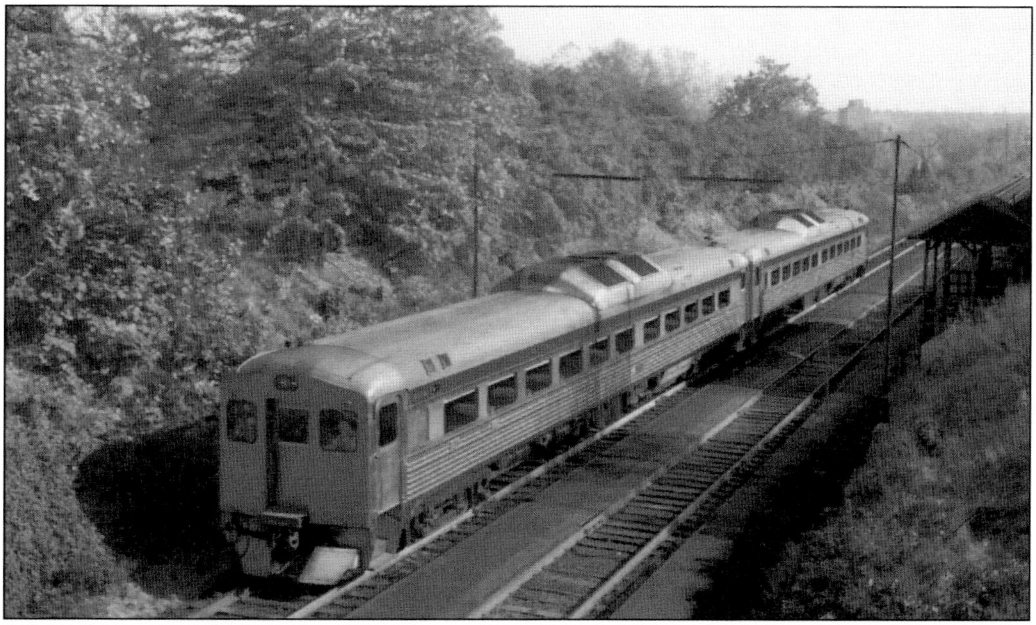

When the new Budd-built Rail Diesel Cars were delivered in 1950, they were posed in several locations along the NYS&W for publicity photographs. The most commonly used scenes in advertisements were those taken in the Red Hill Cut at the Prospect Avenue station in Hackensack. This view was adapted from one of the original publicity photographs of NYS&W M-1 and M-2 and was used as a postcard during the 1950s. (Author's collection.)

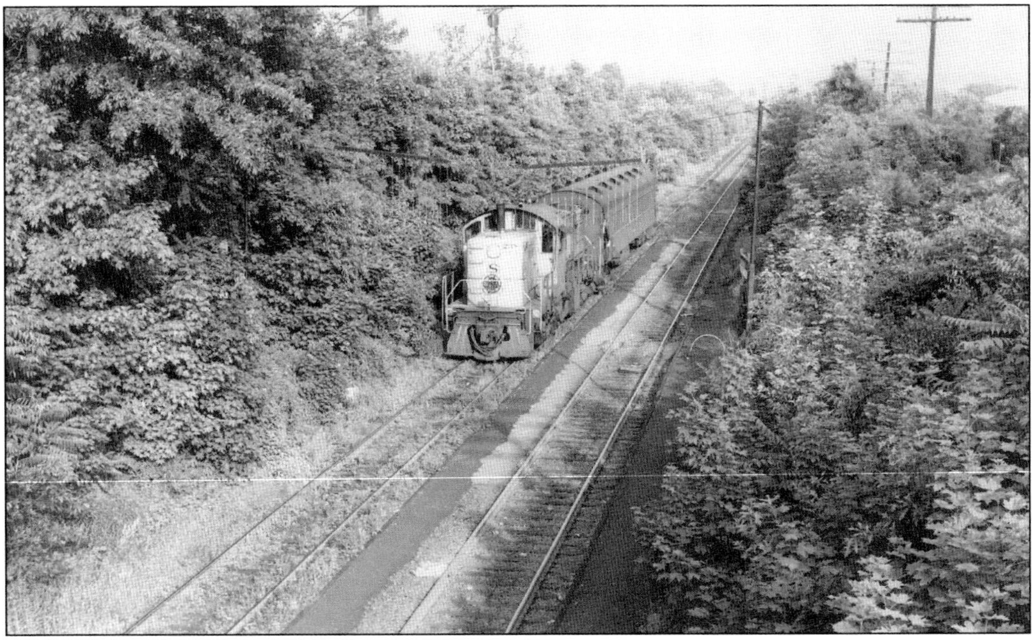

NYS&W RS-1 No. 238 is shown here, leading one passenger car westbound near the Prospect Avenue station in Hackensack during a late afternoon in July 1963. Just above No. 238 are "tell tales" hanging down to warn any crew member who may be riding on top of the train to duck, as they will be approaching a bridge and they might not have enough height clearance. (Author's collection.)

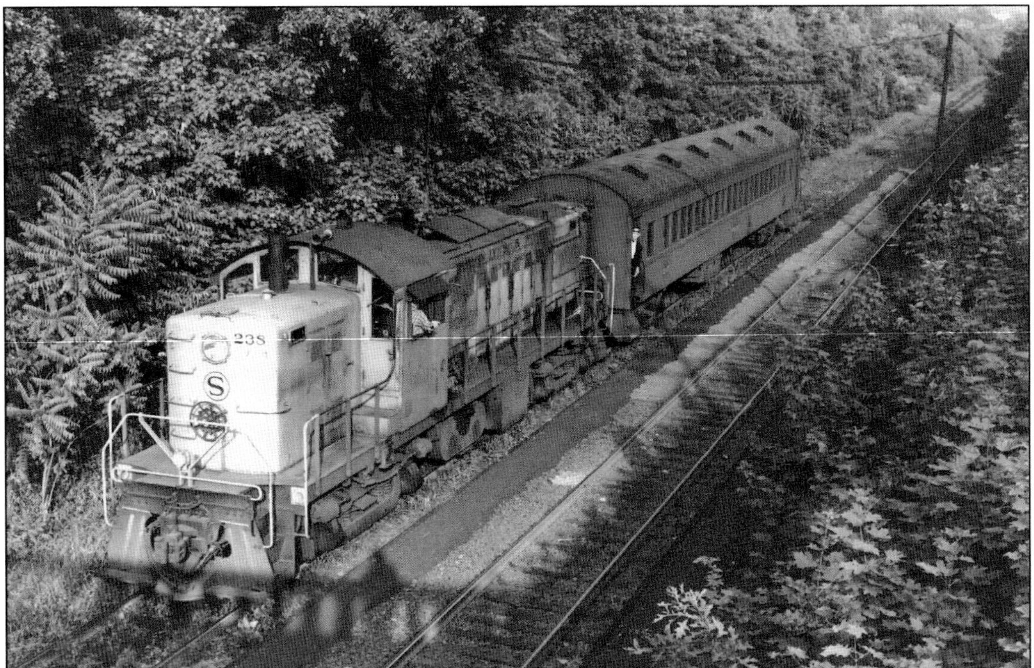

The same one-car passenger train led by NYS&W RS-1 No. 238, as seen in the previous photograph, is shown from a different angle as it works west from the Prospect Avenue station in Hackensack in July 1963. (Author's collection.)

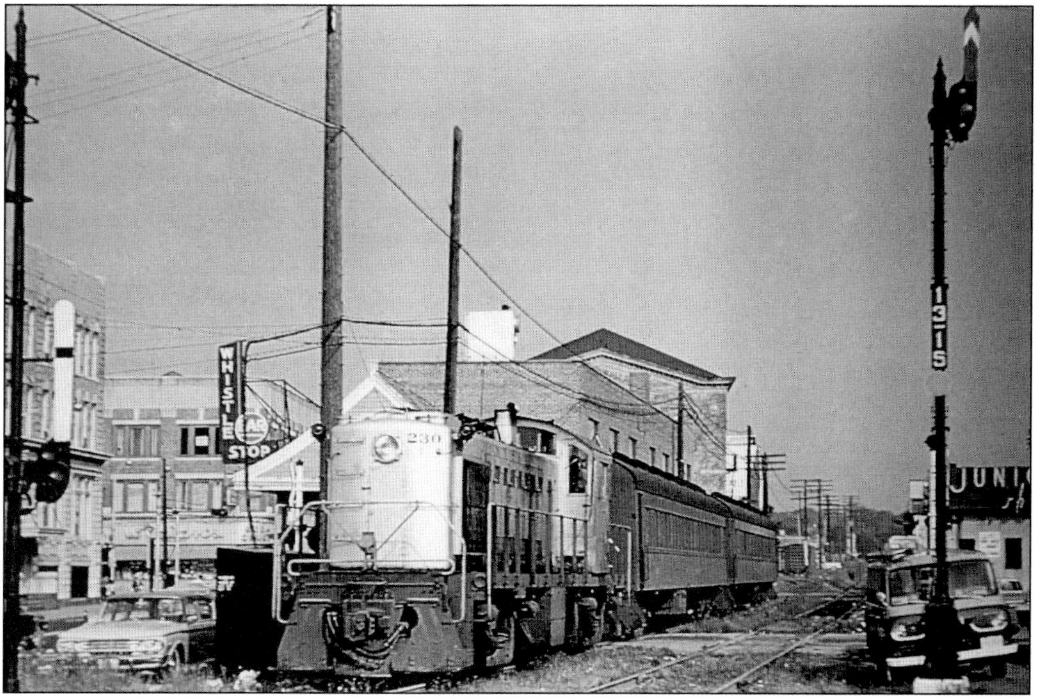

It is October 1964, and NYS&W RS-1 No. 230 has just crossed Main Street in Hackensack, heading east with a two-car passenger train. Visible in the photograph just above and to the left of the nose of No. 230 is part of the old NYS&W Main Street station. (Author's collection.)

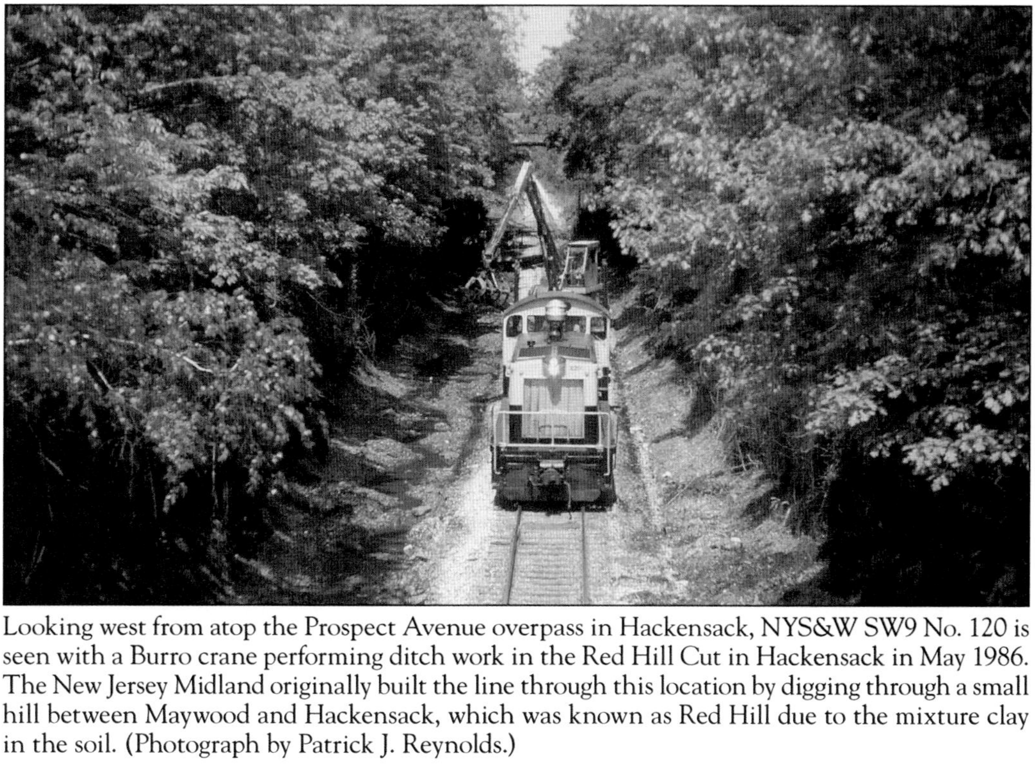

Looking west from atop the Prospect Avenue overpass in Hackensack, NYS&W SW9 No. 120 is seen with a Burro crane performing ditch work in the Red Hill Cut in Hackensack in May 1986. The New Jersey Midland originally built the line through this location by digging through a small hill between Maywood and Hackensack, which was known as Red Hill due to the mixture clay in the soil. (Photograph by Patrick J. Reynolds.)

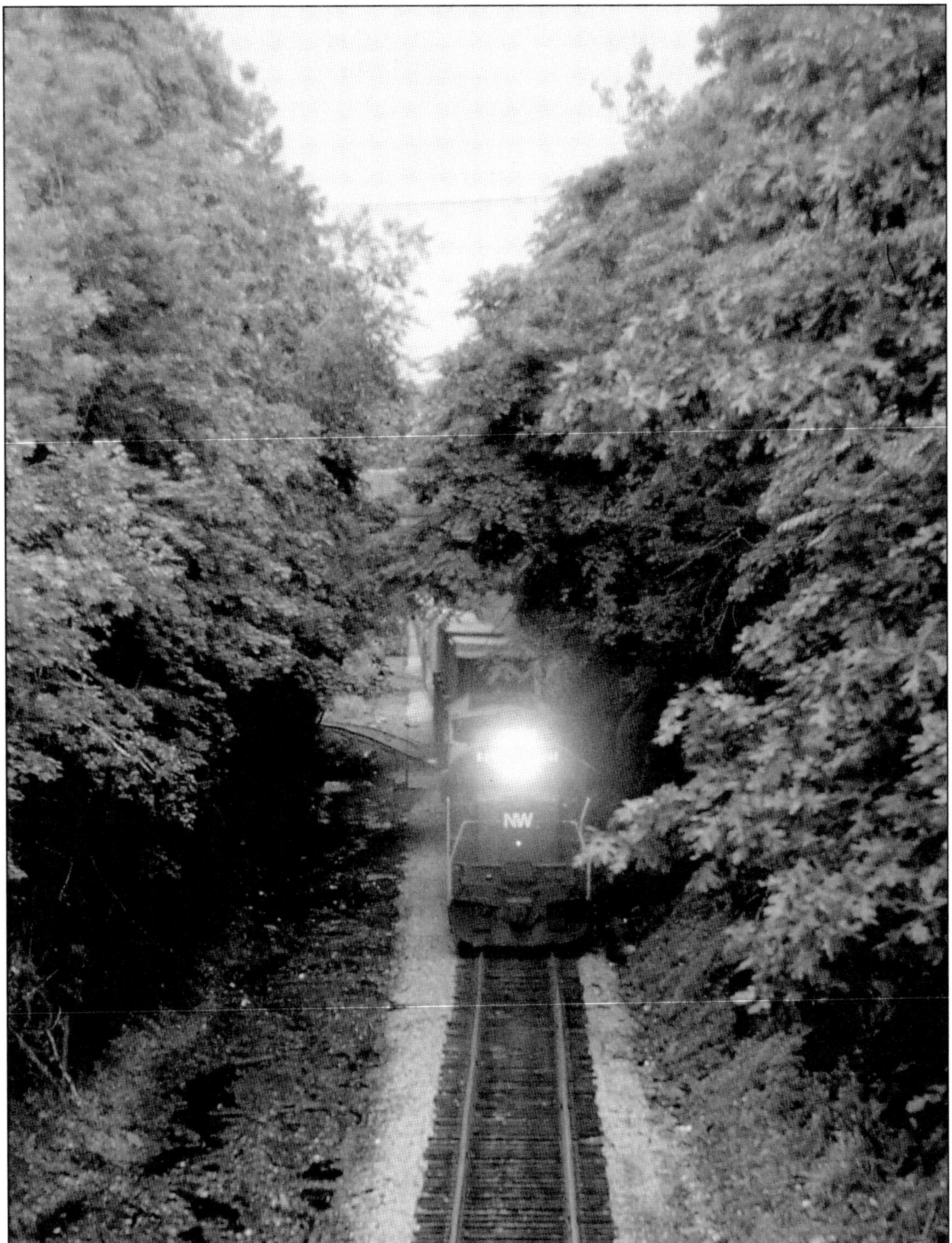

In this view looking west from the Summit Avenue overpass in Hackensack, a Norfolk & Western C30-7 leads and intermodal train eastbound en route to Little Ferry in August 1988. Visible to the left of the first car is the switch for the Lodi branch, which originally ran off in a southerly direction for approximately 3 miles into the borough of Lodi. (Photograph by Patrick J. Reynolds.)

Three

Maywood to Elmwood Park (East Paterson)

The NYS&W continues west out of Hackensack towards Maywood through a cut, and the Lodi branch (originally the Hackensack & Lodi Railroad) begins at a location known as Lodi Junction and heading in a south direction. Maywood is a residential area, but it has industry near the NYS&W tracks, including the Maywood Chemical Works (today Stepan Chemical), with its 2400-foot siding that begins in Rochelle Park and Malt Products located just west of Lodi Junction. The first grade heading west from Jersey City begins near the Hackensack River bridge in Hackensack and crests at Maywood Avenue in Maywood. The ruling grade is 0.79 percent. Heading west from Maywood, the NYS&W enters Rochelle Park as it travels under the New Jersey State Route 17 highway overpass. The 1872-built Rochelle Park station was rebuilt by the NYS&W in the late 1980s and now serves as their southern division offices. Rochelle Park has limited industry, and what there is has been in the vicinity near the station, including a grain and coal company.

Immediately leaving Rochelle Park, the NYS&W continues west under Interstate Route 80, which was built in the mid-1960s and enters Passaic Junction yard in the township of Saddle Brook. Passaic Junction is also known as "BT" for Bergen Transfer, where an interchange was conducted with the Erie and, later, Erie Lackawanna Railway. Passaic Junction was also the site of Coalburg yard, which had 10 trimmers and storage capacity for anthracite coal. Coalburg was built in the 1904–1908 period and was replaced by the coal facility in Edgewater by the mid-1930s. Proceeding in a westerly direction, the NYS&W crosses under the Erie Railroad (now New Jersey Transit) and enters Elmwood Park (formerly known as East Paterson until 1973) before entering Passaic County. Elmwood Park is mainly residential but has had its share of industry located within its borders, most notably the large Marcal Paper Products plant on the western end of town.

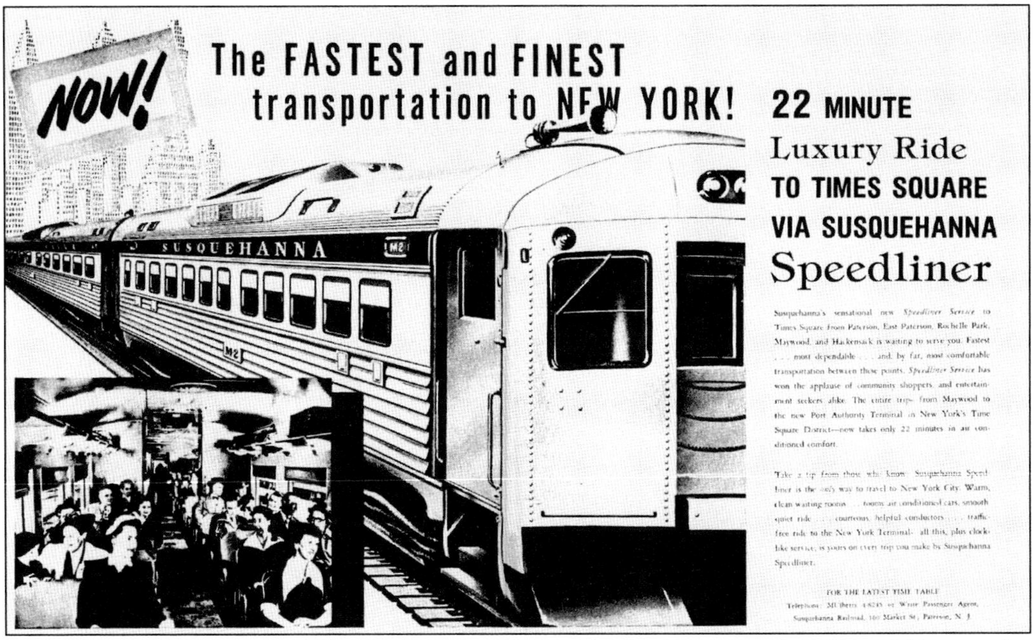

The four new NYS&W Budd-built Rail Diesel Cars that were acquired in late 1950 were the theme of several advertisements. This advertisement boasts the luxury and speed of the new self-propelled cars, including an air-conditioned trip to Times Square in New York City from Maywood—in only 22 minutes. (Author's collection.)

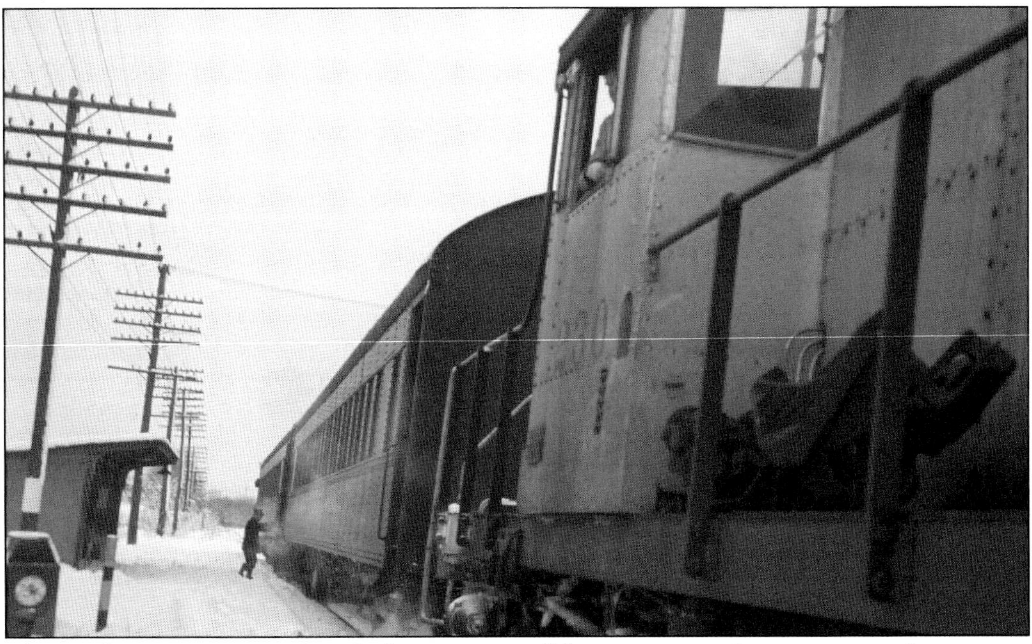

The conductor prepares to board after ensuring all his commuters have gotten on his two-car eastbound passenger train led by NYS&W RS-1 No. 230 in this scene taken in Maywood on a cold and snowy February 20, 1964. The passenger shelter for eastbound passenger trains is shown to the left. (Photograph by George Berisso; courtesy of Thomas J. Callan and the Maywood Station Museum Collection.)

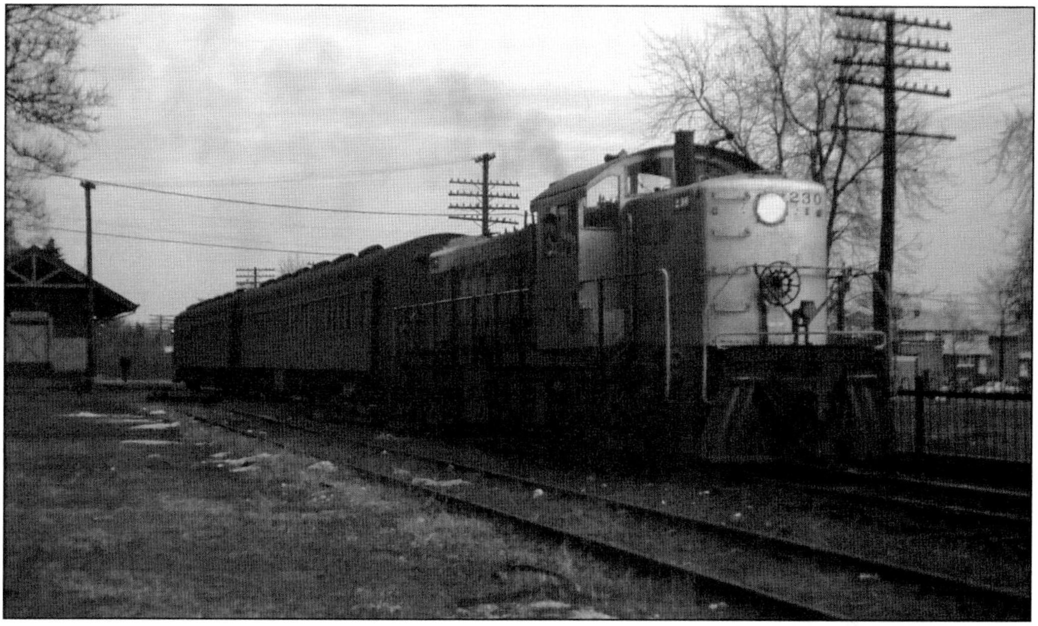

The engineer looks back at his two-car passenger train led by NYS&W RS-1 No. 230 and gets ready to depart Maywood Station, westbound in this view recorded on a gloomy March 31, 1964. Maywood station's siding track is visible in the foreground of the photograph. It once extended 440 feet and was used to load and unload freight cars for local consignees. (Photograph by George Berisso; courtesy of Thomas J. Callan and the Maywood Station Museum Collection.)

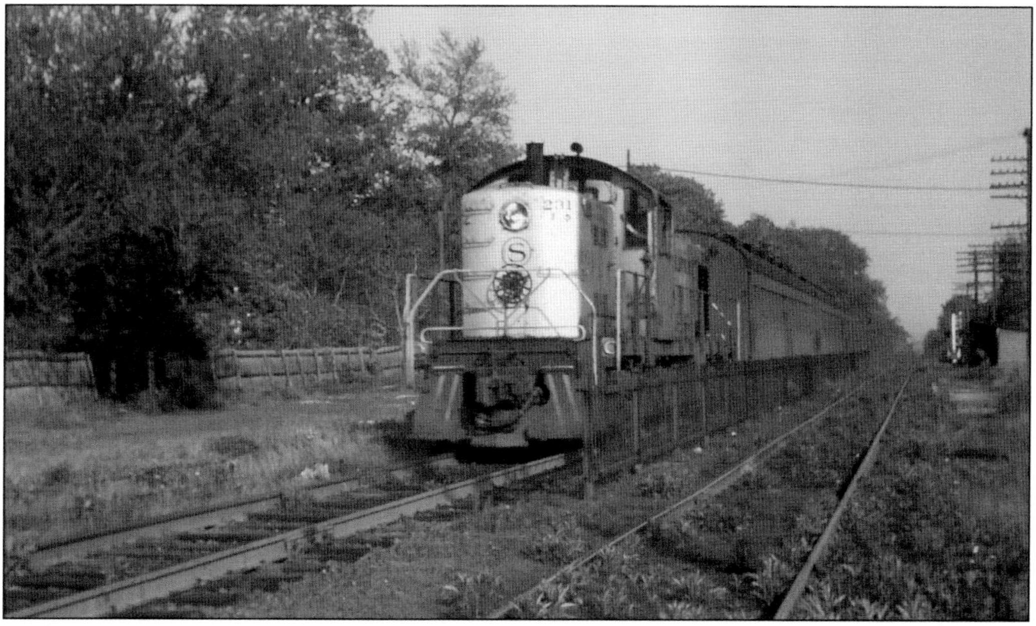

In this view taken on a sunny May 20, 1964, NYS&W RS-1 No. 231 makes its way west with Train No. 923's two-passenger cars after just leaving Maywood station. The vegetation growth between the rails is a sign of the deferred maintenance that the railroad was conducting at the time in order to survive. (Photograph by George Berisso; courtesy of Thomas J. Callan and the Maywood Station Museum Collection.)

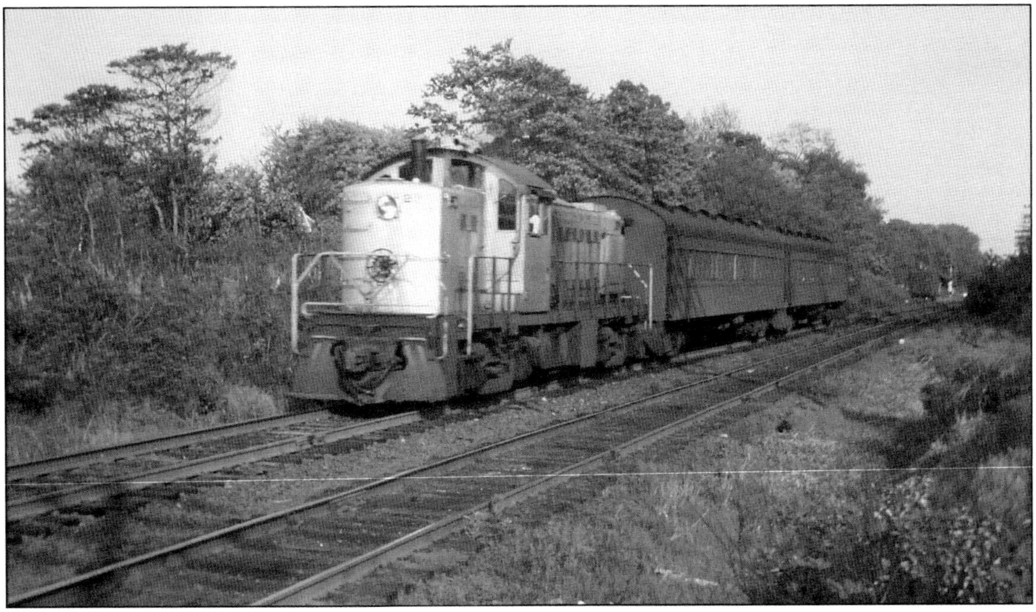

In this scene looking east on May 20, 1964, NYS&W RS-1 No. 230 has just departed Maywood and is heading west with its two-car passenger train. Just visible in the distance is Maywood station, and a boxcar can be seen on the station siding. (Photograph by George Berisso; courtesy of Thomas J. Callan and the Maywood Station Museum Collection.)

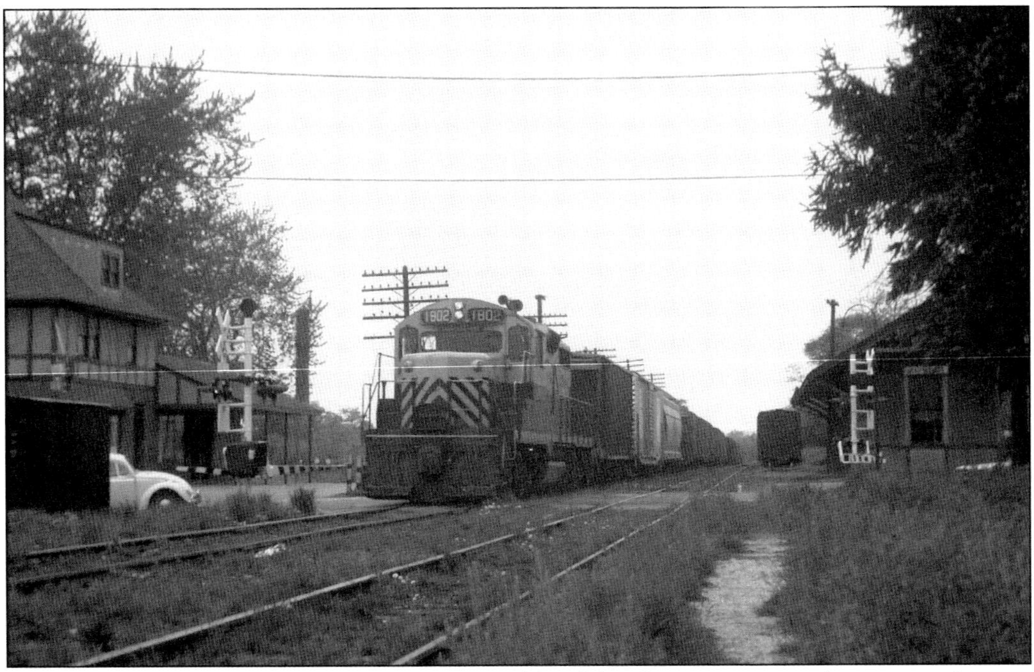

NYS&W GP18 No. 1802 leads a long eastbound local freight past Maywood station and across Maywood Avenue in this perspective shot on May 21, 1967. In the distance, a boxcar sits on the Maywood station siding. At this date, the railroad is providing freight service only. The NYS&W ceased passenger operations on June 30, 1966. (Photograph by George Berisso; courtesy of Thomas J. Callan and the Maywood Station Museum Collection.)

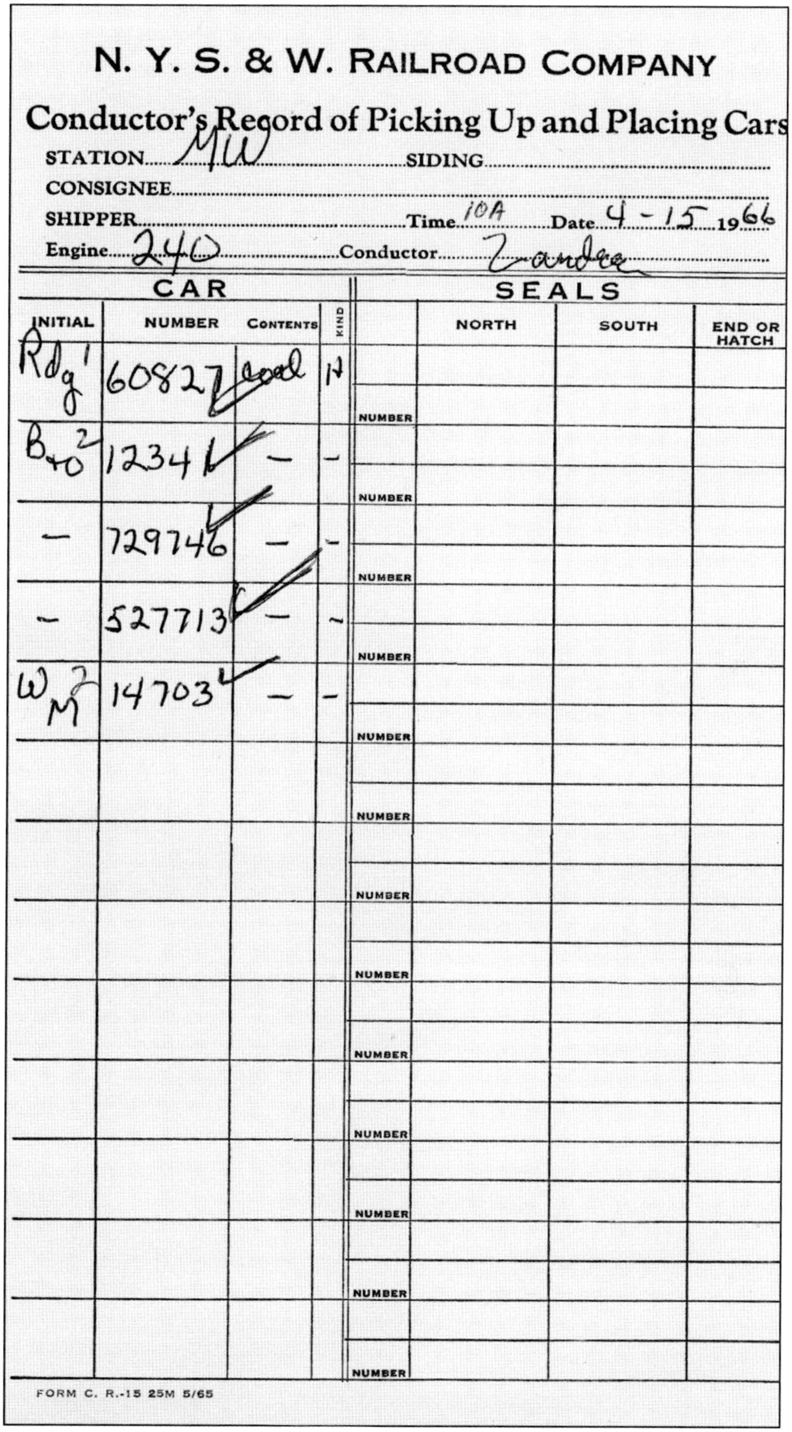

N. Y. S. & W. RAILROAD COMPANY

Conductor's Record of Picking Up and Placing Cars

STATION MW SIDING

CONSIGNEE

SHIPPER Time 10A Date 4-15 1966

Engine 240 Conductor Zandee

CAR				SEALS			
INITIAL	NUMBER	CONTENTS	KIND		NORTH	SOUTH	END OR HATCH
Rdg 1	60827	coal	H	NUMBER			
B+O 2	12341	–	–	NUMBER			
–	729746	–	–	NUMBER			
–	527713	–	–	NUMBER			
WM 2	14703	–	–	NUMBER			
				NUMBER			
				NUMBER			
				NUMBER			
				NUMBER			
				NUMBER			
				NUMBER			
				NUMBER			
				NUMBER			
				NUMBER			

FORM C. R.-15 25M 5/65

This is an example of an NYS&W "Conductor's Record of Picking Up and Placing Cars" filled out at 10 a.m. on April 15, 1966, at Maywood. According to the report, NYS&W RS-1 No. 240 and its crew set out five coal hoppers on the Maywood station siding that morning. (Courtesy of Kevin Quinn and the Maywood Station Museum Collection.)

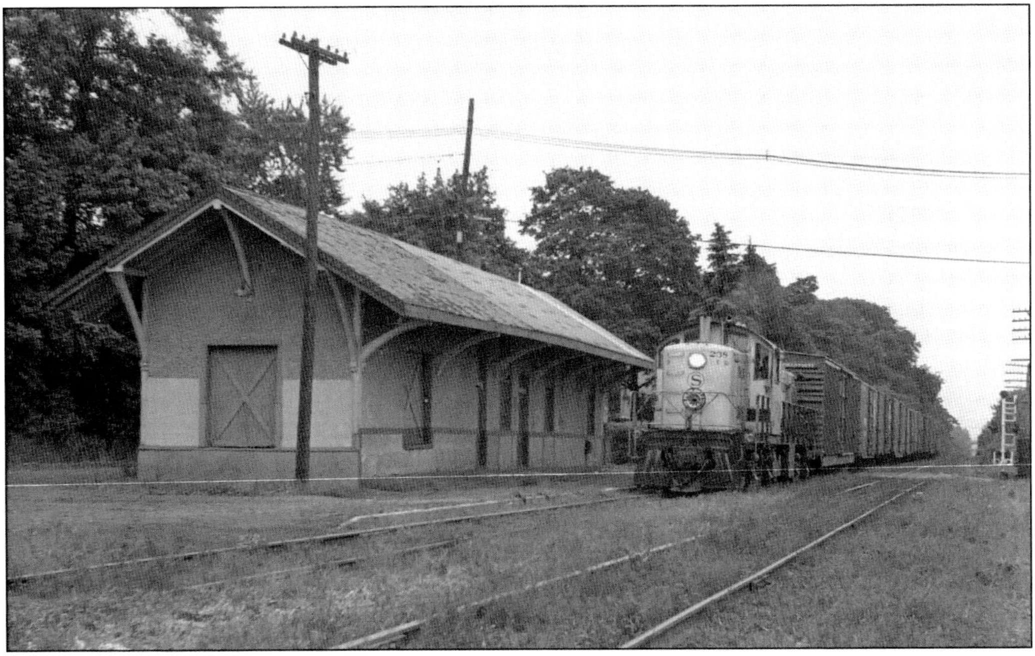

NYS&W RS-1 No. 238 proceeds west with its local freight as it passes Maywood station in July 1968. The station is vacant and beginning to show signs of neglect, judging by the condition of its roof. The tracks are overgrown with weeds, a sign of deferred maintenance by the railroad. (Photograph by John Krause; author's collection.)

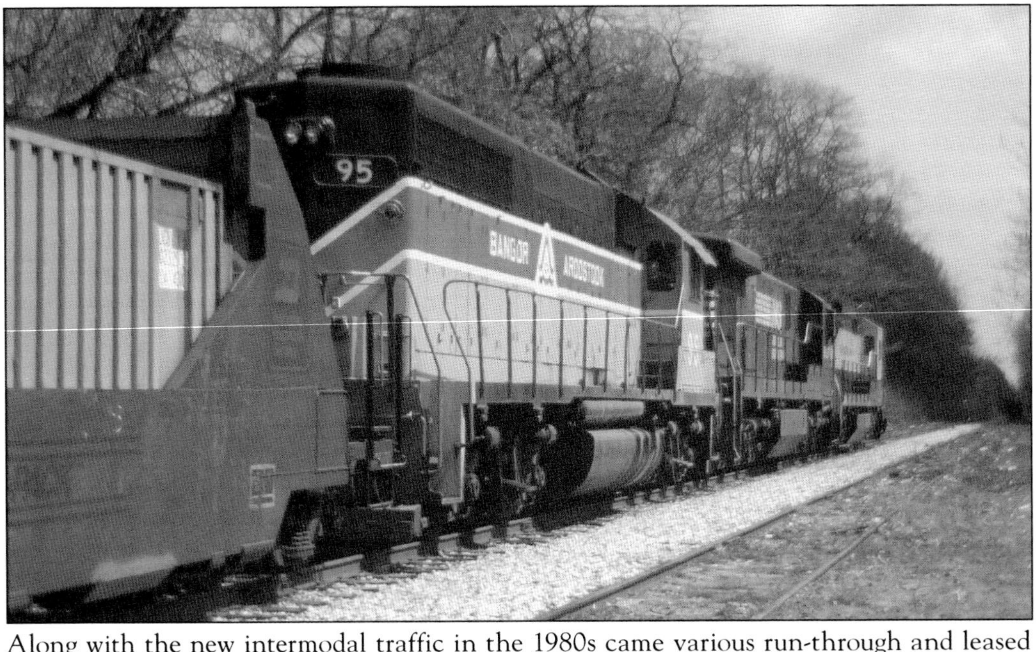

Along with the new intermodal traffic in the 1980s came various run-through and leased locomotives. This intermodal train led by a NYS&W B40-8 brought with it a Norfolk Southern C30-7 and Bangor & Aroostook GP38 No. 95 as it heads east through Maywood in December 1988. A portion of the second mainline track is still visible, although it is out of service and would be removed shortly afterward. (Photograph by Patrick J. Reynolds.)

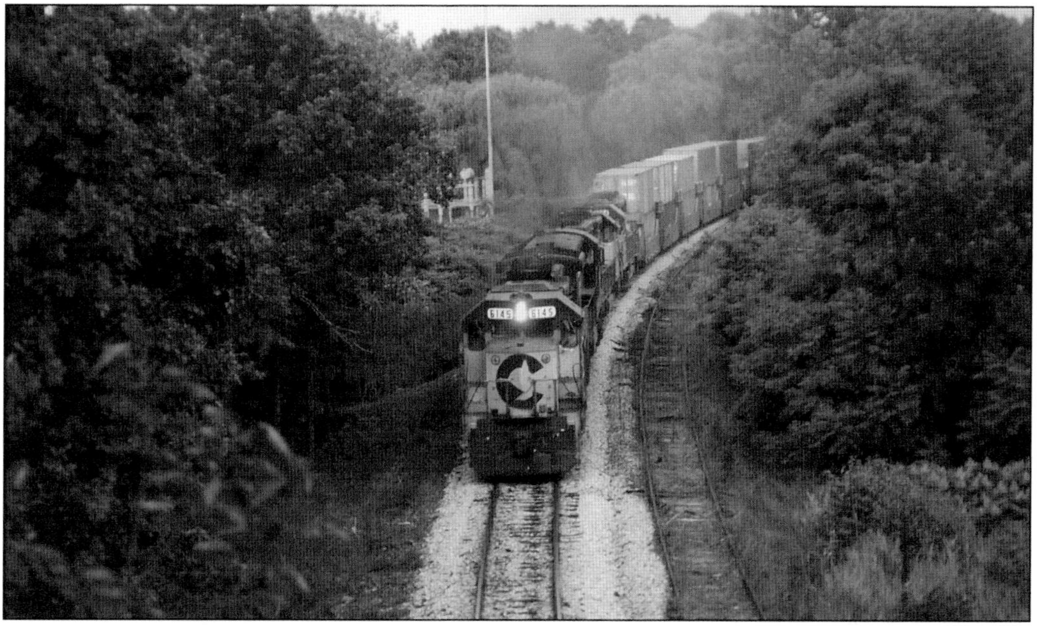

Chessie System GP40-2 No. 6145 leads an intermodal train westbound through Maywood as it approaches Rochelle Park in this view taken in July 1987. The photograph was taken looking east toward Maywood from the Route 17 overpass at the Maywood/Rochelle Park border. (Photograph by Patrick J. Reynolds.)

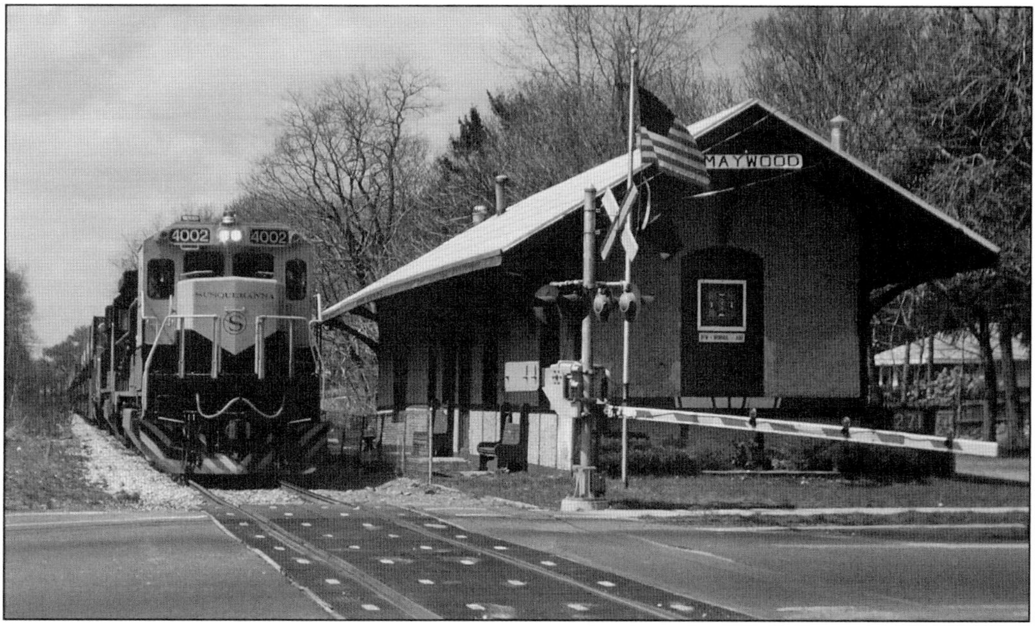

NYS&W B40-8 No. 4002 leads an intermodal train eastbound past Maywood station in this view taken in December 1988. Maywood station, built 1872, has been recently restored by the all-volunteer, 501C3 nonprofit Maywood Station Historical Committee Division of the New York, Susquehanna & Western Technical & Historical Society and now operates as a museum. At the time of this photograph, the station was leased by the Veterans of Foreign Wars Post No. 7408. (Photograph by Barbara Logue Reynolds.)

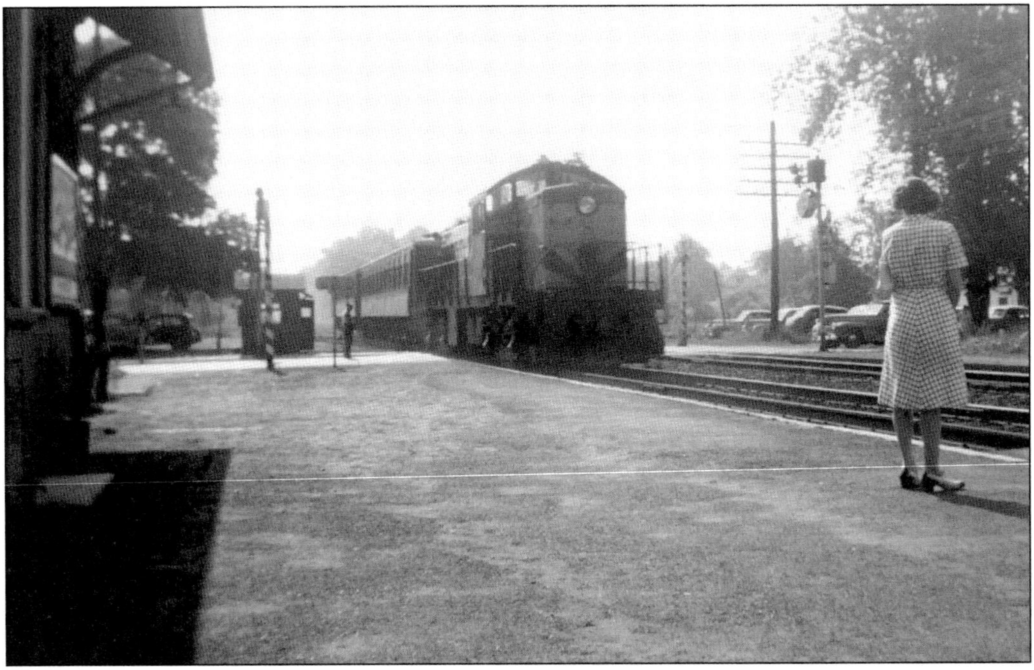

In this backlit photograph taken in July 1945, a woman waits to board a westbound passenger train led by NYS&W RS-1 No. 234 and two former Erie Railroad Stillwell coaches at Rochelle Park station. Note the guard shanty to the left of the first passenger car, which was used by the grade crossing guard. The guard can also be seen in the street, to the left of No. 234, halting automobile traffic. (Author's collection.)

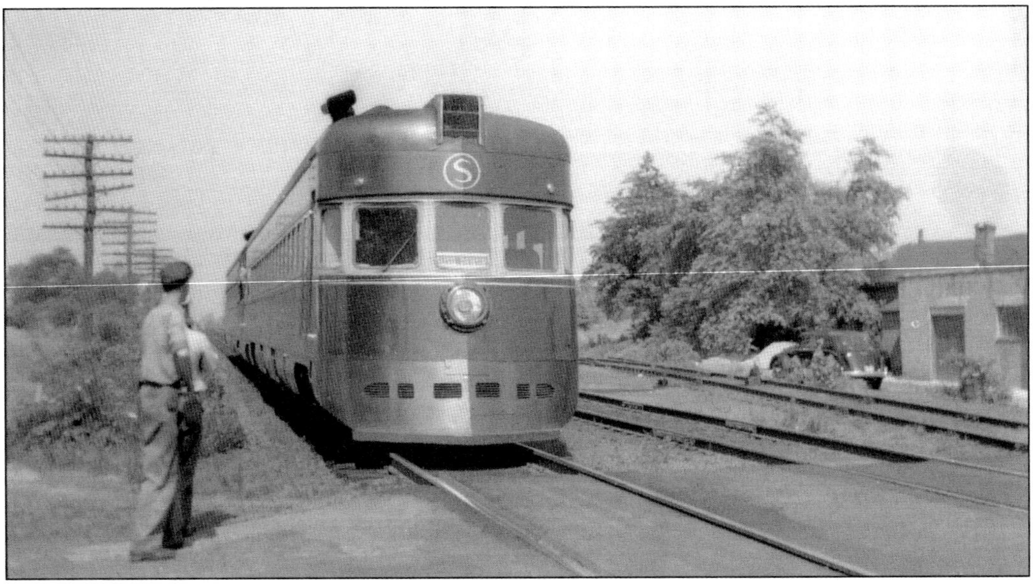

American Car & Foundry–built Motorailers, NYS&W Nos. 1005 and 1006 with train No. 818 are about to cross Saddle River Road in Rochelle Park as they work east on July 17, 1948. Interstate 80 was built through here in the 1960s and now crosses above the NYS&W tracks, making this scene hard to recognize. (Photograph by John L. Treen; courtesy of Thomas J. Callan and the Maywood Station Museum Collection.)

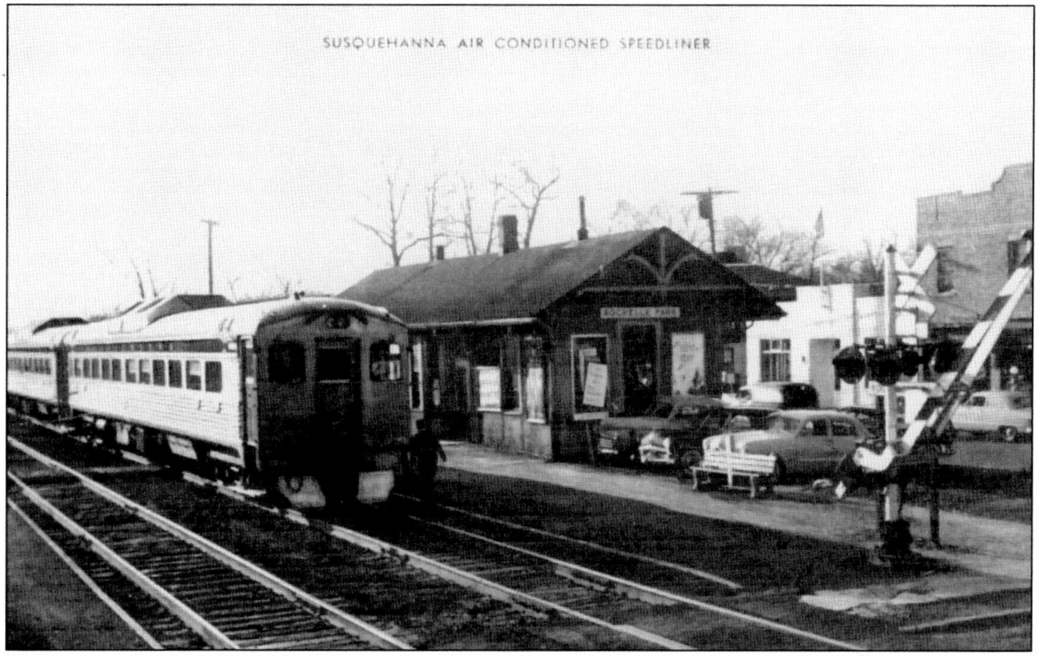

Two of the four NYS&W Budd-built Rail Diesel Cars are shown at Rochelle Park station in this 1951 photograph/postcard view. The RDCs usually ran as single units but occasionally would be run in pairs as needs dictated. (Author's collection.)

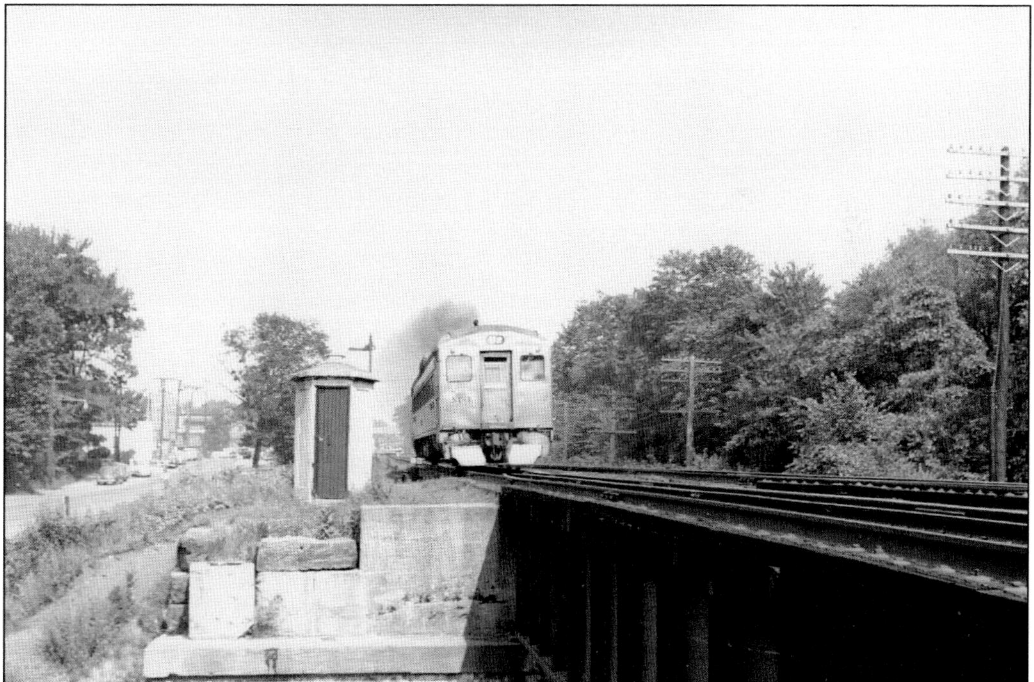

In this image photographed in June 1956, NYS&W Budd-built Rail Diesel Car M-1 is about to cross the bridge over the Saddle River in Rochelle Park as it proceeds westbound. Out of view, about 100 yards behind M-1, is Rochelle Park station. (Courtesy Maywood Station Museum Collection.)

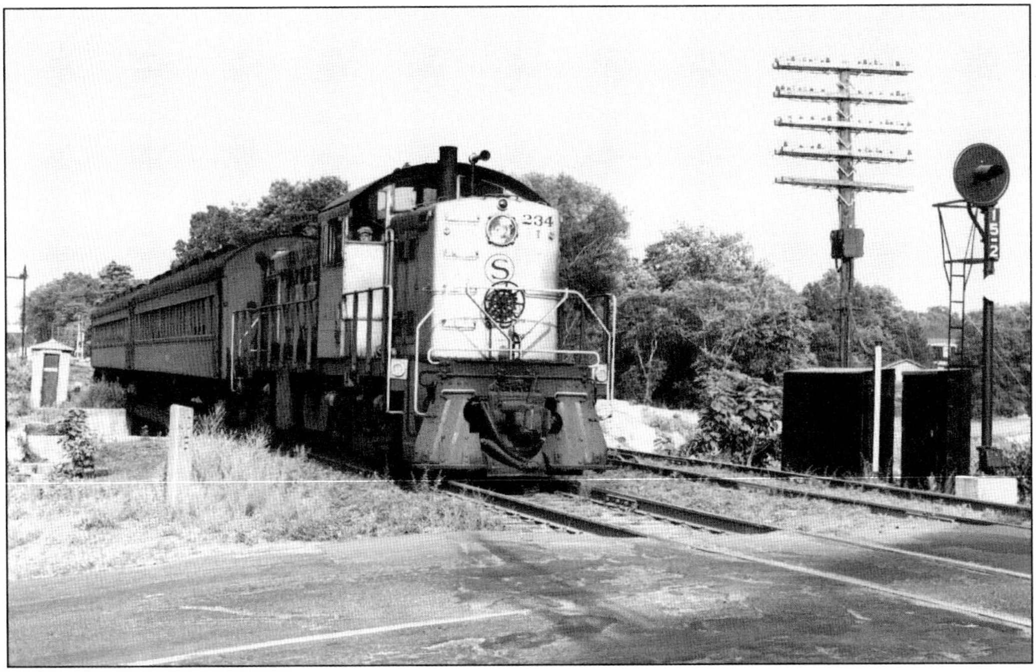

NYS&W RS-1 No. 234 leads two passenger cars westbound as it heads across the bridge over the Saddle River in Rochelle Park and is about to cross Saddle River Road in this image photographed in September 1964. (Author's collection.)

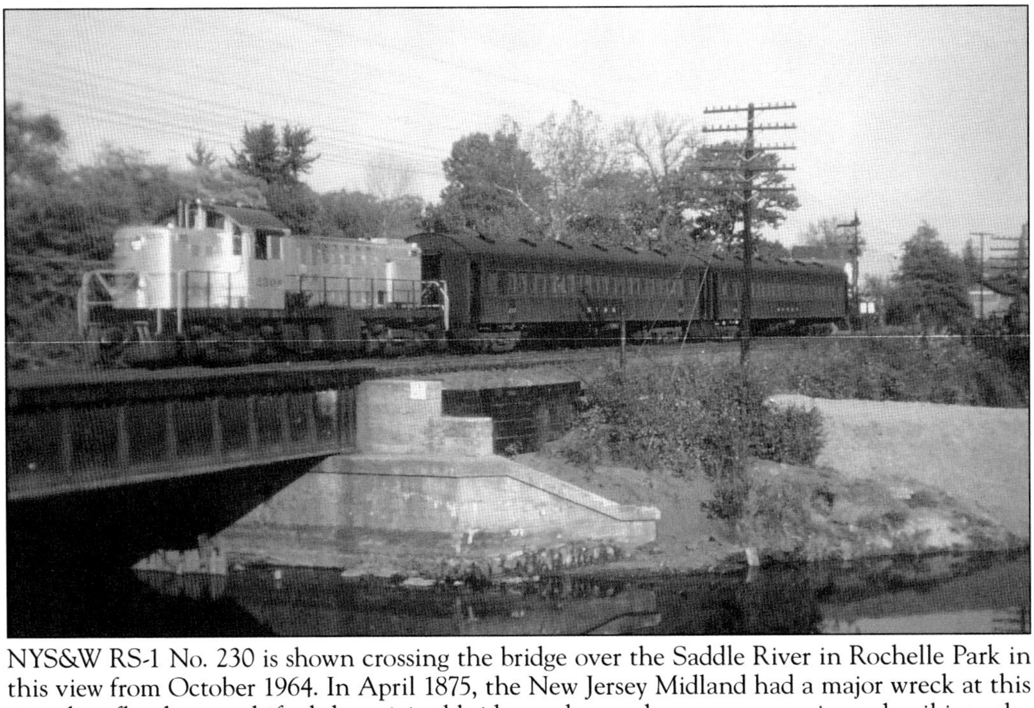

NYS&W RS-1 No. 230 is shown crossing the bridge over the Saddle River in Rochelle Park in this view from October 1964. In April 1875, the New Jersey Midland had a major wreck at this site when floodwaters shifted the original bridge and caused a passenger train to derail into the river. Just visible in the far right of the photograph is the Rochelle Park station and freight house. (Author's collection.)

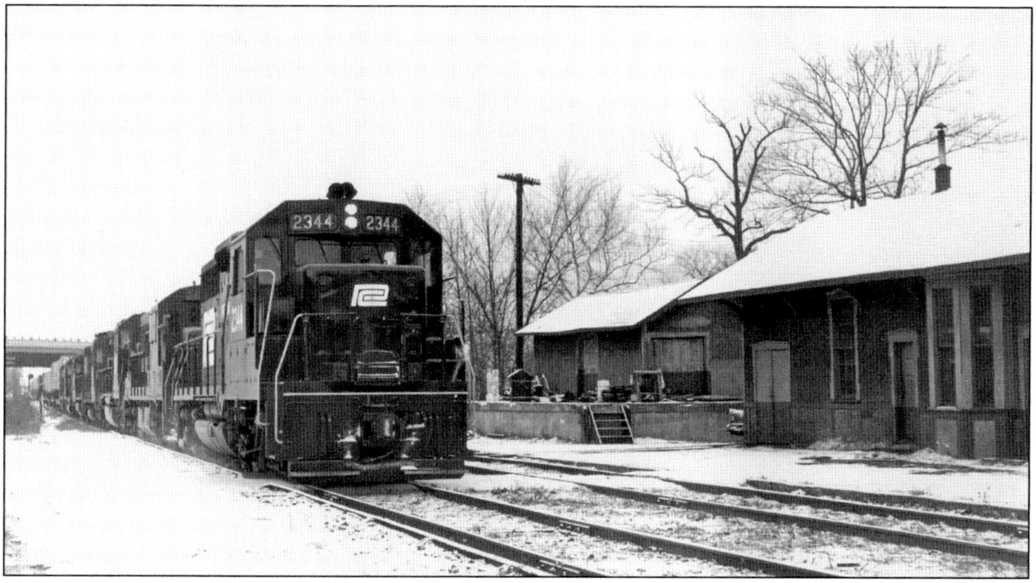

Penn Central GP35 No. 2344 leads six additional Penn Central locomotives and its train eastbound past Rochelle Park station on March 2, 1969. Due to a derailment on its own line in New York State, the hot piggyback train was detoured over the Erie Lackawanna from Maybrook, New York, to Passaic Junction in Saddle Brook and traveled NYS&W rails to Jersey City, where it regained Penn Central rails again. (Photograph by Donald P. Wallworth; author's collection.)

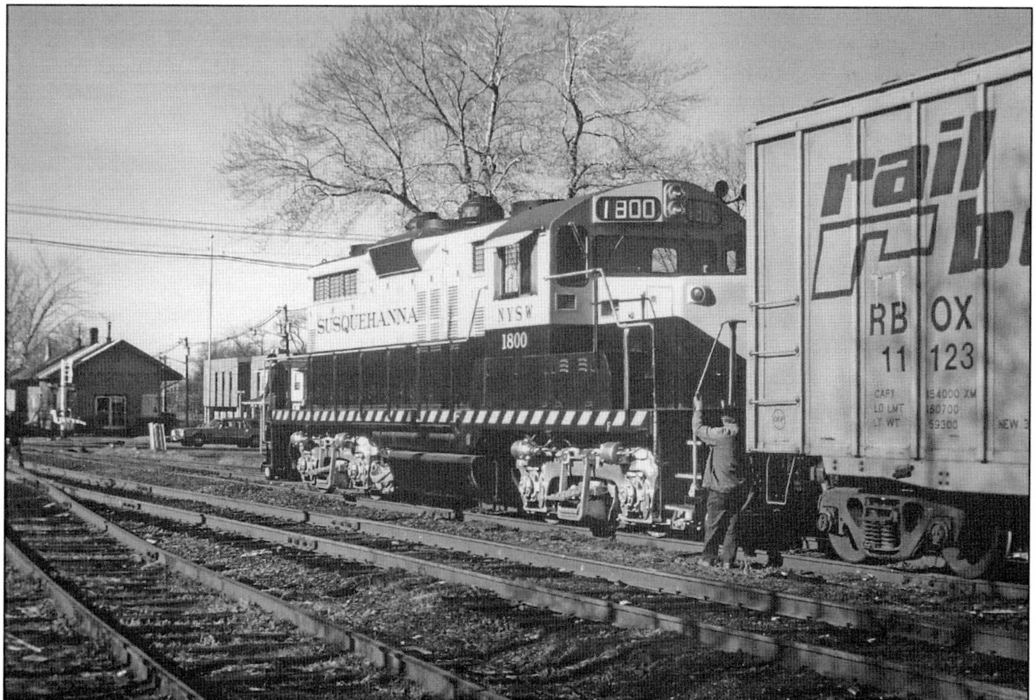

Freshly repainted NYS&W GP18 No. 1800 is shown performing a switching assignment in Rochelle Park in March 1979. In the background is the Rochelle Park station, which was built in 1872 and now serves as the NYS&W's southern division offices. (Photograph by Edwin D. Quinn.)

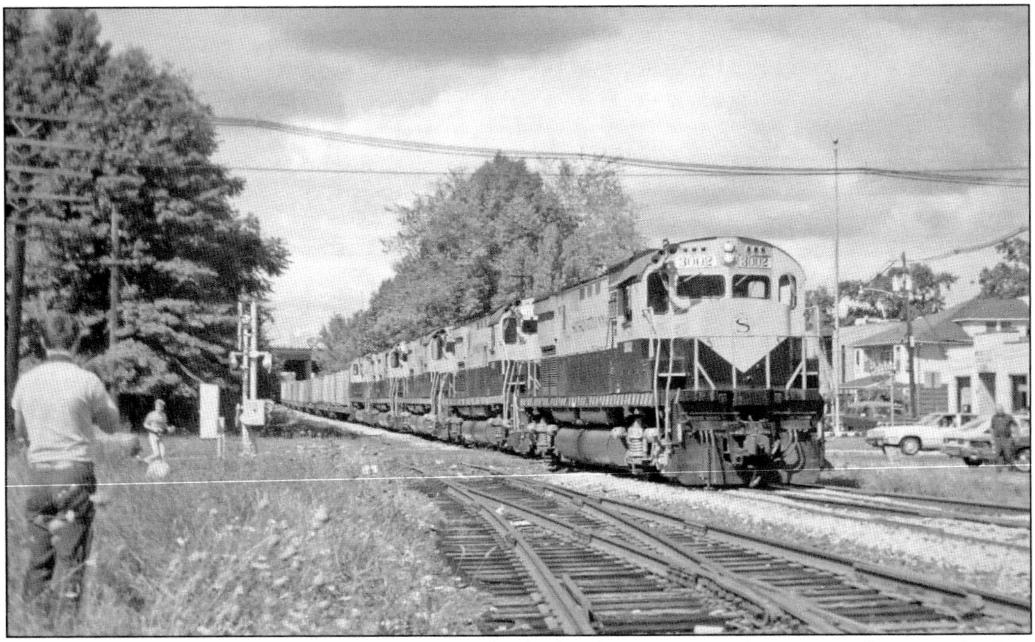

All five of NYS&W's fleet of ALCO C-430s lead a haulage train in this scene photographed in Rochelle Park in August 1985. In 1982, the NYS&W purchased the five C-430s from Conrail and repainted and renumbered them NYS&W Nos. 3000, 3002, 3004, 3006, and 3008. The train originated on the NYS&W in Binghamton, New York, and came east on Conrail trackage rights to Passaic Junction in Saddle Brook, where it regained NYS&W rails to its destination in Little Ferry. (Photograph by Patrick J. Reynolds.)

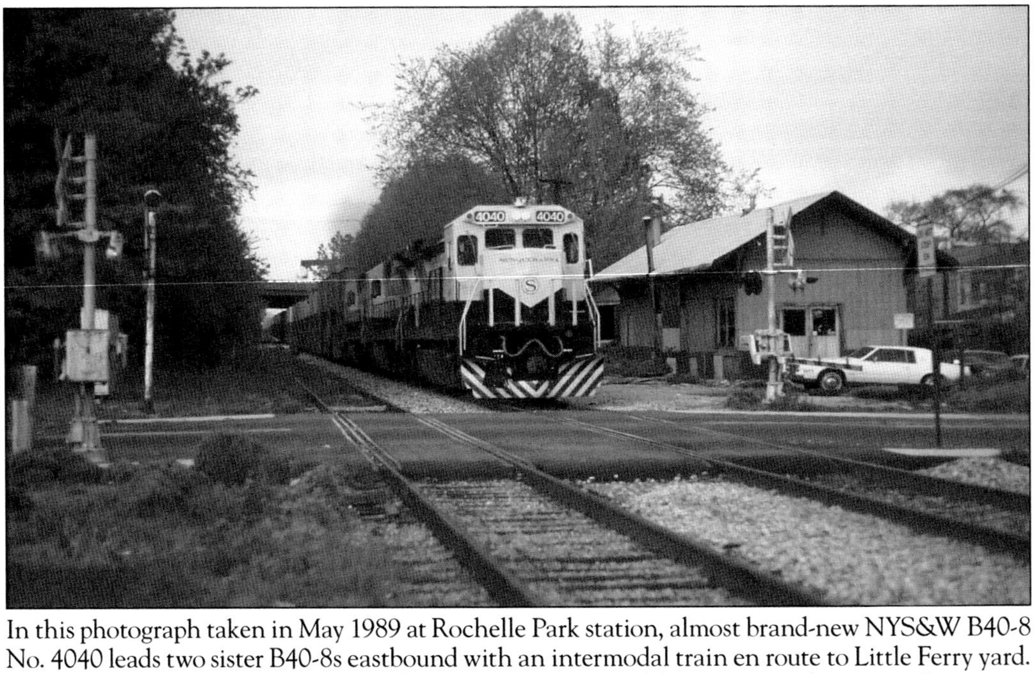

In this photograph taken in May 1989 at Rochelle Park station, almost brand-new NYS&W B40-8 No. 4040 leads two sister B40-8s eastbound with an intermodal train en route to Little Ferry yard. Shortly after this photograph was taken, the NYS&W would renovate and convert the station into their southern division offices. (Photograph by Patrick J. Reynolds.)

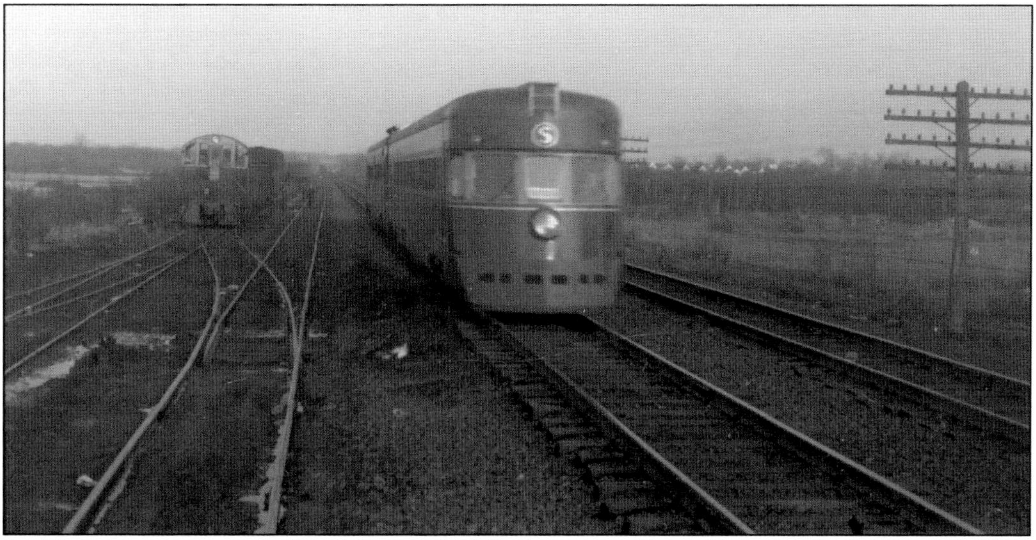

In this image photographed on March 18, 1949, American Car & Foundry–built Motorailer No. 1005 and a sister Motorailer make their way through Passaic Junction yard in Saddle Brook with westbound Train No. 831. On the adjacent track, NYS&W S-2 No. 208 switches freight cars in the yard. The surrounding area appears desolate as compared to today. (Photograph by John L. Treen; courtesy of Thomas J. Callan and the Maywood Station Museum Collection.)

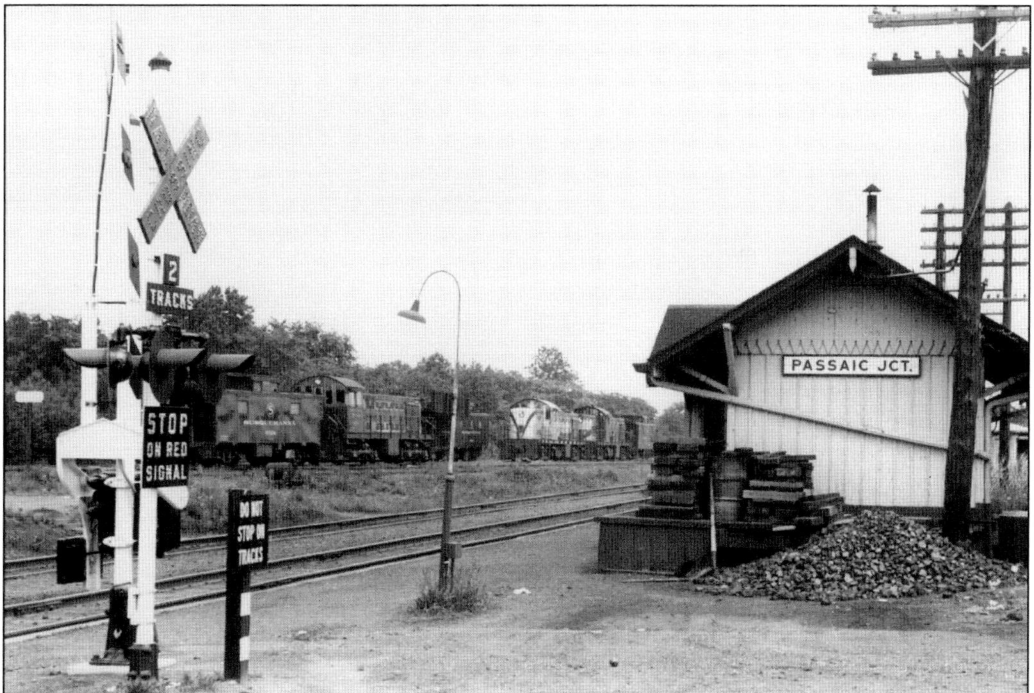

Passaic Junction station at Midland Avenue in Saddle Brook is in the foreground while two NYS&W RS-1s, an S-2, and three cabooses dominate the scene in the background in this view taken in August 1952. The cabooses are less than two years old, and one of the RS-1s wears the new, simplified aluminum and maroon stripe paint scheme. (Courtesy of Railroad Avenue Enterprises; author's collection.)

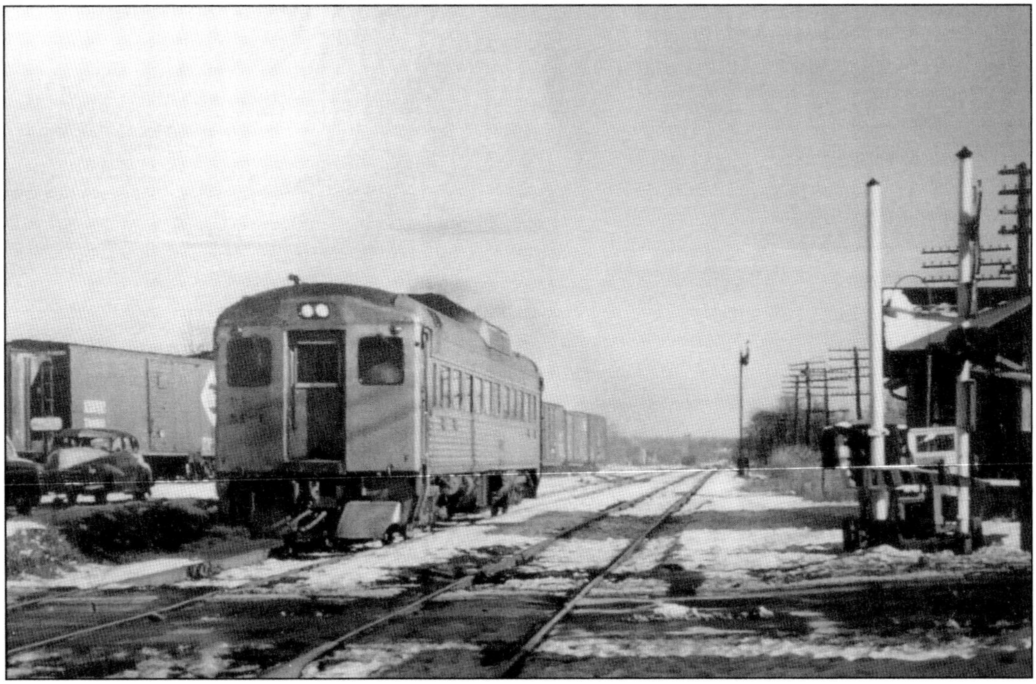

NYS&W Budd-built Rail Diesel Car M-1 accelerates westbound as it departs Passaic Junction station in Saddle Brook in this scene photographed in February 1955. Interchange cars destined to the Erie Railroad are in the yard. (Author's collection.)

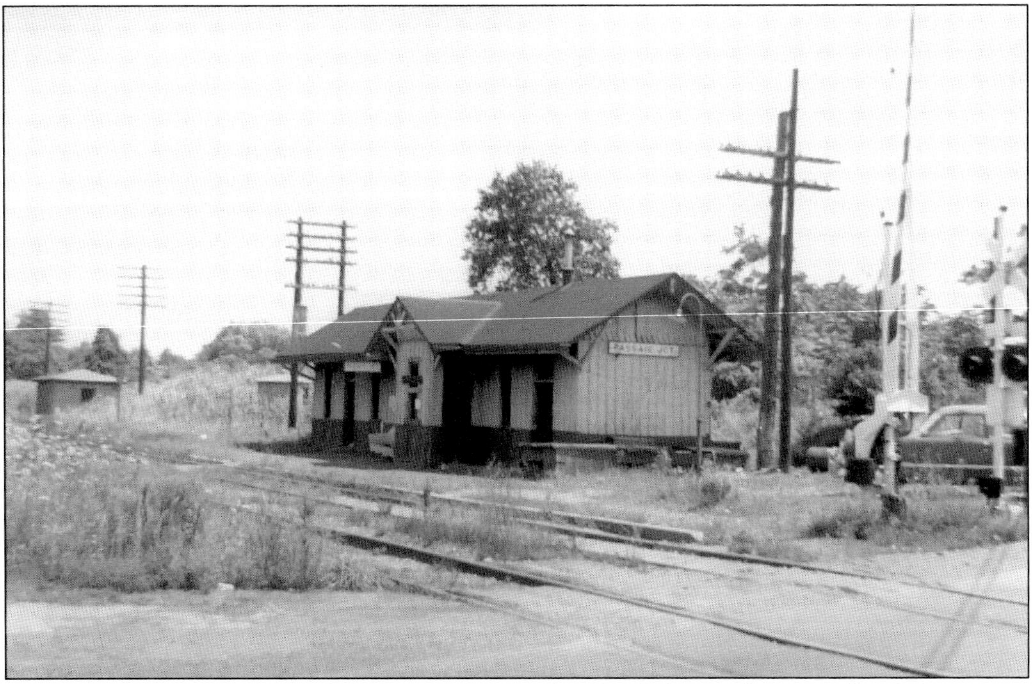

Passaic Junction station was located on the south side of the tracks at Midland Avenue in Saddle Brook. This view was taken on July 24, 1960. (Courtesy of Railroad Avenue Enterprises; author's collection.)

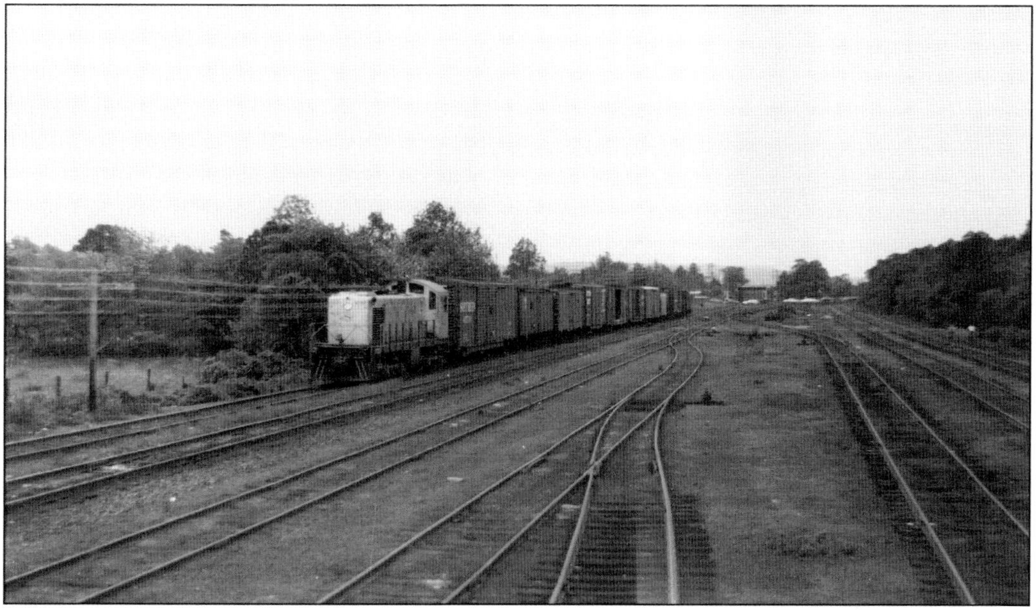

In this photograph looking east toward Rochelle Park from Saddle Brook, NYS&W S-2 No. 202 brings a cut of cars into Passaic Junction yard on June 14, 1961. The NYS&W mainline is to the far right. This scene has changed very much in the ensuing years. Interstate Route 80 was built over this section of the yard, and the track layout is much different. (Courtesy of Railroad Avenue Enterprises; author's collection.)

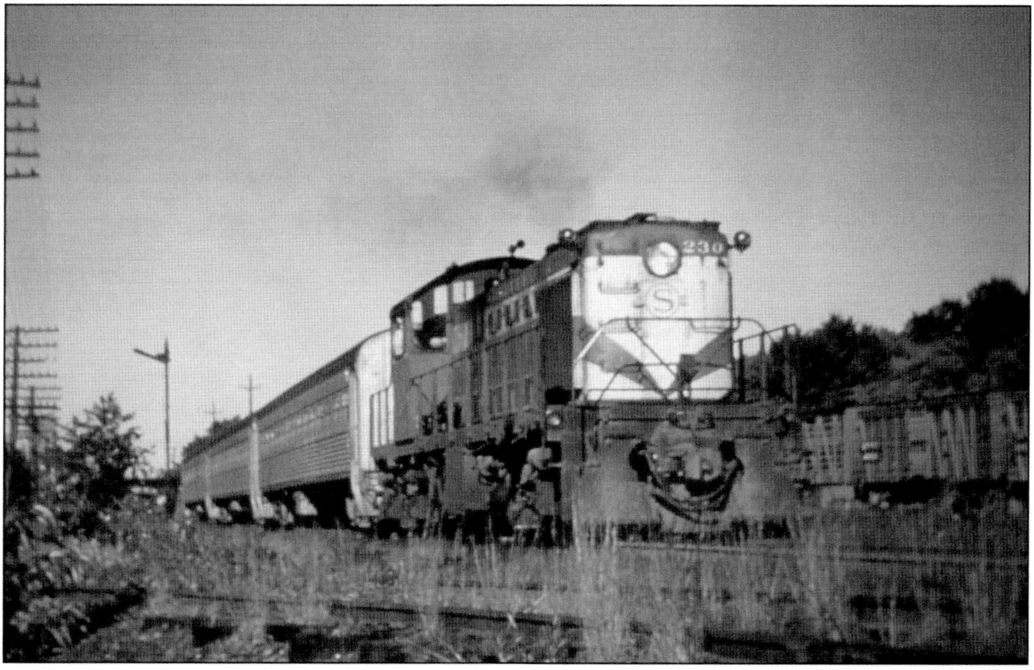

NYS&W RS-1 No. 230 rolls through Passaic Junction yard in Saddle Brook with an eastbound passenger train consisting of three of the NYS&W's new 85-seat stainless steel Budd-built cars in this view taken in October 1952. The stock cars shown to the right in the photograph were used at the Charles Miller Slaughterhouse in North Bergen. (Courtesy of the Patrick J. Reynolds collection.)

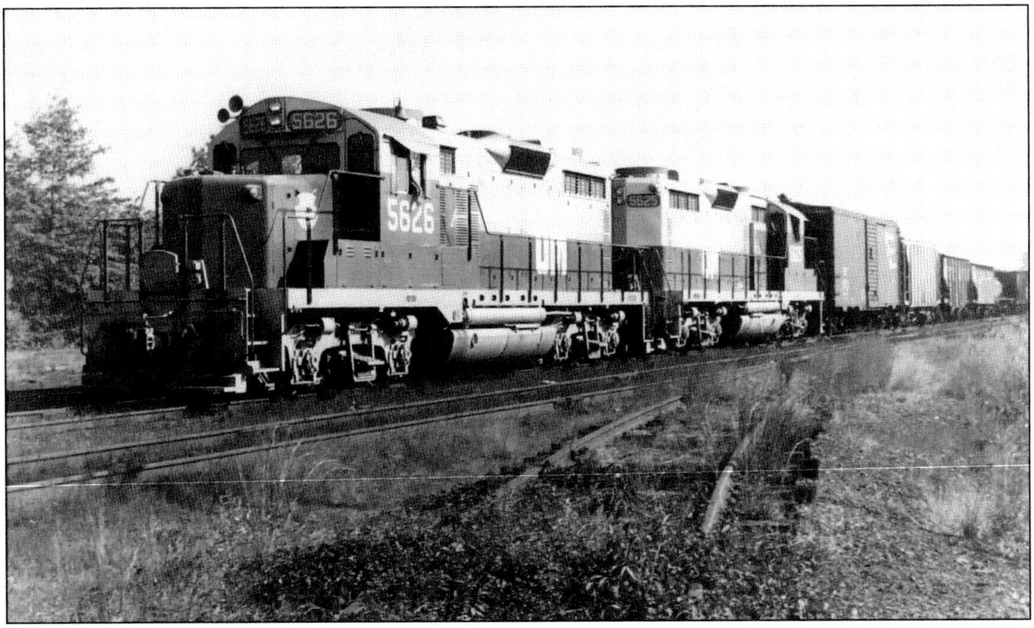

Electro-Motive Division of General Motors GP20 *Demonstrators* Nos. 5626 and 5625 prepare to get a westbound train underway in Passaic Junction yard in Saddle Brook in December 1961. The NYS&W tested the new prototype units and placed an order in 1962 for three GP18 models: NYS&W Nos. 1800, 1802, and 1804. (Courtesy Railroad Avenue Enterprises; author's collection.)

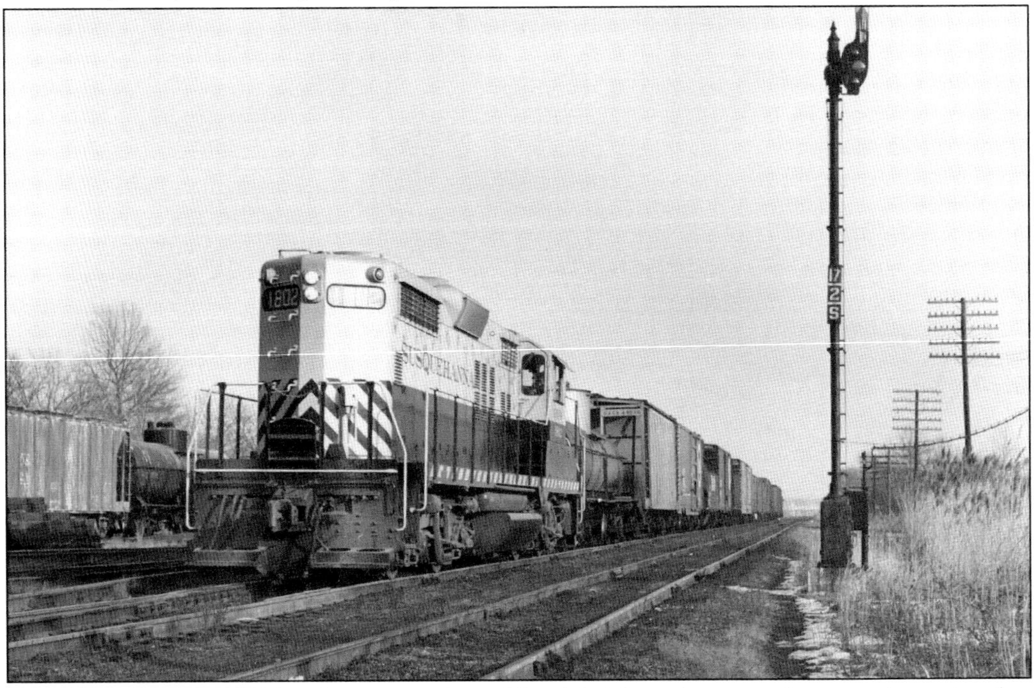

NYS&W GP18 No. 1802 heads up a westbound local freight as it passes the semaphore signal at milepost 17.2 in Passaic Junction yard in Saddle Brook in this view taken in January 1963. The locomotive was only four months old when this photograph was taken. (Photograph by Donald P. Wallworth; courtesy of Patrick J. Reynolds and the Maywood Station Museum Collection.)

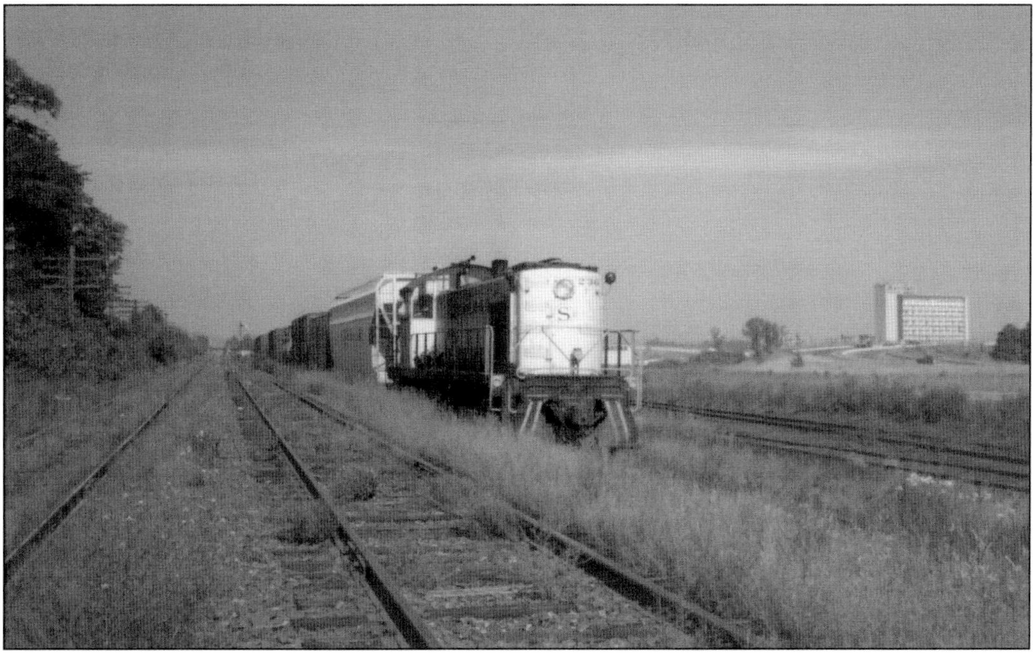

NYS&W RS-1 No. 236 heads east through Passaic Junction yard in Saddle Brook in this scene taken on June 30, 1969. The open area to the right was once part of Coalburg yard. Today any trace of Coalburg yard has been obliterated by the building of Interstate Route 80 in the late 1960s. The large Marriott Hotel that is visible in the right distance is still there. (Author's collection.)

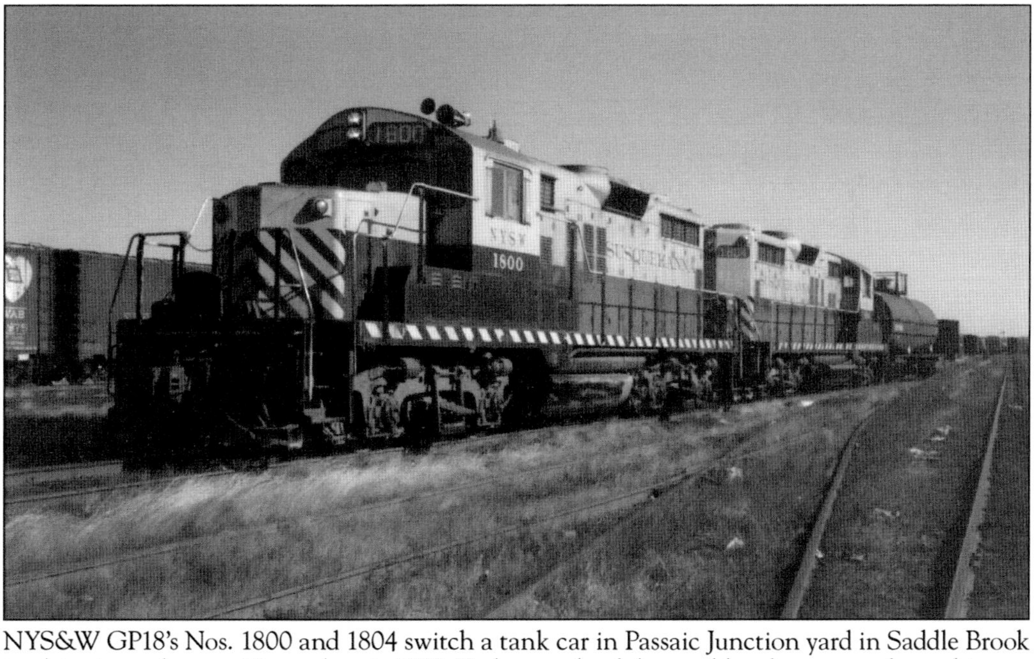

NYS&W GP18's Nos. 1800 and 1804 switch a tank car in Passaic Junction yard in Saddle Brook in this view taken on November 6, 1970. Today much of the yard has been transformed into a bulk transload facility where covered hopper cars containing plastic pellets and other food-grade commodities are off-loaded into trucks for local delivery. (Photograph by Donald P. Wallworth; author's collection.)

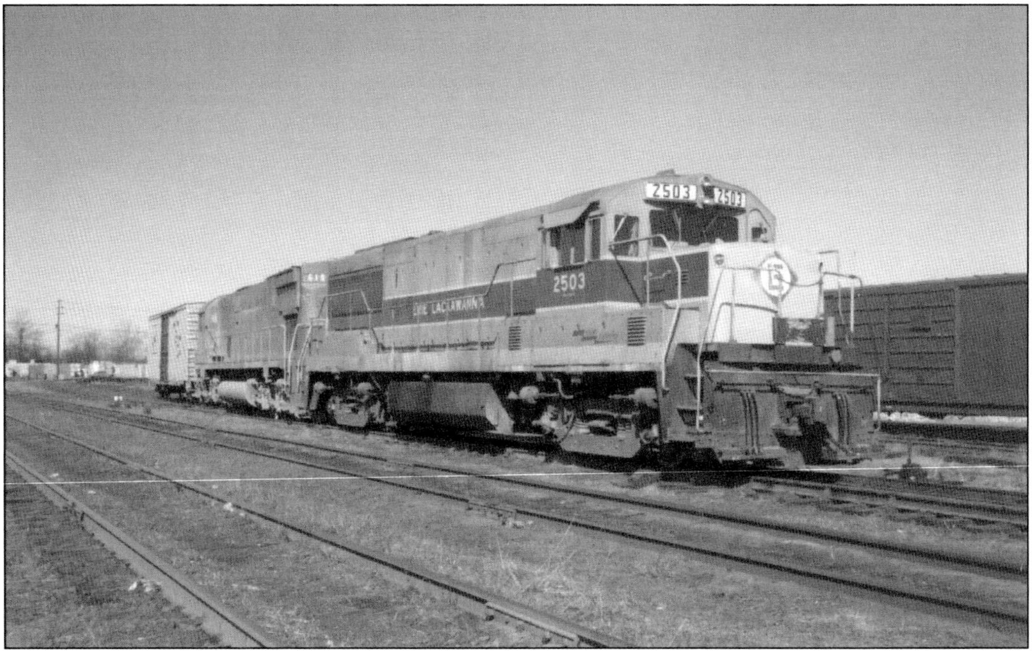

Through the years, the Erie and, later, Erie Lackawanna; Conrail; and Norfolk Southern have all conducted interchange of traffic at Passaic Junction in Saddle Brook. On March 27, 1971, Erie Lackawanna U25B No. 2503 with Delaware & Hudson C-628 No. 618 have just set off a cut of cars in the yard and are returning to their train on the former Erie Bergen County line with one boxcar from the NYS&W. (Author's collection.)

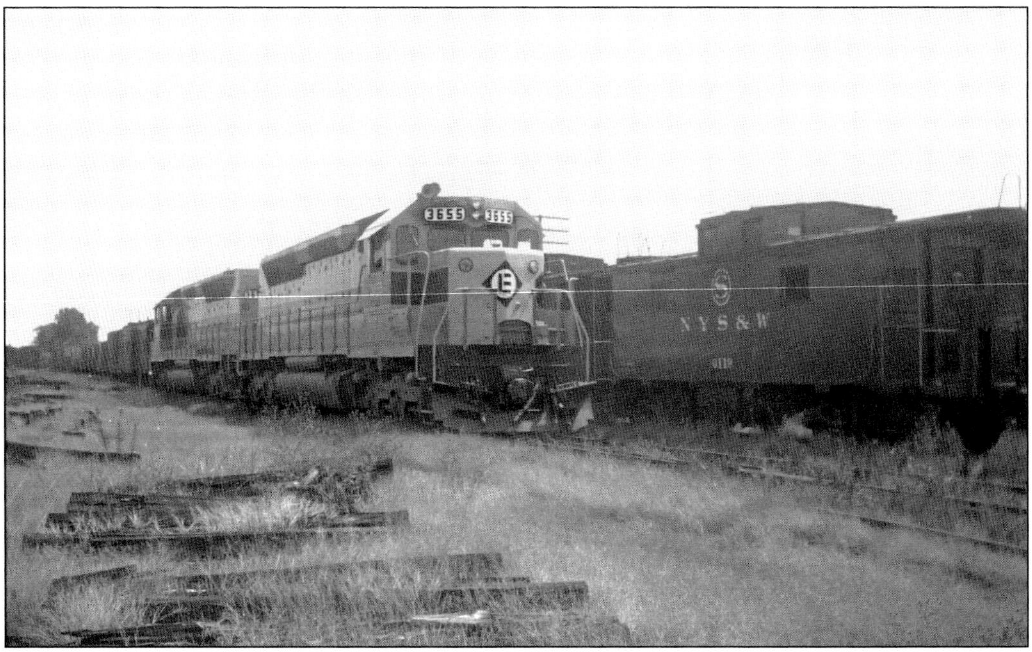

Erie Lackawanna SDP45 No. 3655 and a sister unit are shown in this view passing NYS&W caboose No. 0119 as they prepare to drop off interchange cars at Passaic Junction yard in Saddle Brook in October 1972. (Author's collection.)

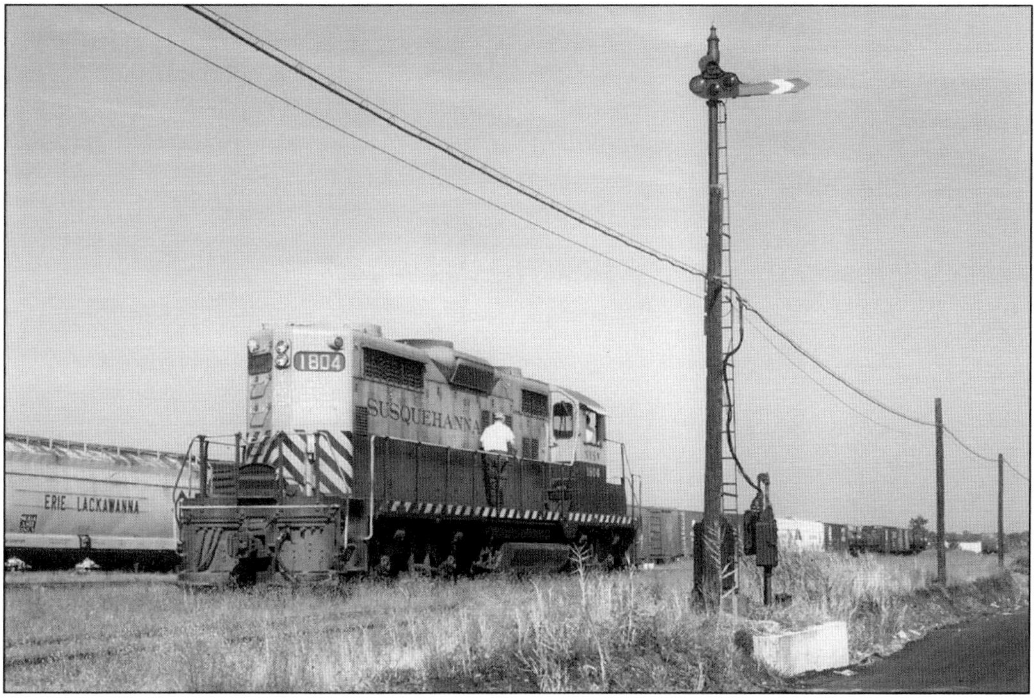

NYS&W GP18 No. 1804 drifts through Passaic Junction yard in Saddle Brook in this scene taken on September 7, 1974. Interchange cars from the Erie Lackawanna dominate the background. The semaphore signal still remains. (Author's collection.)

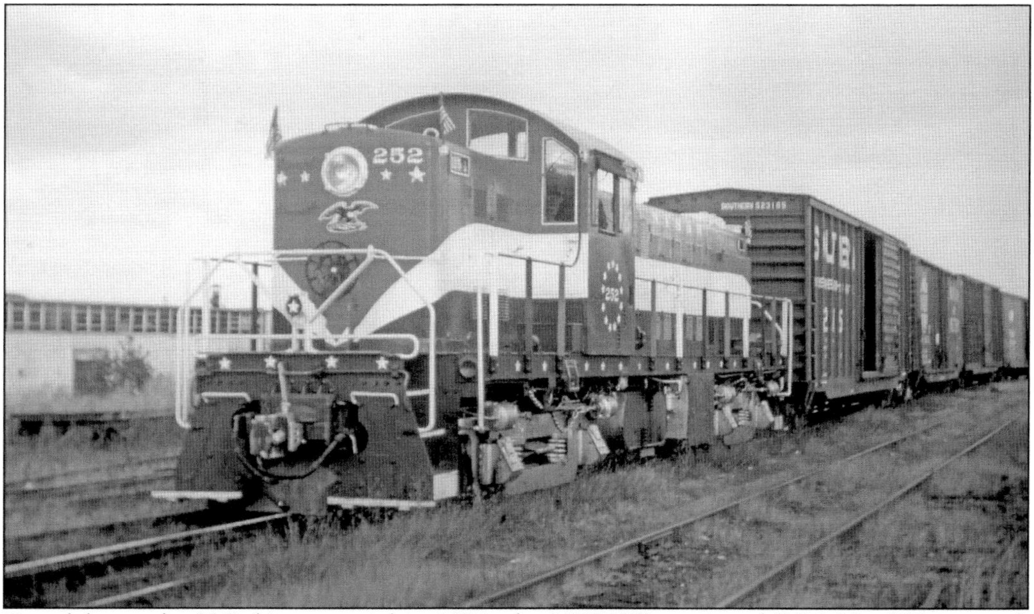

To celebrate the U.S. bicentennial in 1976, the NYS&W repainted RS-1 No. 252 in a red, white, and blue patriotic scheme with classy silver trucks. The shiny locomotive is seen in this photograph switching boxcars in Passaic Junction yard in December 1976. During its career, No. 252 wore a total of five different paint schemes, more than any other locomotive on the NYS&W. (Author's collection.)

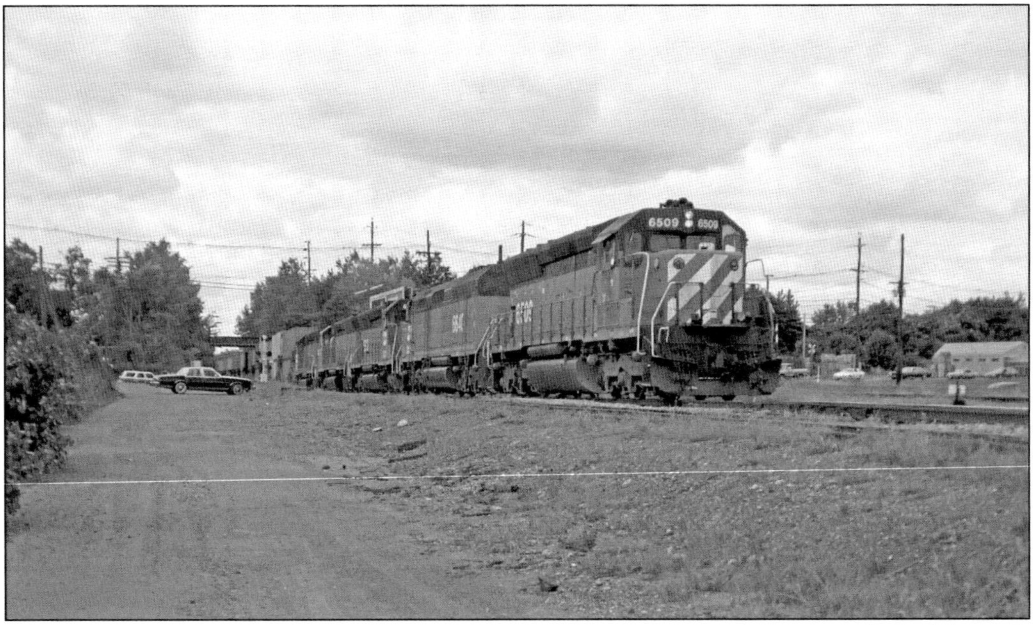

NYS&W SD45 No. 6509 is shown here leading three sister SD45s and an F45 eastbound through Passaic Junction yard en route to Little Ferry yard in October 1986. This train was the first Sealand intermodal train to travel on the recently rebuilt 25 miles of the west end of the railroad between Butler and Sparta. All five locomotives were recently acquired from Burlington Northern and have yet to be repainted in NYS&W colors. (Photograph by Patrick J. Reynolds.)

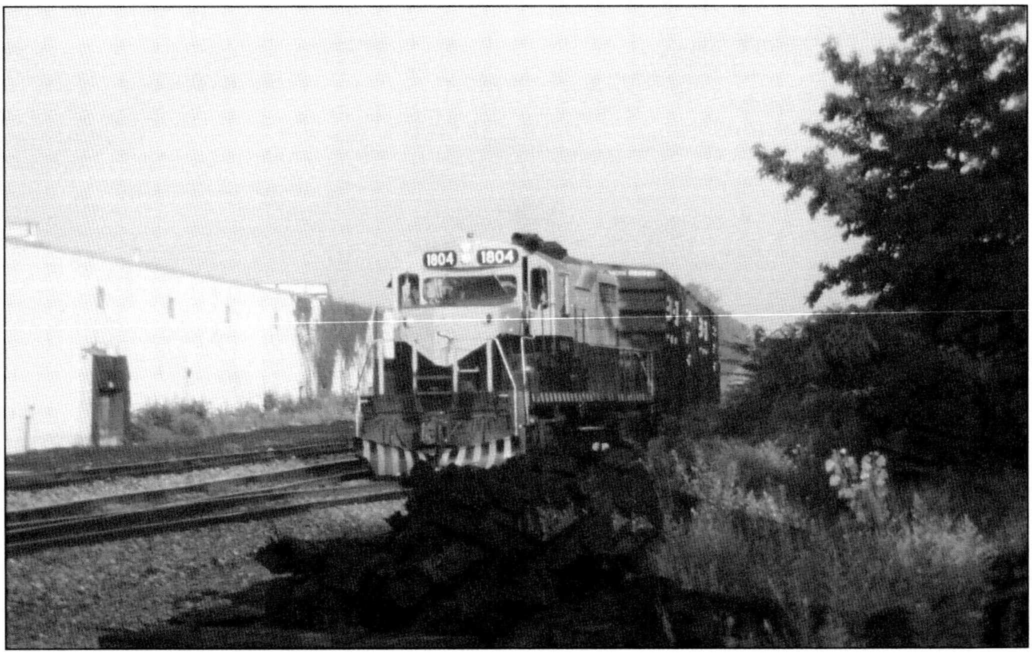

NYS&W GP18 No. 1804 switches two boxcars for an industry located adjacent to Passaic Junction yard in Saddle Brook in this view taken in June 1989. A number of industries and warehouses have been located next to the yard with direct access to the railroad. (Photograph by Patrick J. Reynolds.)

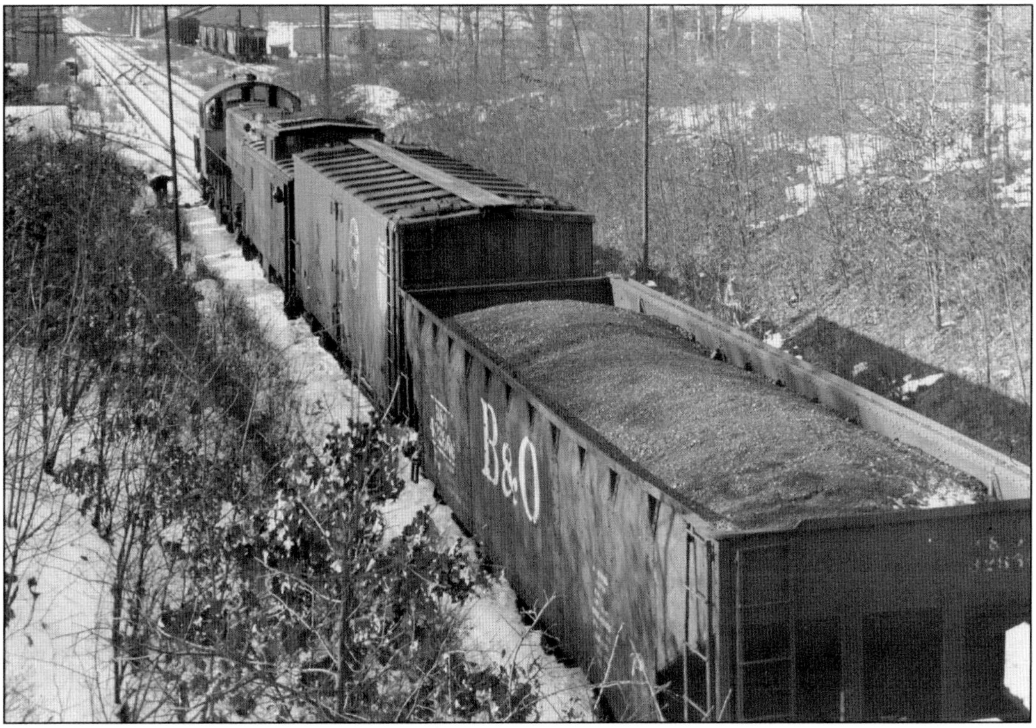

In this scene looking west and taken from the Erie Railroad bridge over the NYS&W at Passaic Junction, NYS&W RS-1 No. 244 and its freight are about to take the switch onto the Passaic branch in East Paterson (Elmwood Park) on December 31, 1960. (Photograph by Donald P. Wallworth; courtesy of Patrick J. Reynolds and the Maywood Station Museum Collection.)

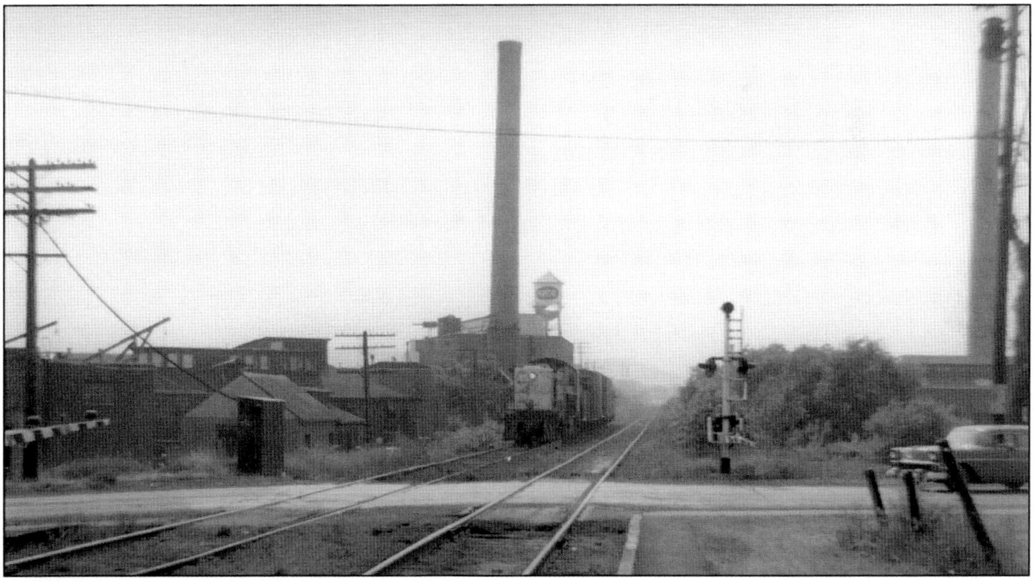

NYS&W S-2 No. 208 approaches the River Drive crossing in East Paterson (Elmwood Park) in this view taken from the East Paterson station platform on June 19, 1961. The industries in the background are part of the Marcal Paper plant, which is still a customer of the NYS&W today. (Courtesy of Railroad Avenue Enterprises; author's collection.)

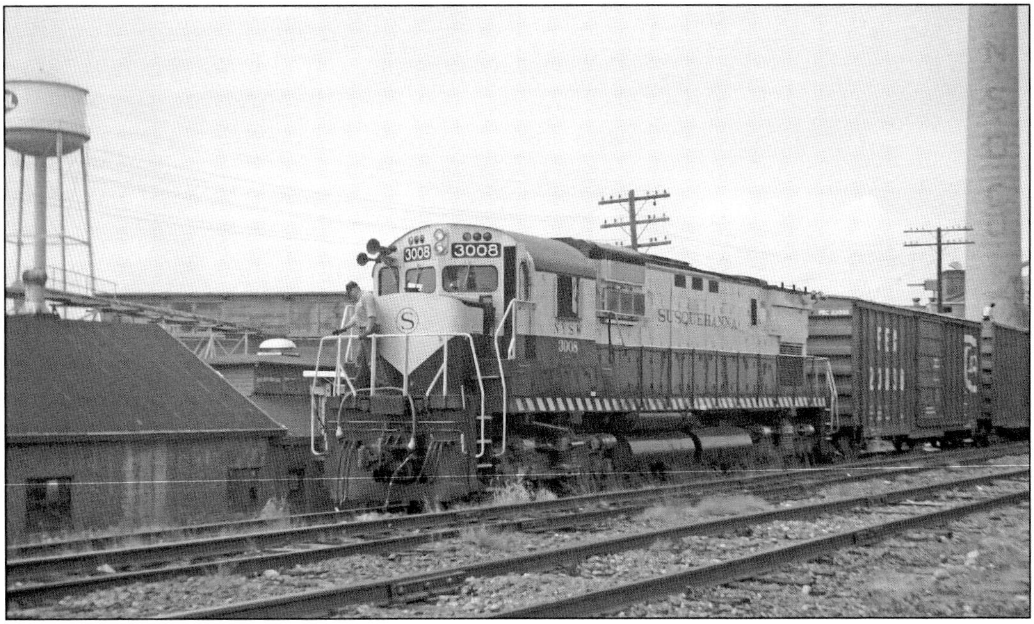

In this view, NYS&W C-430 No. 3008 switches boxcars at the sprawling Marcal Paper plant in Elmwood Park (East Paterson) in October 1986. The paper plant located near Interstate Route 80 has been a longtime customer of the NYS&W. (Photograph by Patrick J. Reynolds.)

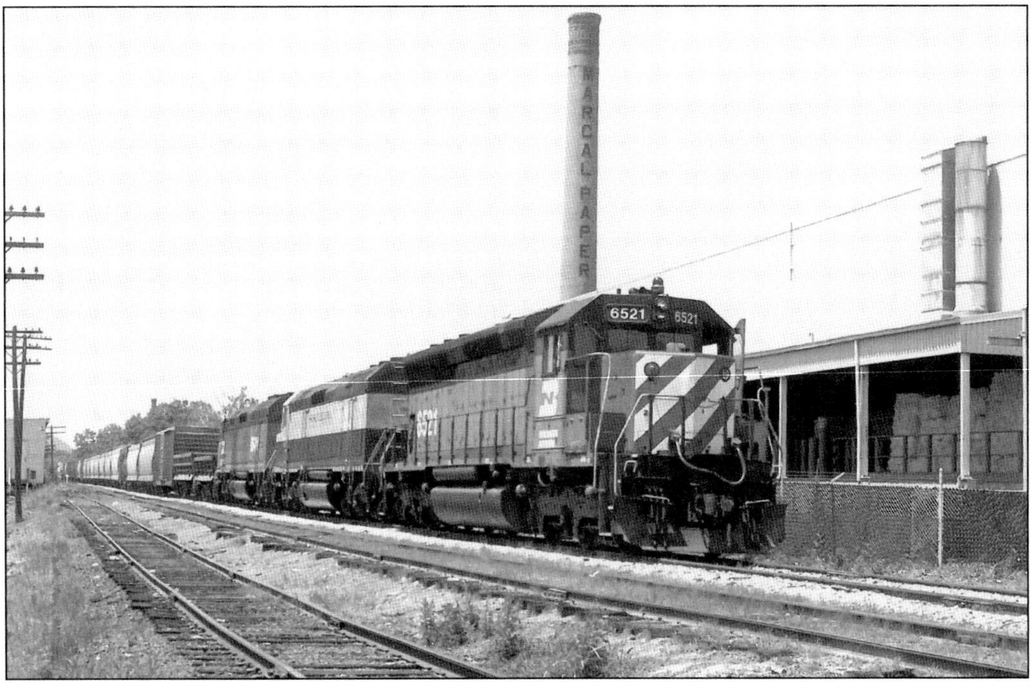

NYS&W SD45 No. 6521, F45 No. 6370, and F45 No. 6640 lead eastbound road freight SU-100 past the Marcal Paper plant in Elmwood Park (East Paterson) in this image taken on June 29, 1987. All three locomotives were recently purchased secondhand from Burlington Northern, and the first and third units still are in their full former BN paint schemes. (Courtesy of Railroad Avenue Enterprises; author's collection.)

Four

Paterson to Wyckoff

The city of Paterson has manufacturing roots tracing back to the late 18th century, and it became one of the centers of the American Industrial Revolution. Until the 1960s, Paterson was a great source of passenger and freight revenue for the railroad, and its general offices were based there. Proceeding west, Hawthorne was an important location on the NYS&W for many years. Numerous industries were located there, but the majority of them were located on the north end of the borough, which was known as North Hawthorne. In the late 1800s, the NYS&W established their passenger and freight car repair shops in North Hawthorne, which survived into the 1950s. A yard with a turntable was also found near the shops. Today very little evidence of a bustling rail-served area exists in North Hawthorne except for various buildings that were once served by the NYS&W and some of the old shops, which have been converted to other uses. A .047 percent westbound ruling grade begins in Hawthorne and increases to 1.21 percent at North Hawthorne.

The NYS&W reenters Bergen County and begins to climb at an accelerated pace upon entering Midland Park, with an average westbound ruling grade of 1.24 percent. The line also begins to curve with greater consistency as it works west. Wortendyke is a small residential community that had a strong presence in the early history of the NJM/NYS&W. Original NJM Pres. Cornelius Wortendyke established the principle shops for the railroad here, which was later replaced by North Hawthorne and Little Ferry. Through the years, Wortendyke has also had a fair share of shippers served by the NYS&W, and at one time had a passing siding. Today Wyckoff is an affluent township, and industry has always been minimal, but several shippers have been located along the NYS&W in the vicinity of Wyckoff Avenue. The ruling grade of the NYS&W levels off briefly while heading west through town but begins to climb once again at the western edge of town, where it crests after achieving a ruling grade of .087 percent.

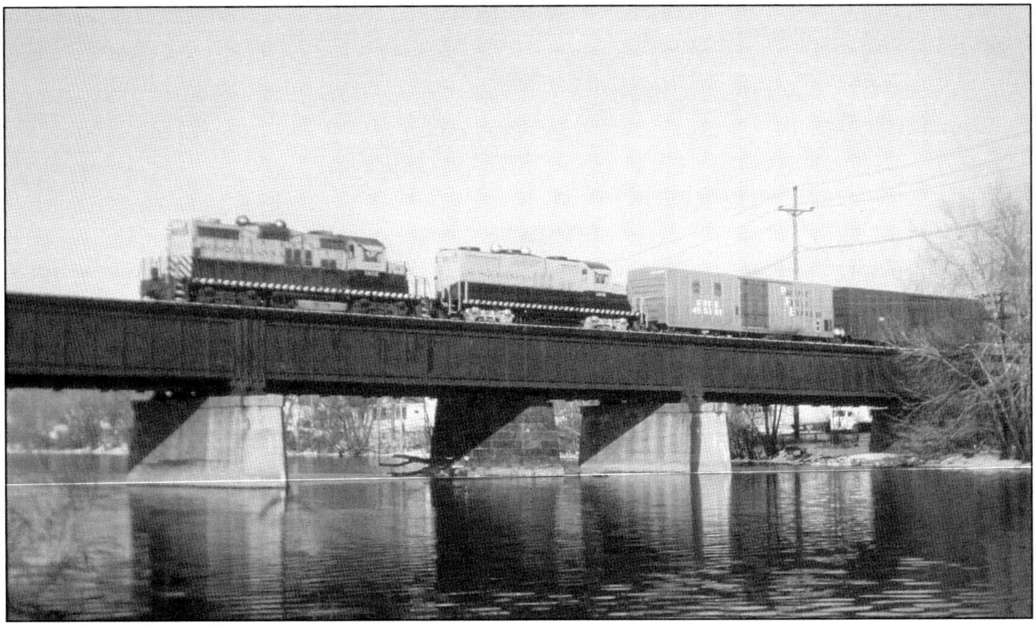

NYS&W GP18s Nos. 1802 and 1804 are shown in this view leading a two-car freight west on the bridge over the Passaic River from Elmwood Park (East Paterson) into Paterson in February 1977. No. 1802 still wears its as-built, 1962 yellow and black paint scheme while No. 1804 wears a modified newer paint scheme with silver trucks and without chevron stripes on its ends. (Author's collection.)

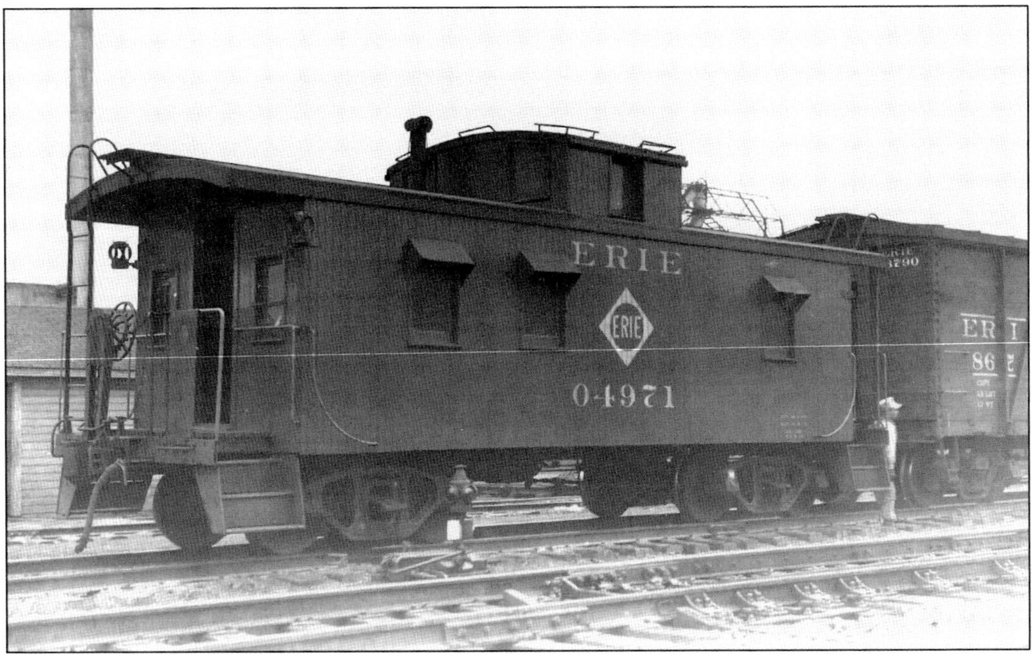

Erie Railroad caboose No. 04971 is seen in this view at the end of an NYS&W train passing through Paterson in the mid-1930s. The caboose was built a few years before in nearby Clifton, New Jersey, by the Magor Car Corporation. Occasionally equipment from NYS&W parent Erie Railroad was loaned or leased during this period. (Photograph by M. D. Carter; courtesy of Robert L. Steele and the Maywood Station Museum Collection.)

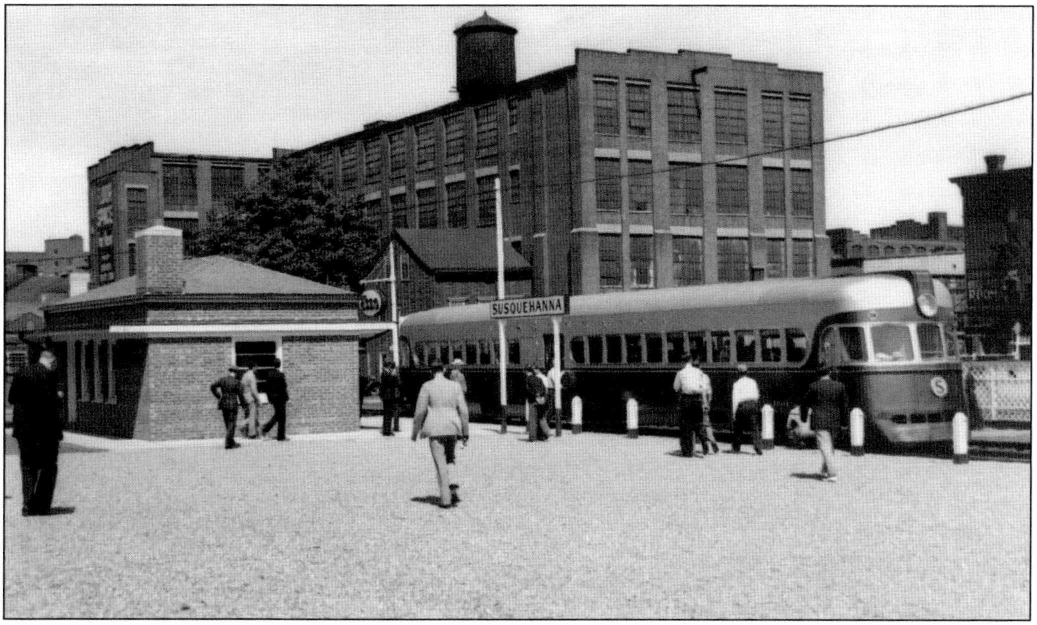

Recently delivered NYS&W No. 1001, a self-propelled American Car & Foundry–built Motorailer, waits to board passengers at the newly built Paterson City branch station in this image taken in May 1940. The Motorailers were something that NYS&W commuters had not experienced before and were a leap forward in luxury and accommodations. (Photograph by Arthur E. Owen; author's collection.)

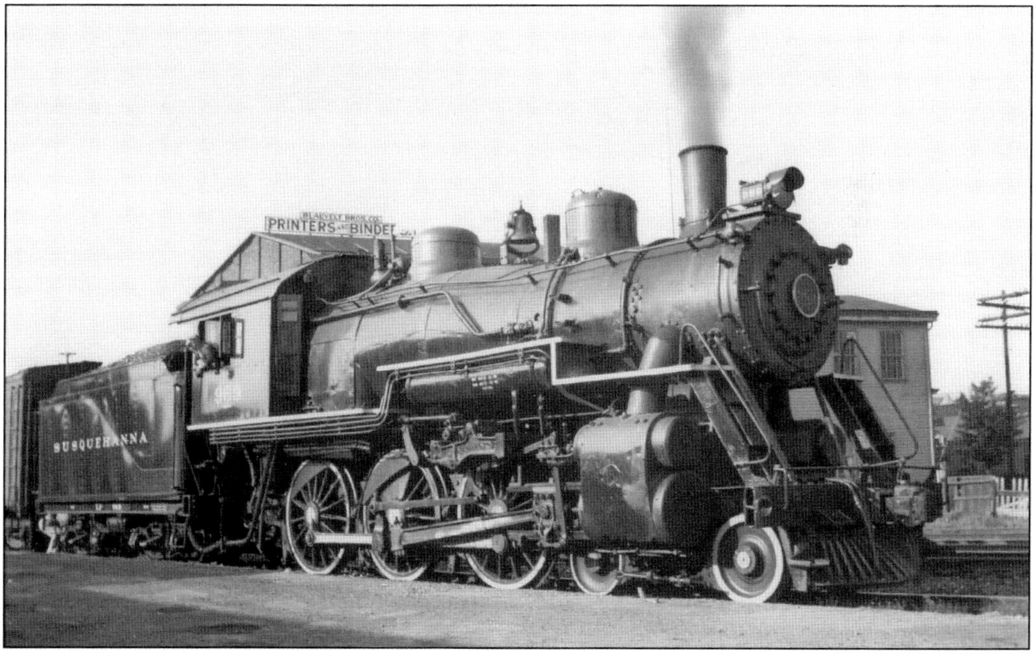

The engineer of NYS&W 4-6-0 No. 969 looks back at his train in this view taken in Paterson in June 1941. Although the NYS&W 4-6-0s were primarily used in passenger service, occasionally they would be used in local freight service, as this photograph illustrates. (Photograph by John Zuidema; author's collection.)

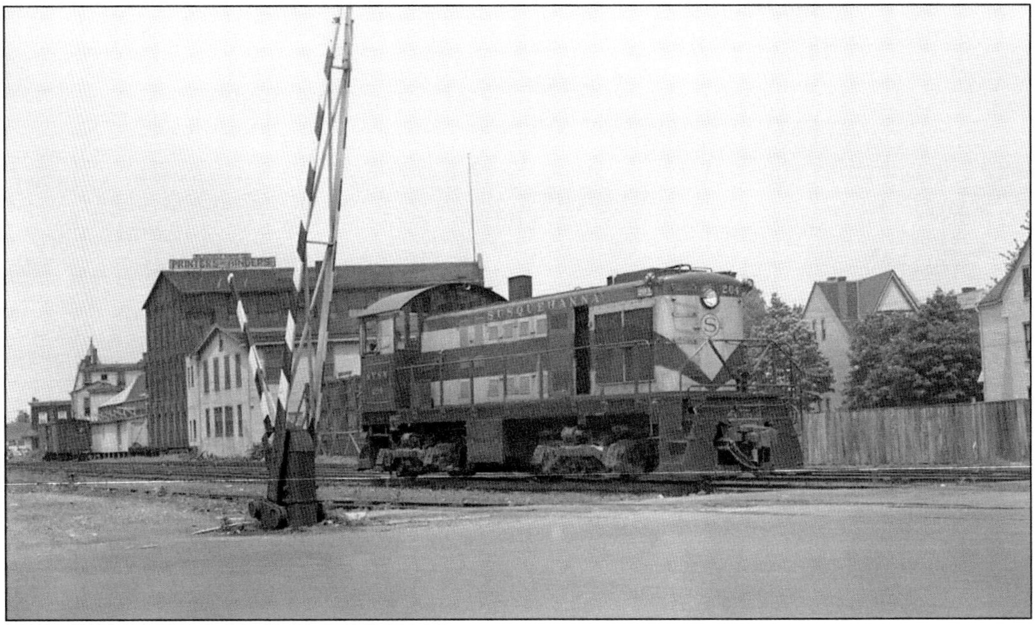

In this scene on June 29, 1946, NYS&W S-2 No. 204 approaches a grade crossing in Paterson on its way to its next assignment. Paterson was home to the Rogers Locomotive Works; Cooke Locomotive Works; Danforth Locomotive Works; and Grant Locomotive Works, which supplied many of the early New Jersey Midland and NYS&W steam locomotives. Both Rogers and Cooke later became part of the American Locomotive Company, the builder of NYS&W S-2 No. 204. (Author's collection.)

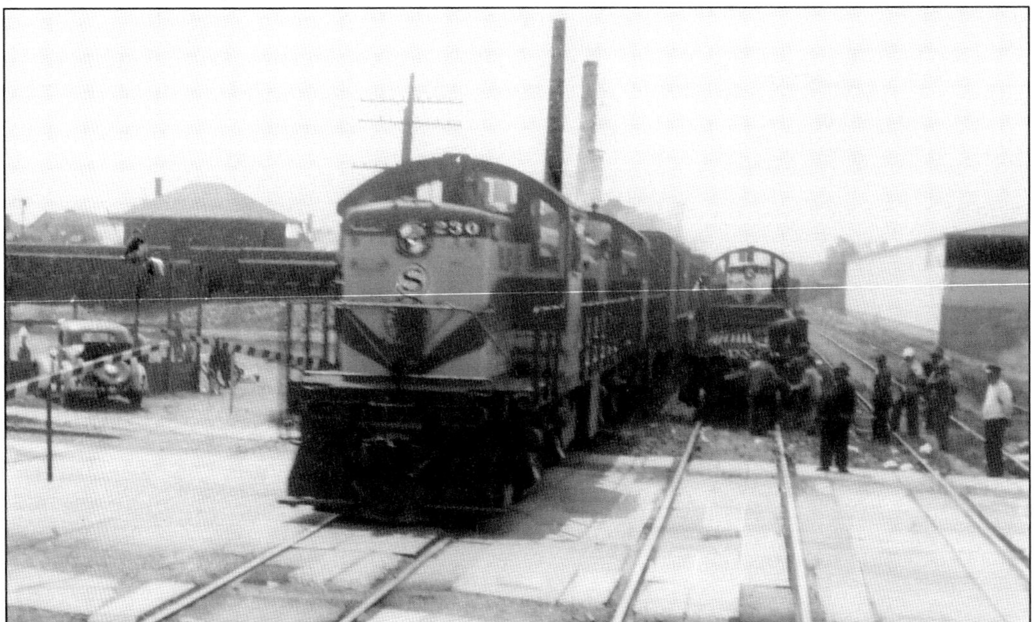

On May 17, 1947, NYS&W RS-1 No. 230 leads a sister RS-1 and its train past a work train and its track crew in this scene recorded at Lafayette Street in Paterson. (Photograph by John L. Treen; courtesy of Thomas J. Callan and the Maywood Station Museum Collection.)

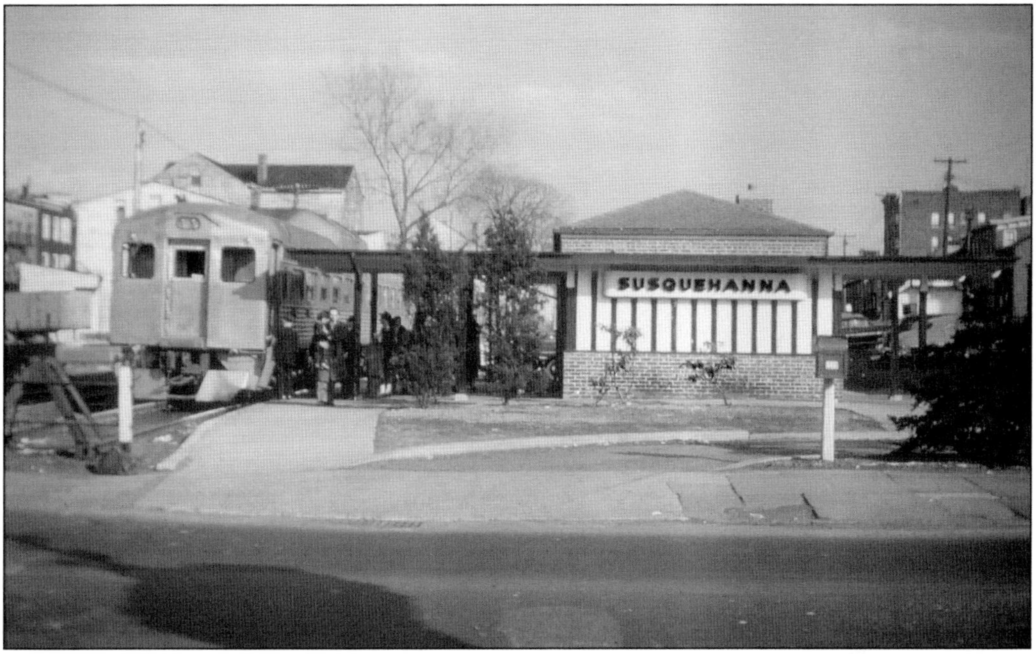

In this image taken in April 1950, a Budd-built Rail Diesel Car *Demonstrator* unit is stopped at the Paterson City branch station to load passengers for its trip east to Susquehanna Transfer in North Bergen. This location marked the end of the branch. (Author's collection.)

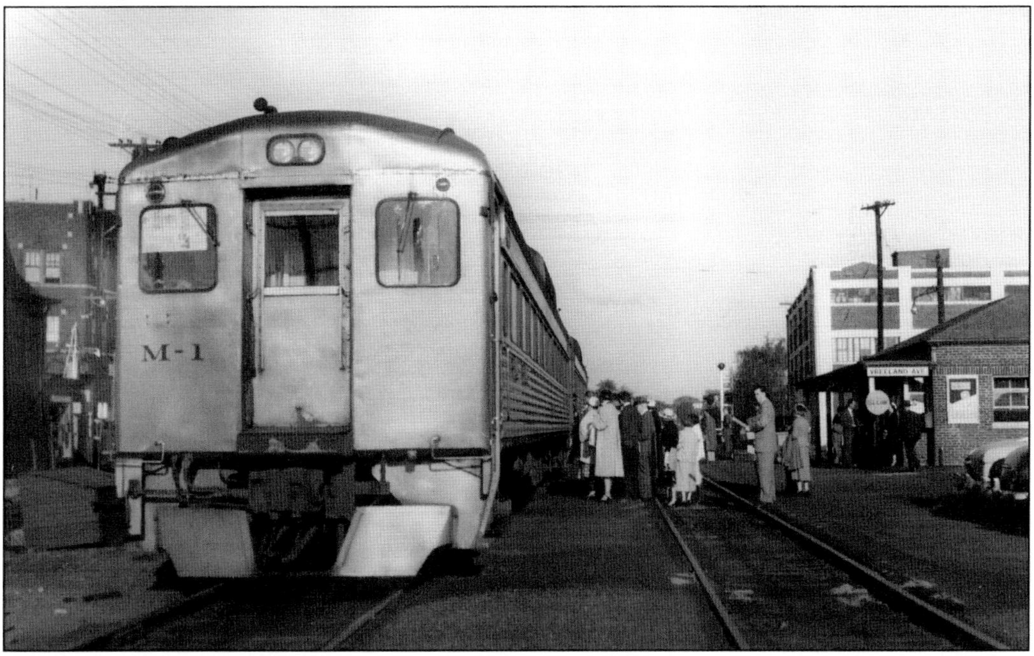

Passengers board NYS&W Budd-built Rail Diesel Car M-1 at the Vreeland Avenue station in Paterson in this scene taken in May 1957. Today M-1 has been restored to operating condition by the New York, Susquehanna & Western Technical & Historical Society. The society has also acquired original NYS&W M-2 and M-4, and their restorations are ongoing. (Courtesy of Railroad Avenue Enterprises; author's collection.)

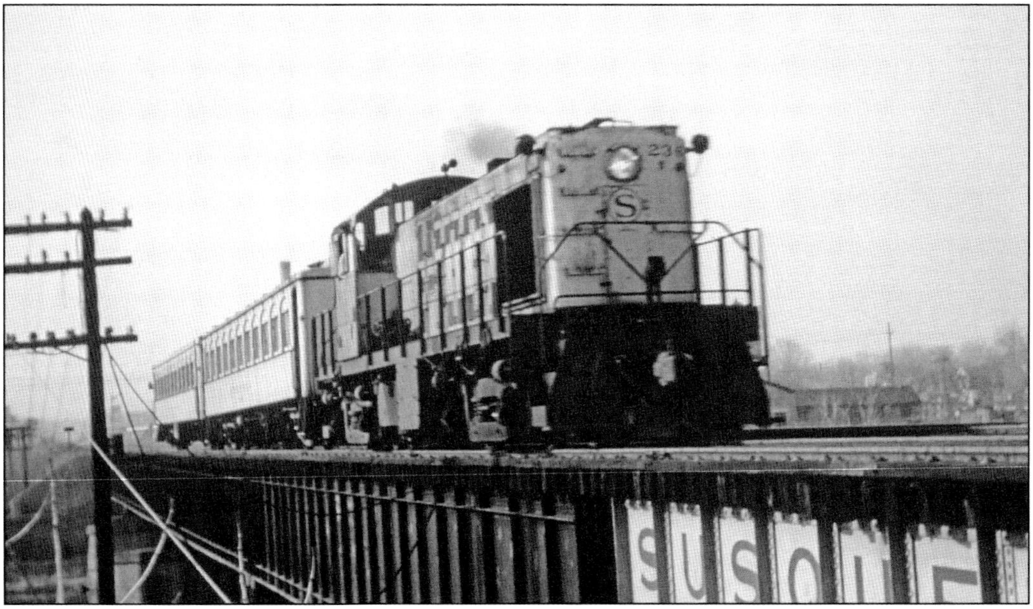

NYS&W RS-1 No. 236 rides high above the Passaic River on the bridge between East Paterson (Elmwood Park) and Paterson with westbound train No. 919 that consists of two ex-Erie Railroad Stillwell coaches in this scene taken in November 1957. The view is looking east from the Paterson side of the river. (Author's collection.)

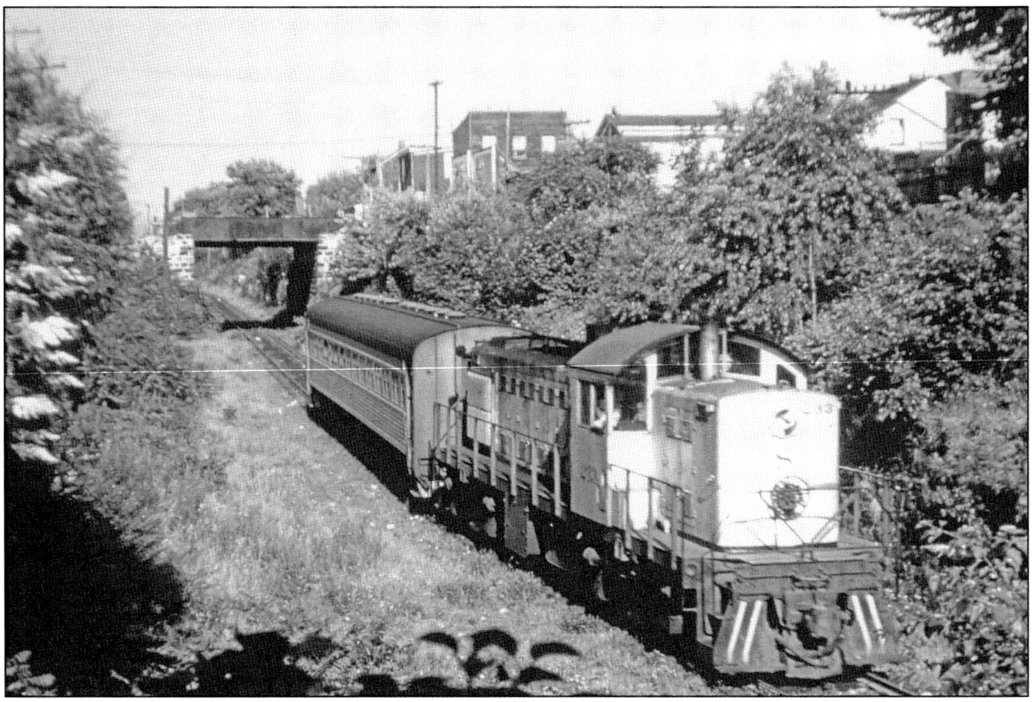

NYS&W RS-1 No. 233 and a passenger car head down the .75-mile Paterson City branch in this image photographed in July 1958. At this date, diesels have taken over for the four Budd-built Rail Diesel Cars, which were sold to the Jersey Central. The branch has about a year left before it is ripped up and the land sold to the City of Paterson. (Author's collection.)

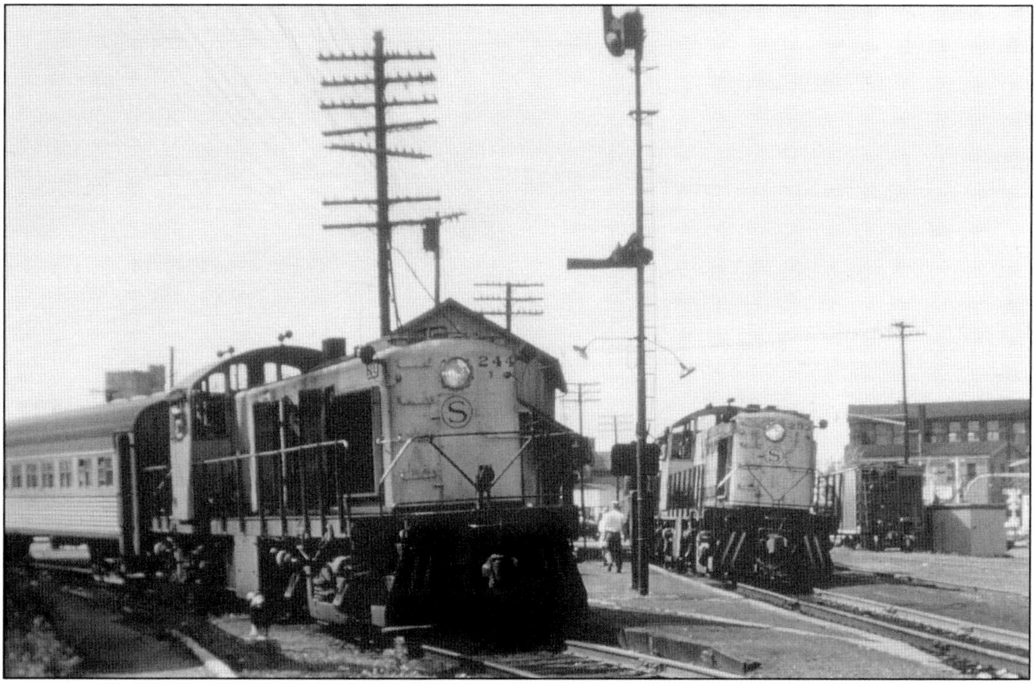

In this image photographed at a busy Broadway station in Paterson in July 1958, NYS&W RS-1 No. 244 is coming off the Paterson City branch to go east onto the mainline with its passenger train while NYS&W RS-1 No. 233 waits on the mainline to head east with its freight train. (Author's collection.)

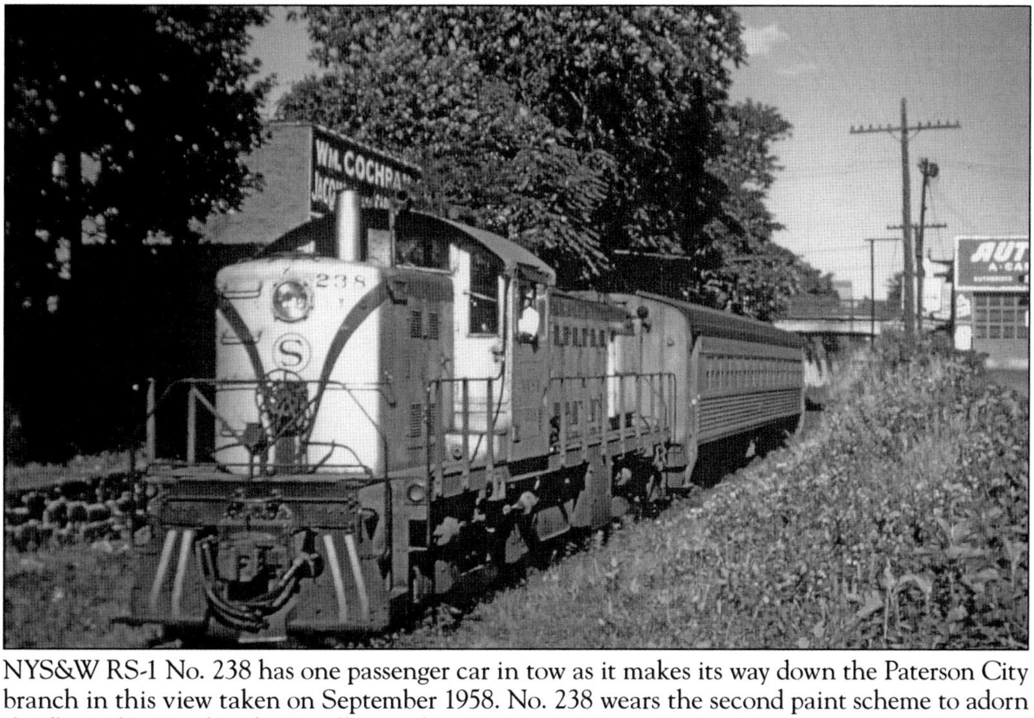

NYS&W RS-1 No. 238 has one passenger car in tow as it makes its way down the Paterson City branch in this view taken on September 1958. No. 238 wears the second paint scheme to adorn the fleet of RS-1s. (Author's collection.)

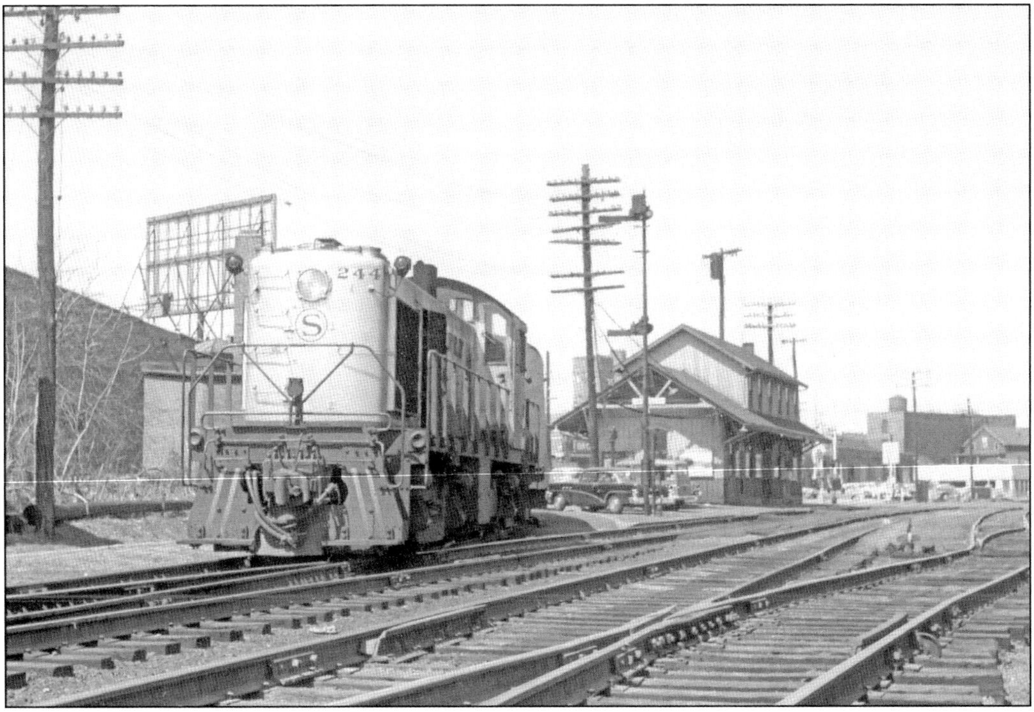

NYS&W RS-1 No. 244 is about to come off the Paterson City branch with one passenger car and proceed east on the NYS&W mainline in this view taken in February 1959. In the background is the NYS&W's Broadway station, which also served as the railroad's headquarters for many years. (Photograph by Donald P. Wallworth; courtesy of Patrick J. Reynolds and the Maywood Station Museum Collection.)

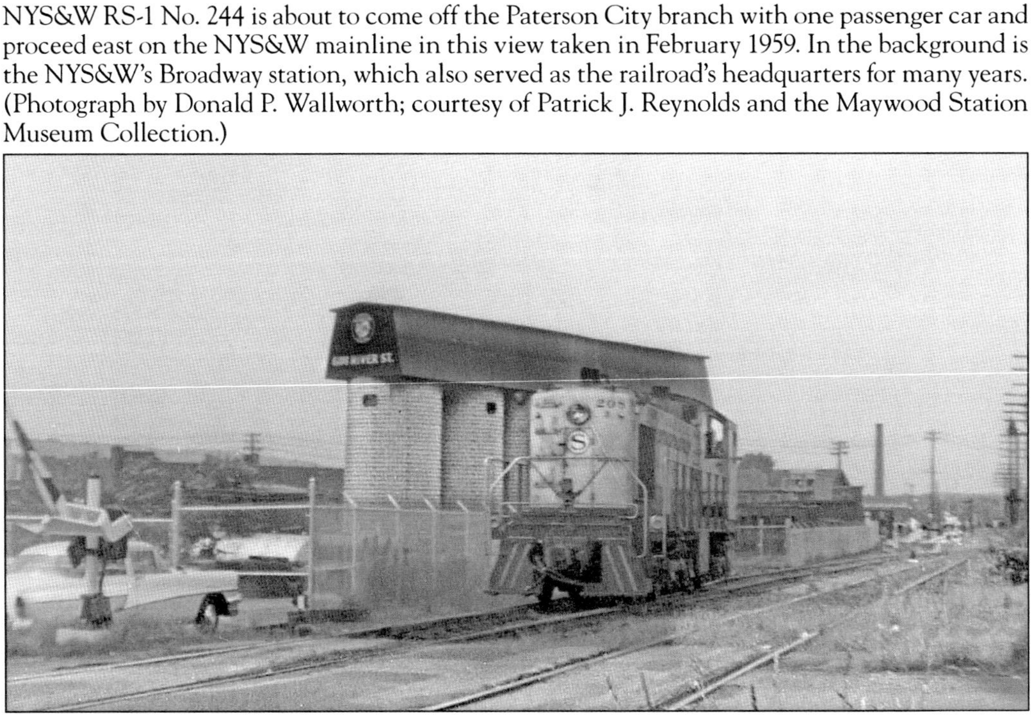

NYS&W S-2 No. 208 is shown approaching the River Street grade crossing in Paterson in June 1961. At one time, Paterson had an extensive array of industrial sidings served by the NYS&W, but much of the city's industrial base either closed or moved away, beginning in the 1950s. (Author's collection.)

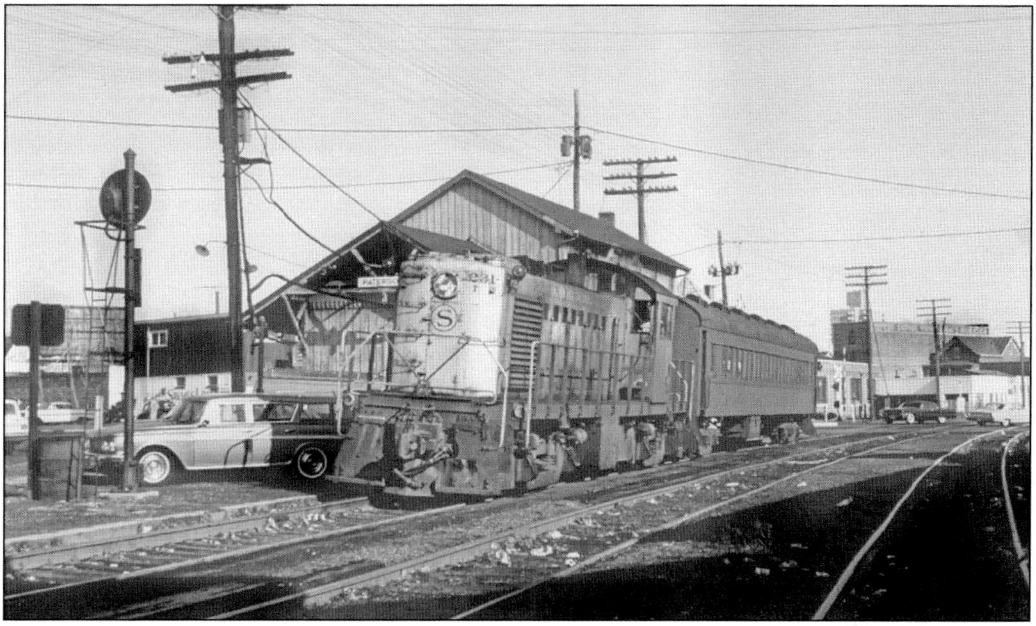

NYS&W RS-1 No. 231 is stopped at Broadway station in Paterson with its one-car passenger train waiting to go east in this perspective taken in May 1964. The two-story station served as NYS&W headquarters for many years. Sadly, the station was razed in the early 1970s. (Author's collection.)

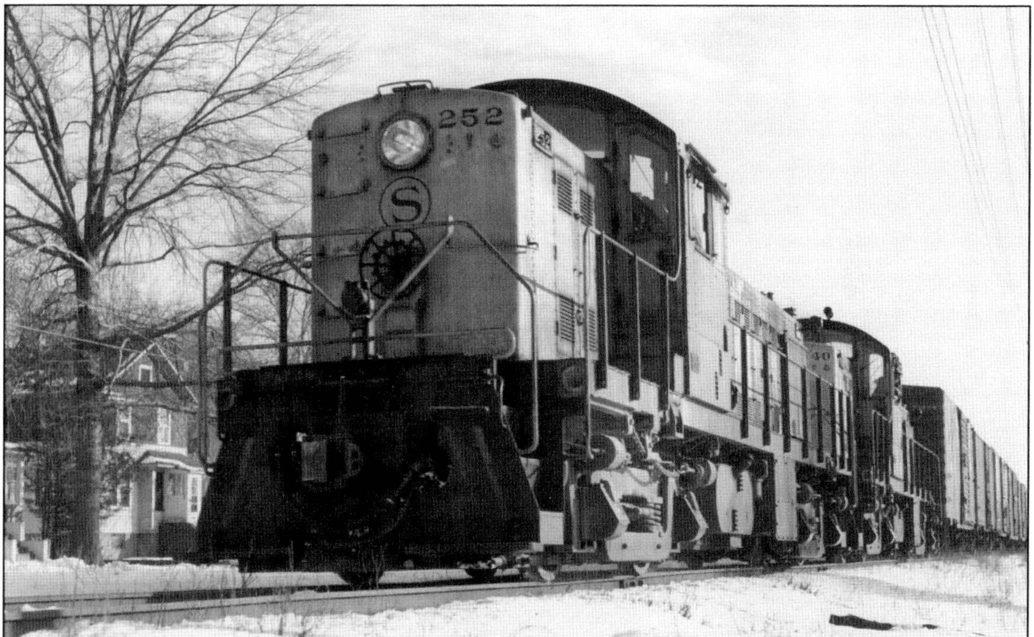

NYS&W RS-1 Nos. 252 and 240 roll westbound with their freight train between Royal Avenue and Grand Avenue in Hawthorne in this image photographed on February 2, 1966. The NYS&W ran between Royal Avenue and Grand Avenue, which paralleled the NYS&W for about a half-mile in this location. (Photograph by Donald P. Wallworth; courtesy of Patrick J. Reynolds and the Maywood Station Museum Collection.)

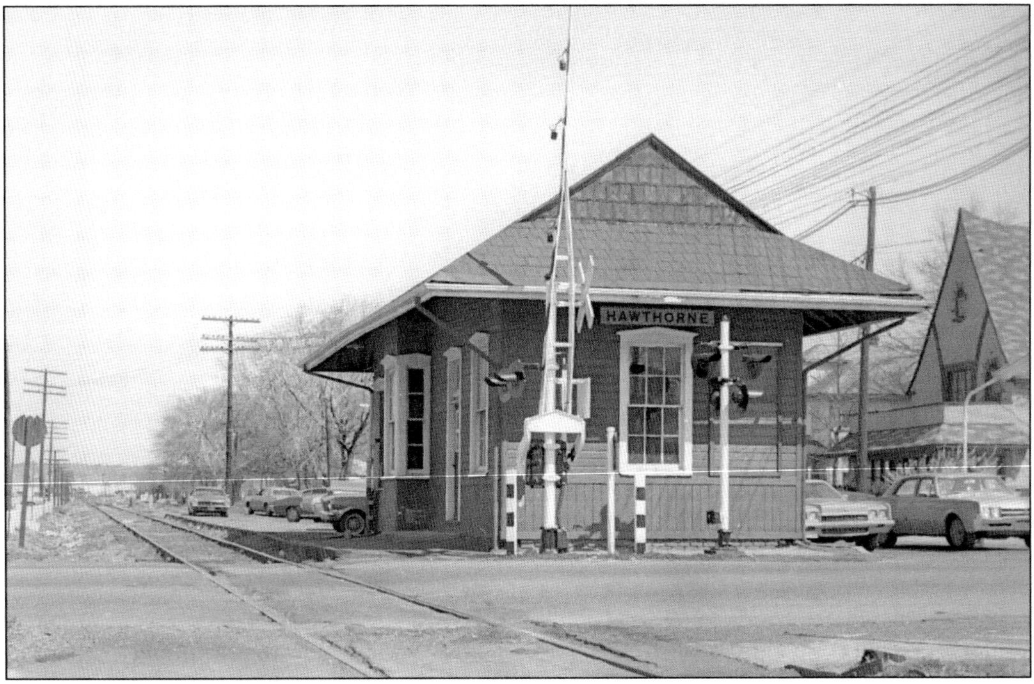

Hawthorne station at Diamond Bridge Avenue in Hawthorne is shown in this view taken on April 7, 1973. The NYS&W mainline once went from one track to two tracks from here to North Hawthorne yard and with a long siding extending to Central Avenue. The station, which was built around 1892, exists today and is maintained by the Volunteer Railroaders Association. (Courtesy of Railroad Avenue Enterprises; author's collection.)

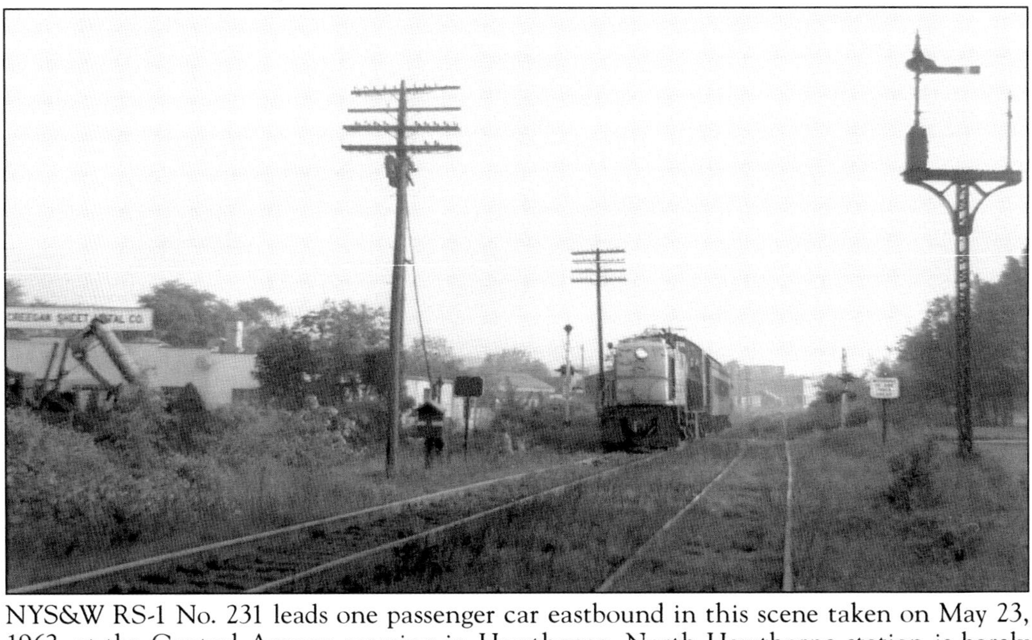

NYS&W RS-1 No. 231 leads one passenger car eastbound in this scene taken on May 23, 1962, at the Central Avenue crossing in Hawthorne. North Hawthorne station is barely visible in the far distance straight down the tracks. (Courtesy of Railroad Avenue Enterprises; author's collection.)

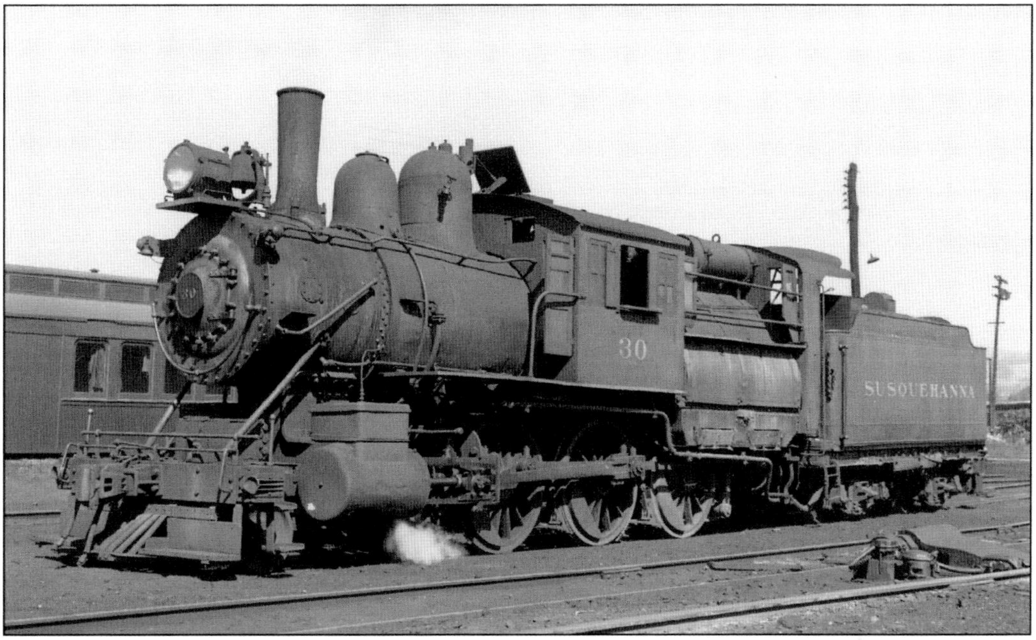

NYS&W 4-6-0 No. 30 rests in North Hawthorne yard in this view taken during the summer of 1935. An old wooden coach is seen behind the locomotive that has been taken off its trucks and is now resting on a foundation, probably being used for yard offices. (Author's collection.)

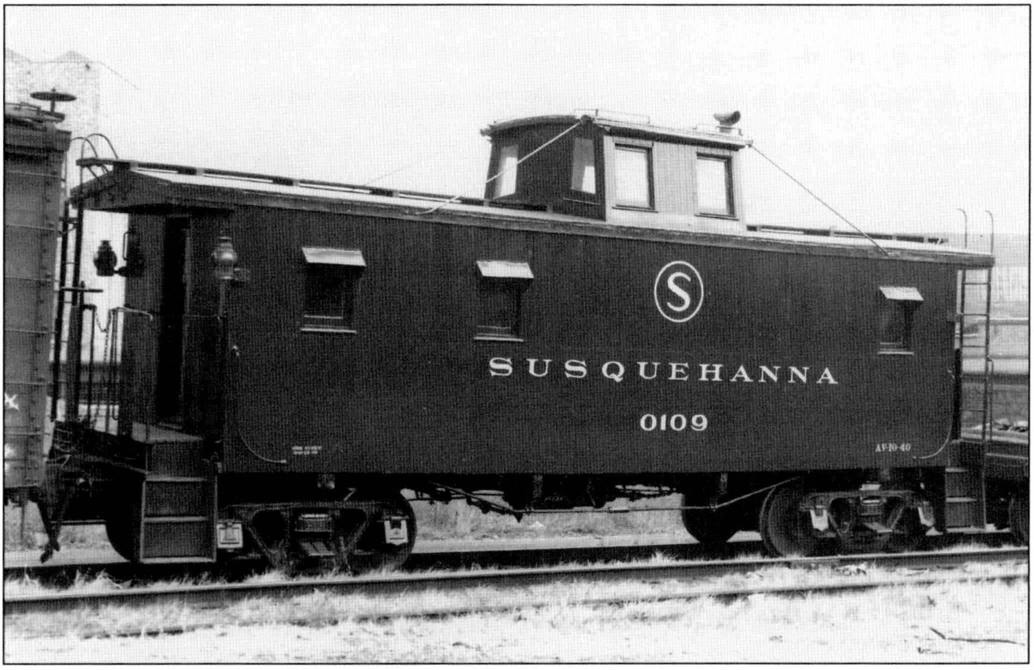

A fresh coat of paint adorns NYS&W caboose No. 0109 in this scene taken in the early 1930s in North Hawthorne. The NYS&W originally had a fleet of wooden four-wheel "bobber" cabooses, which were later replaced by a fleet of wooden eight-wheel cabooses, like the one in this photograph. In the late 1940s, all of the wooden cabooses were replaced by new steel ones. (Photograph by M. D. Carter; courtesy of Robert L. Steele and the Maywood Station Museum Collection.)

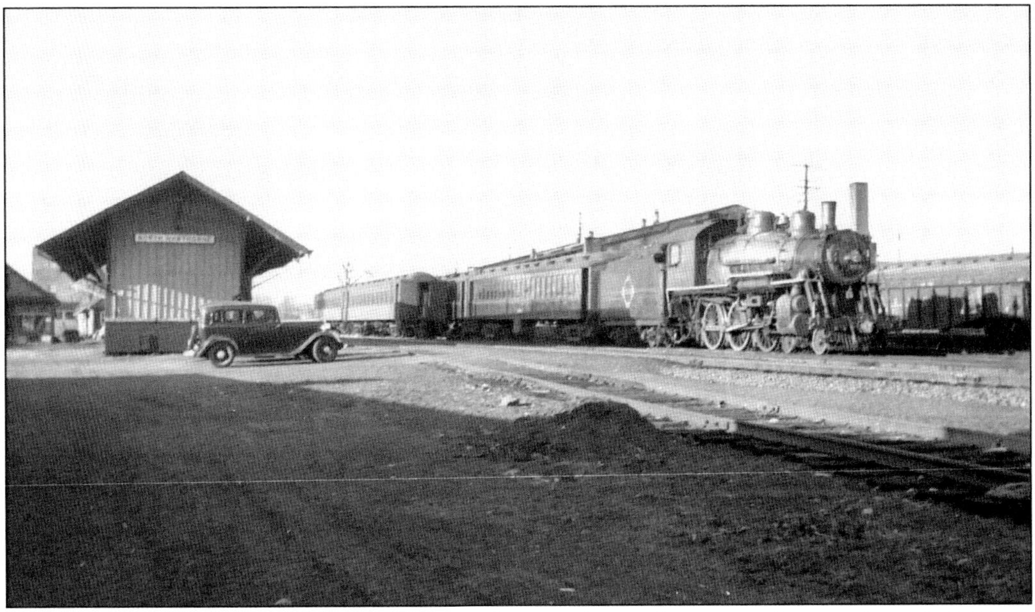

North Hawthorne station and part of the yard are visible in this view taken on April 6, 1940, as Erie 4-6-0 No. 954 gets underway eastbound with a passenger train. (Courtesy of Railroad Avenue Enterprises; author's collection.)

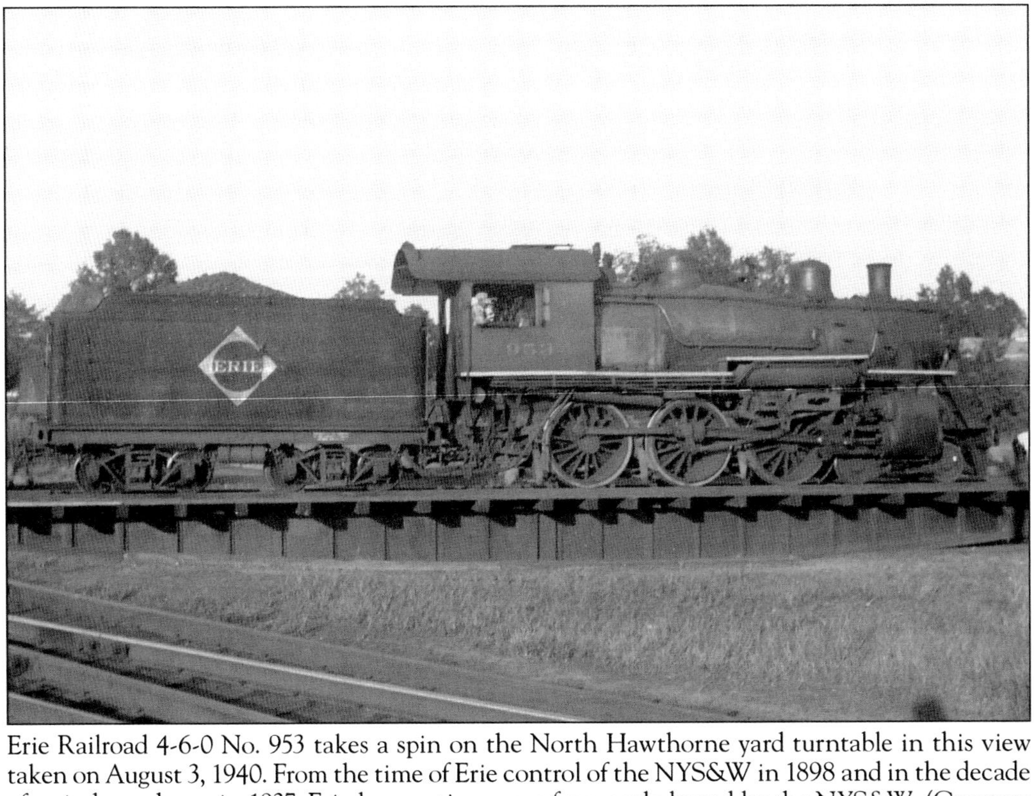

Erie Railroad 4-6-0 No. 953 takes a spin on the North Hawthorne yard turntable in this view taken on August 3, 1940. From the time of Erie control of the NYS&W in 1898 and in the decade after independence in 1937, Erie locomotives were frequently leased by the NYS&W. (Courtesy of Railroad Avenue Enterprises; author's collection.)

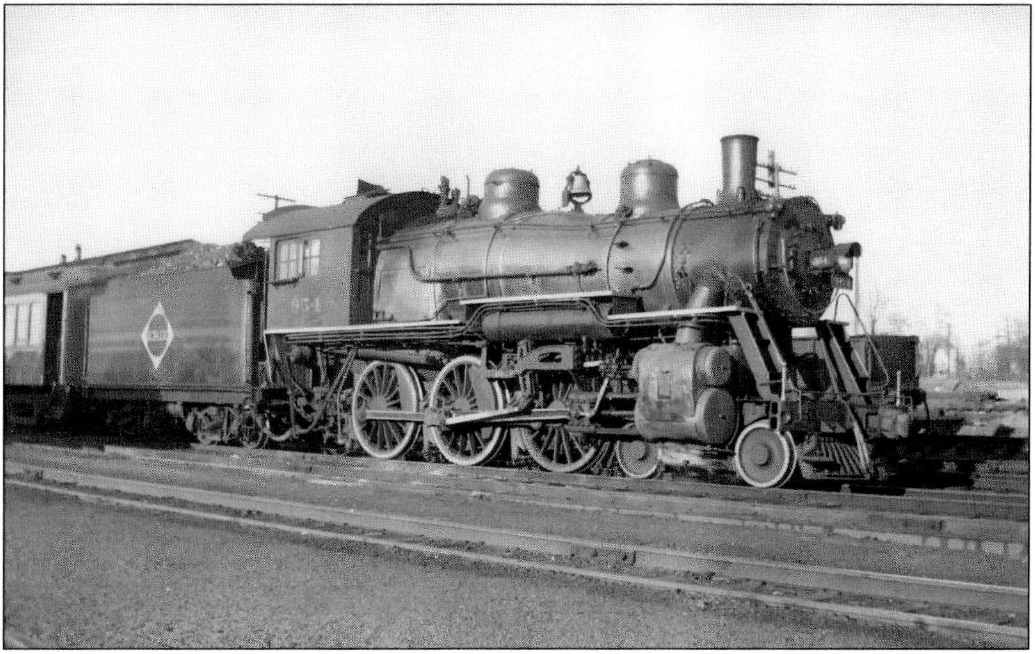

Erie Railroad 4-6-0 No. 954 is seen passing through North Hawthorne yard with an eastbound passenger train in this photograph taken on April 6, 1940. From the 1910s through early 1940s, the 4-6-0s were the backbone of the passenger locomotive fleet. Some locomotives in the 4-6-0 fleet were also purchased or leased by the NYS&W from the Erie Railroad and lettered "Susquehanna." (Courtesy of Railroad Avenue Enterprises; author's collection.)

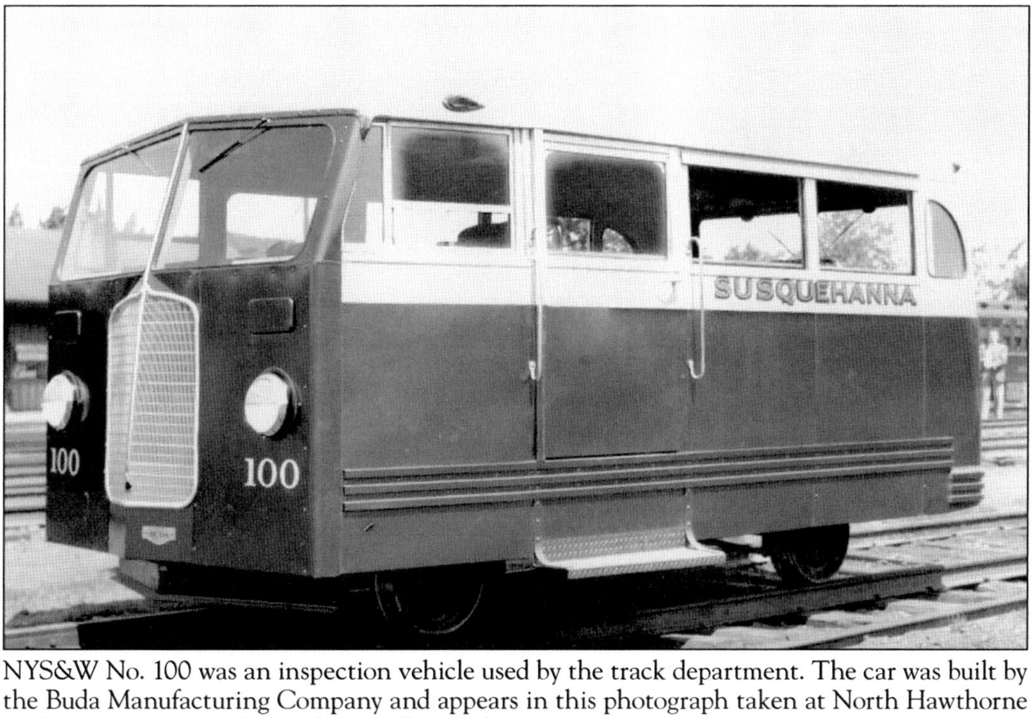

NYS&W No. 100 was an inspection vehicle used by the track department. The car was built by the Buda Manufacturing Company and appears in this photograph taken at North Hawthorne yard on August 3, 1940. (Author's collection.)

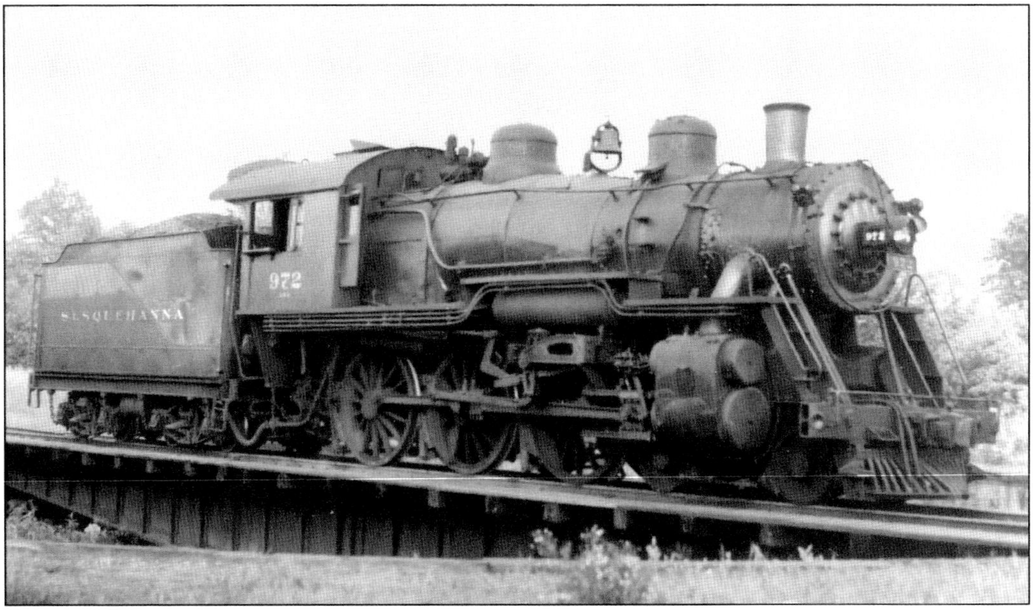

NYS&W 4-6-0 No. 972 is shown taking a ride on the North Hawthorne yard turntable in July 1940. By the time of this photograph, many of the NYS&W 10-wheel 4-6-0s were approaching 40 years of service. With readily available coal supplies in the nearby Poconos, almost all of the steam locomotives that ever operated on the NYS&W burned coal. (Photograph by John L. Treen; author's collection.)

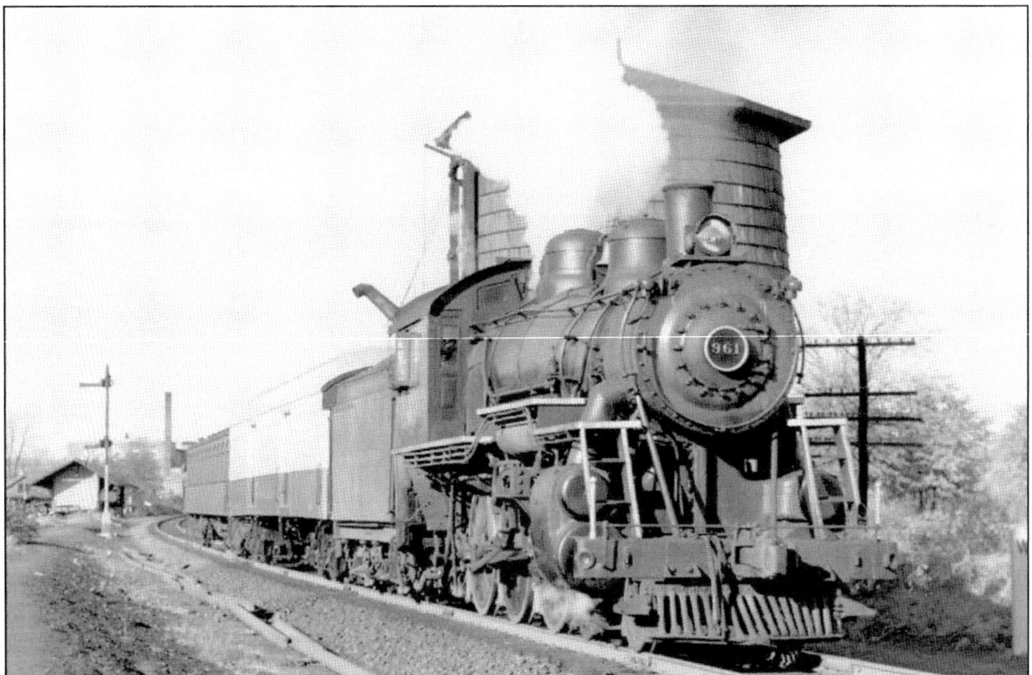

NYS&W 4-6-0 No. 961 chugs eastbound after departing North Hawthorne station, which is visible in the left background in this scene taken on November 2, 1940. Trailing No. 961 this day is a baggage/mail car and one of the ex-Erie Railroad Stillwell coaches. (Author's collection.)

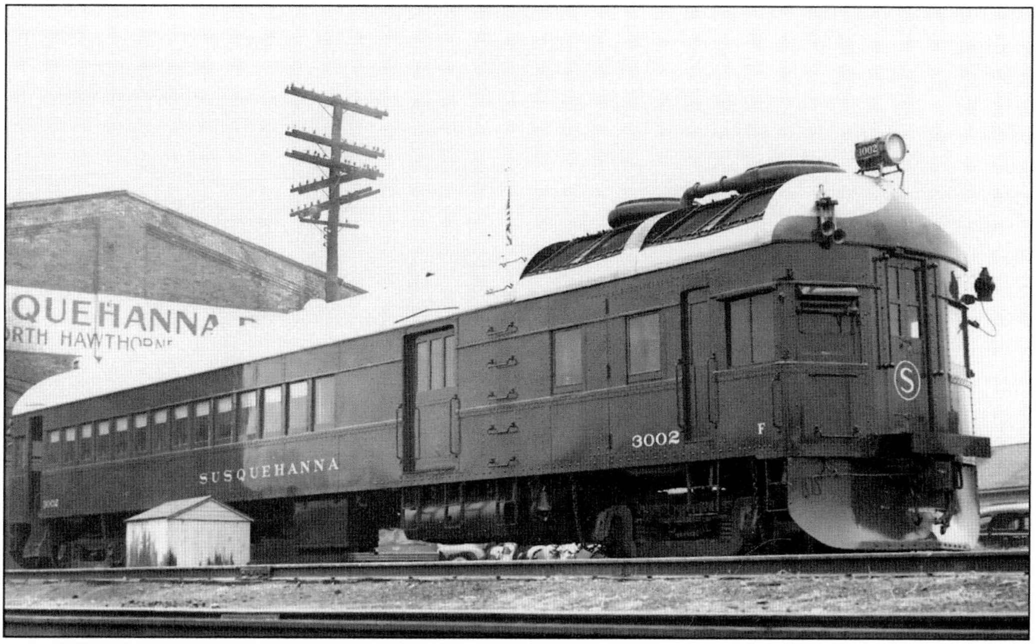

NYS&W No. 3002 was a secondhand, self-propelled, diesel car purchased from the Cumberland & Pennsylvania Railroad that was used for passenger service in the 1940s. Judging by its freshly painted maroon with gray lettering appearance, this view at North Hawthorne probably dates from early 1943, when the car entered service on the NYS&W. (Photograph by M. D. Carter; courtesy of Robert L. Steele and the Maywood Station Museum Collection.)

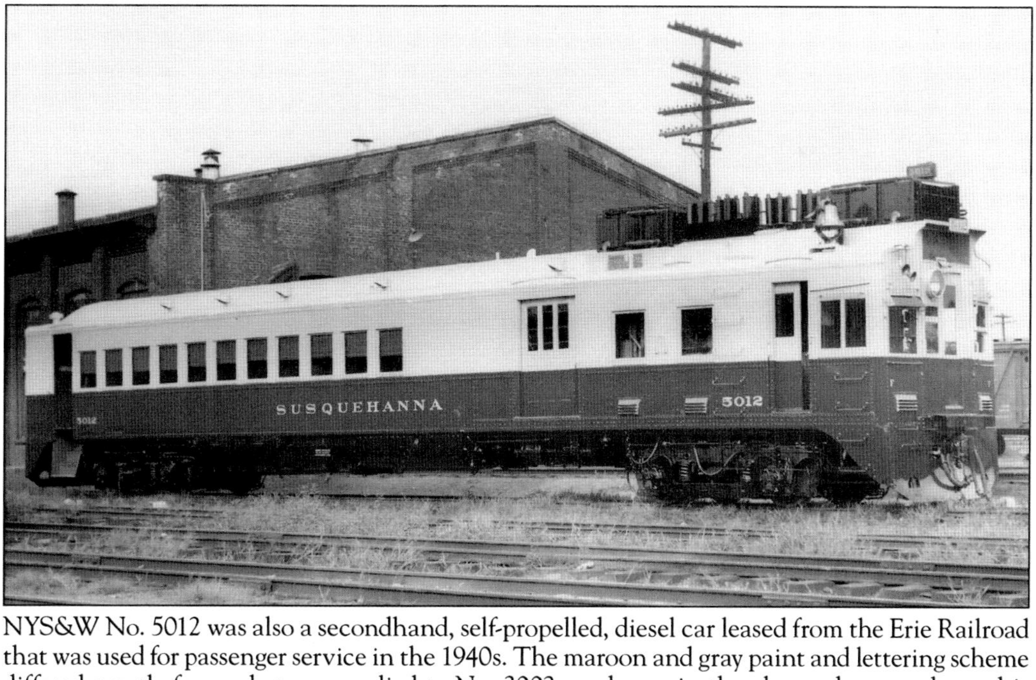

NYS&W No. 5012 was also a secondhand, self-propelled, diesel car leased from the Erie Railroad that was used for passenger service in the 1940s. The maroon and gray paint and lettering scheme differed greatly from what was applied to No. 3002, as shown in the above photograph on this page. No. 5012 survives today in deteriorating condition at a museum in Ohio. (Photograph by M. D. Carter; courtesy of Robert L. Steele and the Maywood Station Museum Collection.)

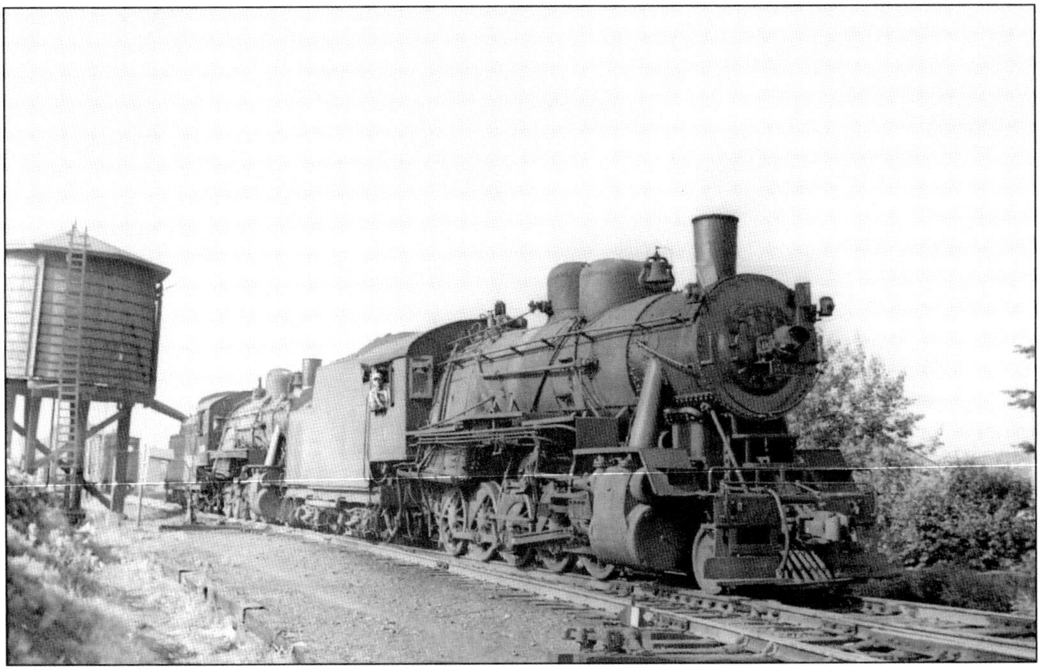

NYS&W 2-10-0 Nos. 2492 and 2490 are shown in this image ready to take on water from the water tower located in North Hawthorne yard in September 1941. The "Russian Decapod" 2-10-0 wheel arrangement were very well suited for the terrain of the NYS&W and served the railroad well in freight service. (Photograph by Vincent DeSantis; author's collection.)

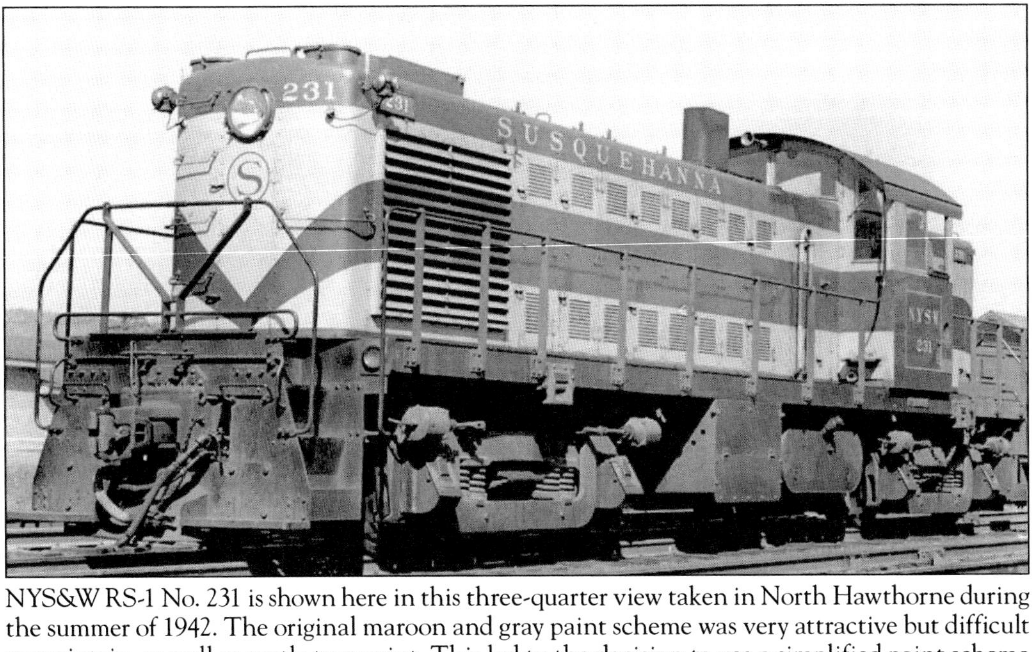

NYS&W RS-1 No. 231 is shown here in this three-quarter view taken in North Hawthorne during the summer of 1942. The original maroon and gray paint scheme was very attractive but difficult to maintain, as well as costly to repaint. This led to the decision to use a simplified paint scheme when these units were due for repainting in the 1950s. (Author's collection.)

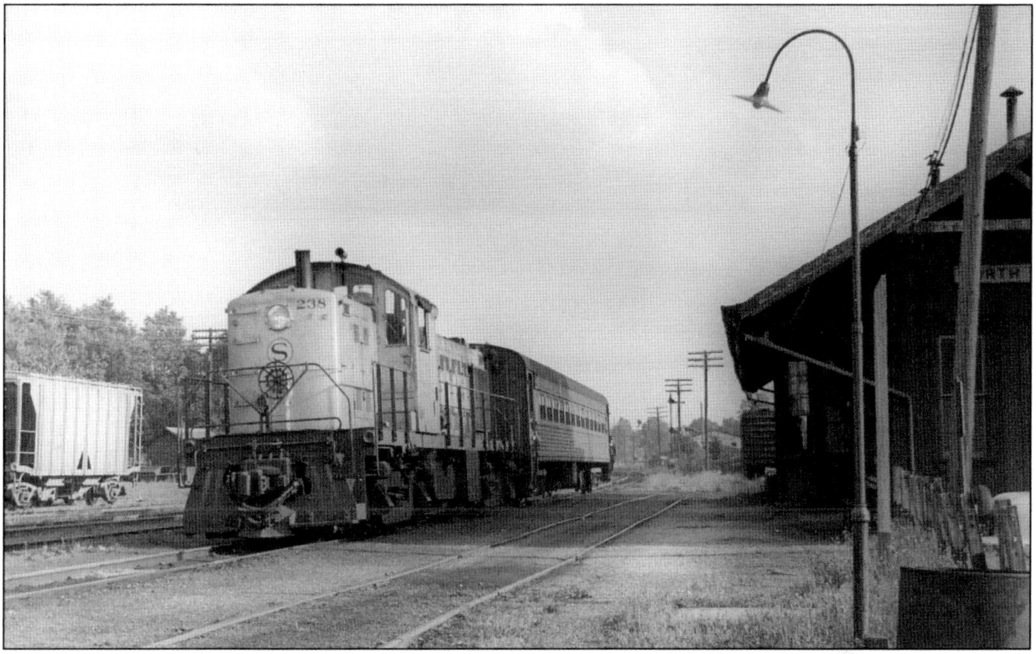

Westbound Train No. 919 consisting of one passenger car and led by NYS&W RS-1 No. 238 has arrived at North Hawthorne station in this image taken in June 1960. There are freight cars in the North Hawthorne yard this day, and a boxcar sits on the station's siding. (Photograph by Donald P. Wallworth; courtesy of Patrick J. Reynolds and the Maywood Station Museum Collection.)

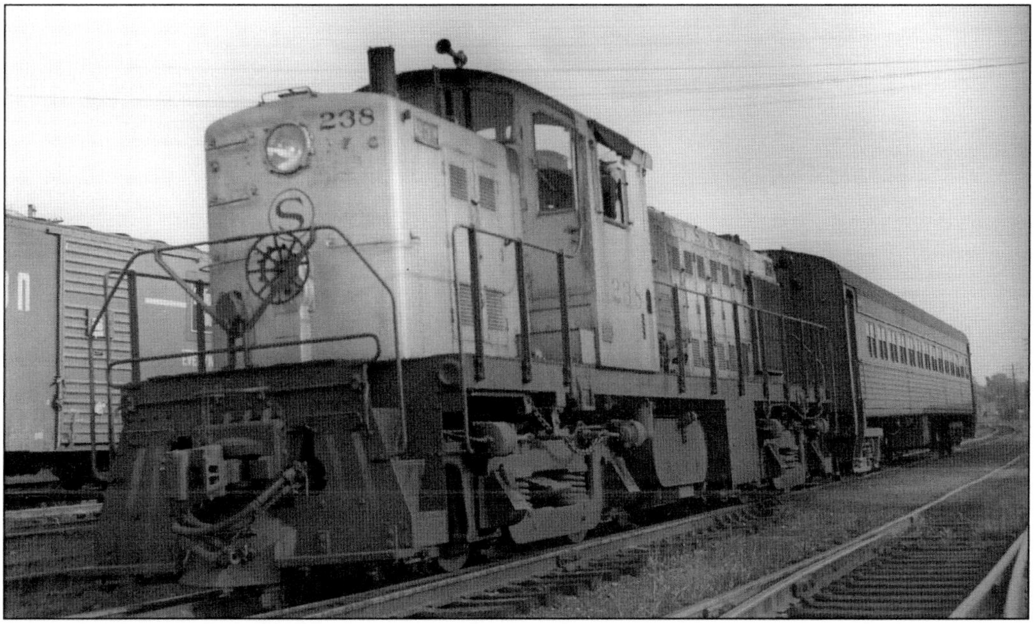

Westbound Train No. 919 (as also seen in the image above) pulls away from North Hawthorne station led by NYS&W RS-1 No. 238 and one passenger car. No. 238 was one of the longest surviving RS-1s on the NYS&W roster. The locomotive lasted into the middle 1980s when it was sold after nearly 40 years of service to the railroad. (Photograph by Donald P. Wallworth; courtesy of Patrick J. Reynolds and the Maywood Station Museum Collection.)

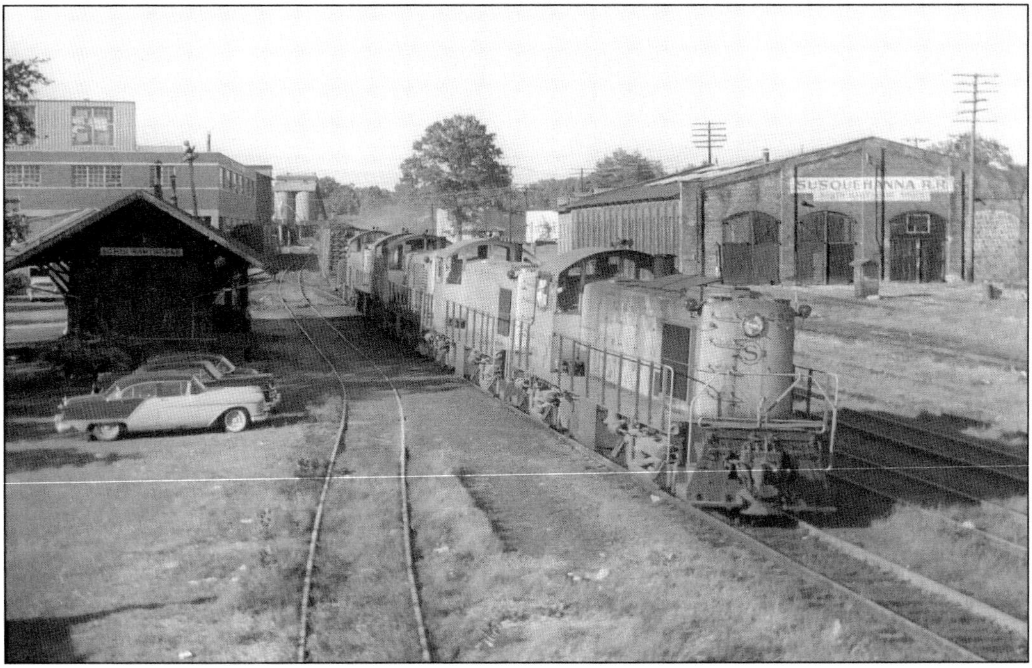

NYS&W RS-1 No. 252 leads three sister RS-1s and one S-2 with an eastbound "Hainesburg Extra" freight train past North Hawthorne station and the former NYS&W shops in this scene captured on September 14, 1960. Today the station is long gone and only a few pieces of the shop complex exist. (This photograph is also on the cover of this book.) (Photograph by Donald P. Wallworth; courtesy of Patrick J. Reynolds and the Maywood Station Museum Collection.)

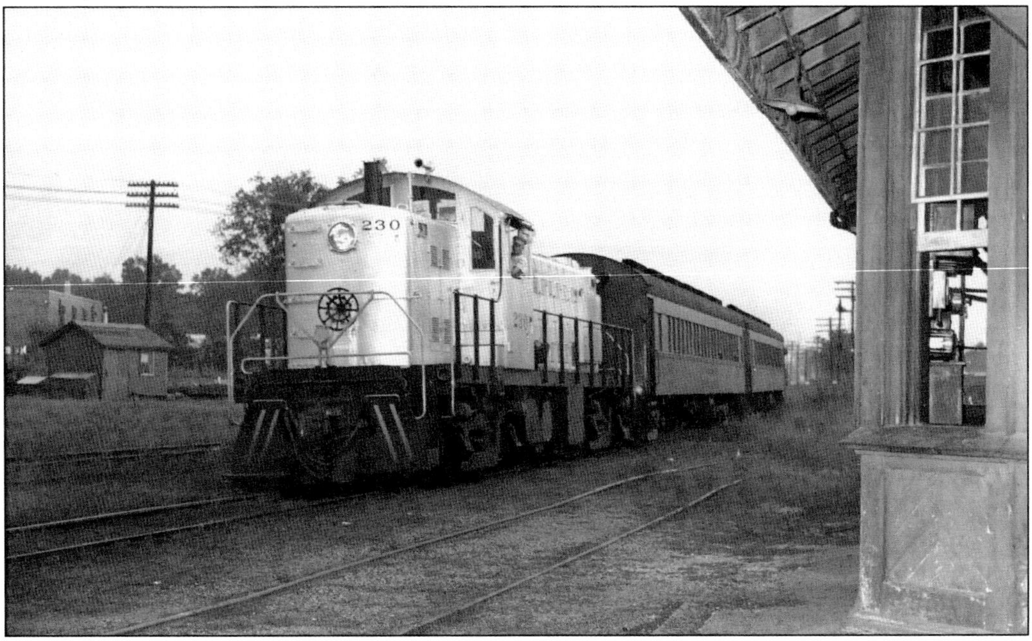

It must be warm out in this view because the bay window on North Hawthorne station is open as NYS&W RS-1 No. 230 arrives from the east with two passenger cars in tow in August 1964. No. 230 looks spiffy in its fresh coat new paint. (Photograph by John Krause; author's collection.)

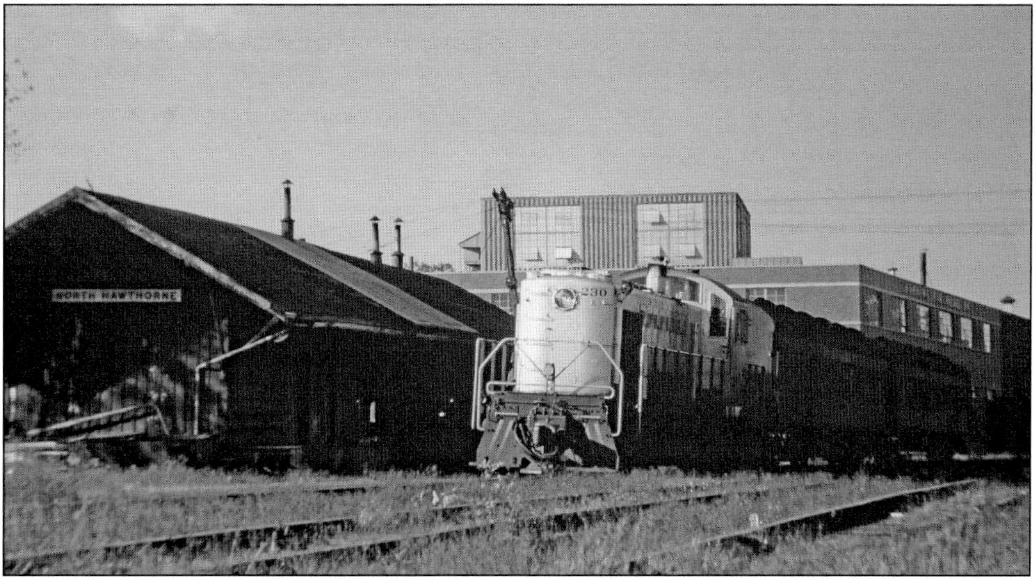

In this photograph, NYS&W RS-1 No. 230 gets ready to depart North Hawthorne station eastbound with two passenger cars in January 1965. The station is beginning to look a little worse for wear but is still being actively used at this date. (Courtesy of Patrick J. Reynolds collection.)

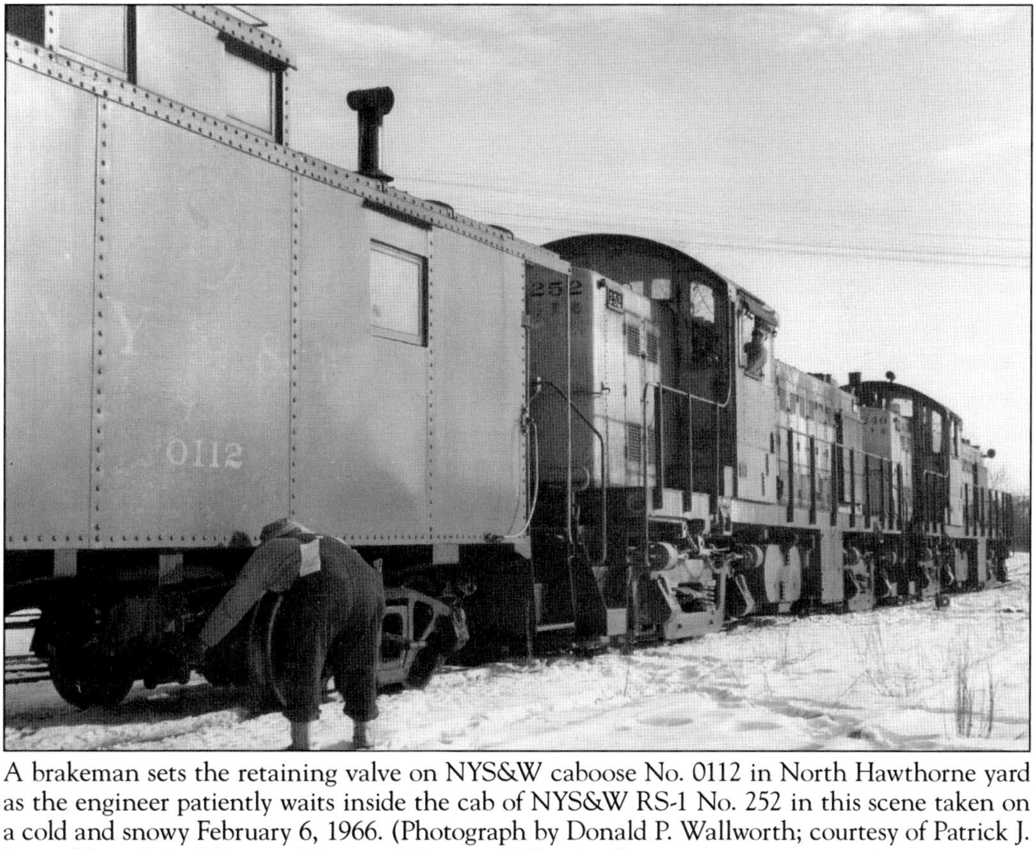

A brakeman sets the retaining valve on NYS&W caboose No. 0112 in North Hawthorne yard as the engineer patiently waits inside the cab of NYS&W RS-1 No. 252 in this scene taken on a cold and snowy February 6, 1966. (Photograph by Donald P. Wallworth; courtesy of Patrick J. Reynolds and the Maywood Station Museum Collection.)

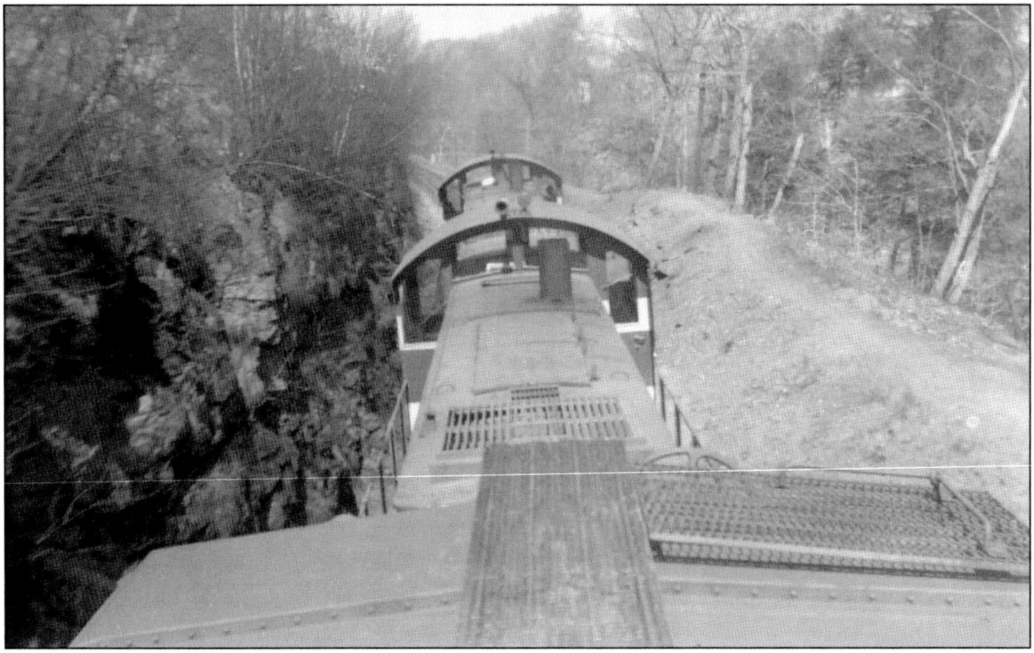

In a photograph taken from the top of the boxcar behind NYS&W RS-1 Nos. 252 and 248, brakeman John L. Treen has captured this unique image of his train going through a cut in Midland Park on March 25, 1948. Treen was a longtime employee of the NYS&W and took many classic photographs of his daily work assignments. (Photograph by John L. Treen; courtesy of Thomas J. Callan and the Maywood Station Museum Collection.)

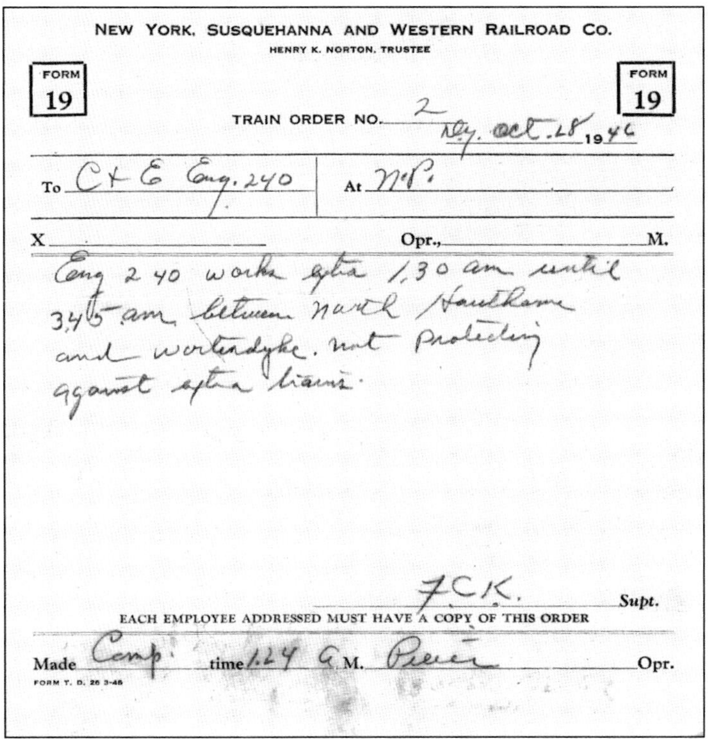

NEW YORK, SUSQUEHANNA AND WESTERN RAILROAD CO.

HENRY K. NORTON, TRUSTEE

FORM 19 | FORM 19

TRAIN ORDER NO. 2 Ny. Oct. 28 1946

To C+E Eng. 240 | At NP.

X ______ Opr., ______ M.

Eng 240 works extra 1.30 am until 3.45 am between North Hawthorne and Wortendyke. not protecting against extra trains.

JCK. Supt.

EACH EMPLOYEE ADDRESSED MUST HAVE A COPY OF THIS ORDER

Made Comp. time 1.24 AM. Pierce Opr.

FORM T. D. 26 3-46

This is an example of a NYS&W Form 19 Train Order that was issued on October 28, 1946, to the conductor and engineer of NYS&W RS-1 No. 240 giving permission to work from 1:30 a.m. to 3:45 a.m. between the locations of North Hawthorne and Wortendyke. (Courtesy of Robert L. Steele and the Maywood Station Museum Collection.)

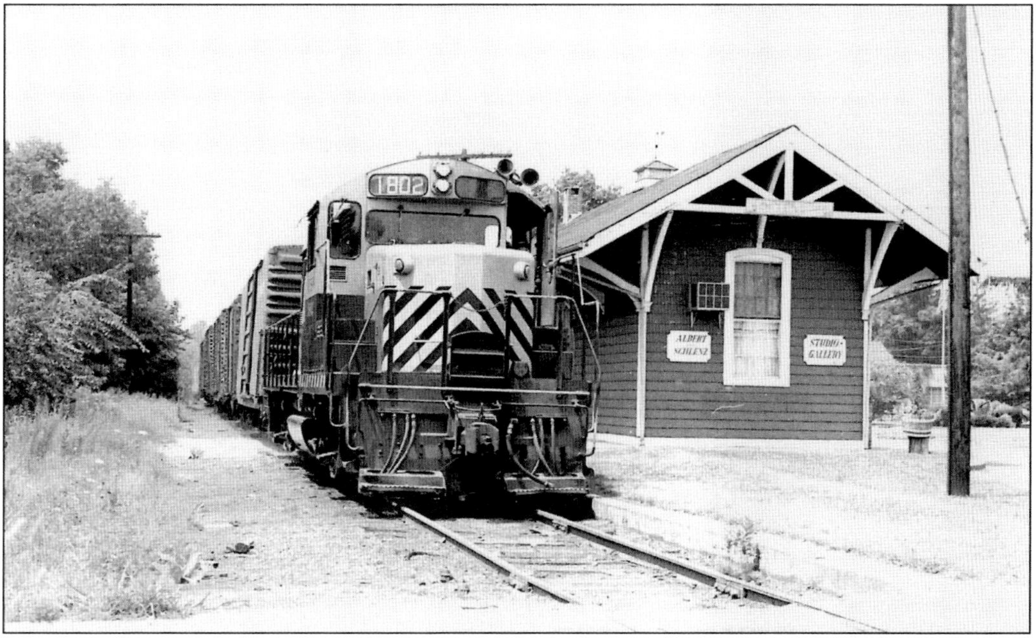

NYS&W GP18 No. 1802 proceeds east with a short train of boxcars in this scene taken at Wortendyke station on July 25, 1973. At the time of this photograph, the station was no longer needed by the railroad and was leased to Albert and Schlenz as an art studio/gallery. (Courtesy Railroad Avenue Enterprises; author's collection.)

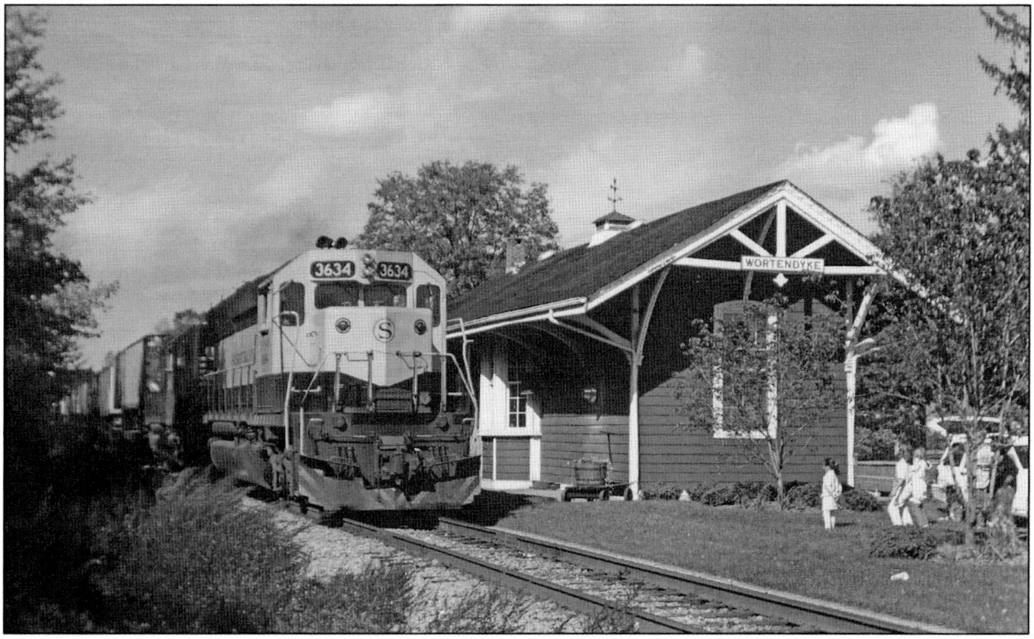

In this view, a group of children look on as NYS&W SD45 No. 3634 leads eastbound intermodal train No. 258 past Wortendyke station en route to Resources Terminal in North Bergen for unloading. The Wortendyke station has been nicely maintained through the years by its private owners. Opened in the early 1990s, Resources Terminal is a warehousing and intermodal facility that is rail served by the NYS&W. (Author's collection.)

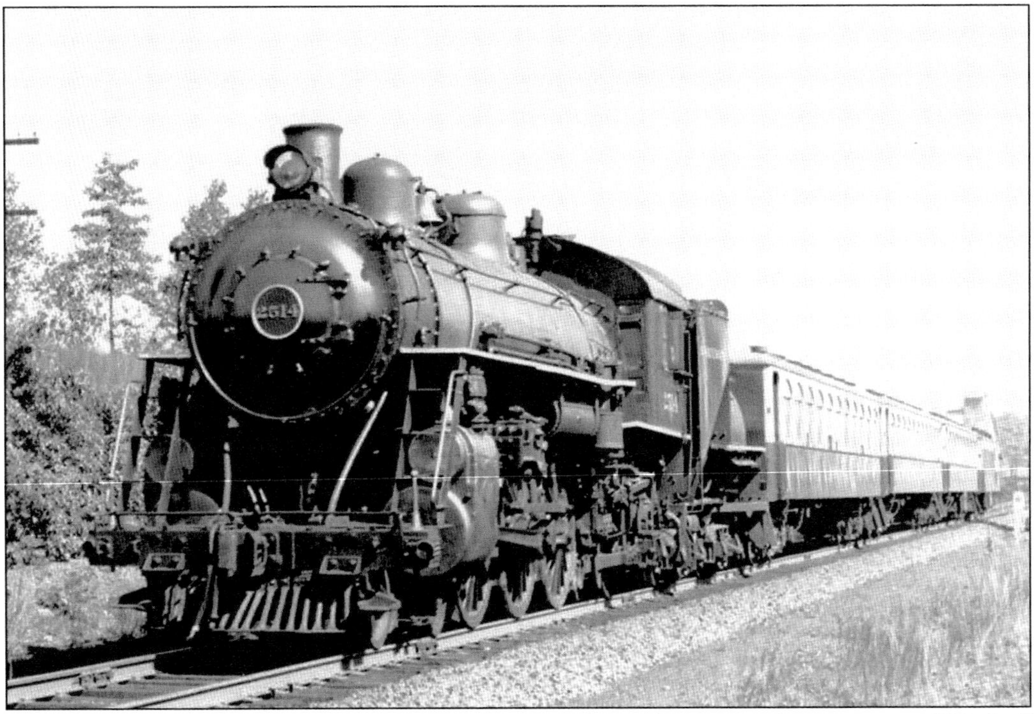

NYS&W 4-6-2 No. 2514 rolls westbound en route to Butler in this scene taken just west of Wyckoff station on September 13, 1940. Three ex-Erie Railroad Stillwell coaches and a combination mail/baggage car trail the Pacific-type steam locomotive. (Author's collection.)

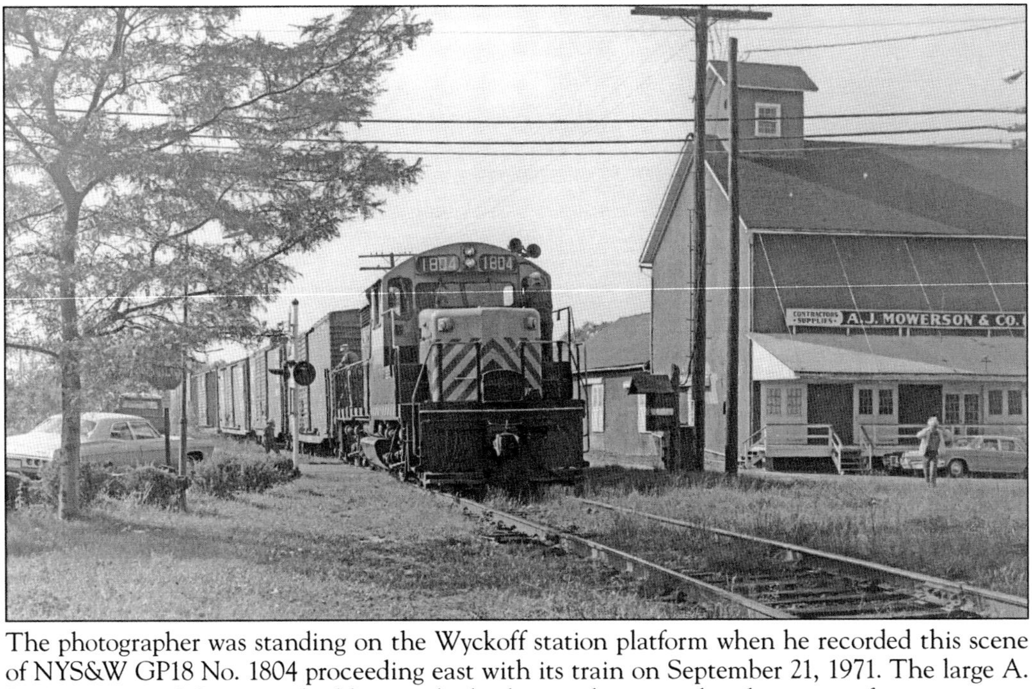

The photographer was standing on the Wyckoff station platform when he recorded this scene of NYS&W GP18 No. 1804 proceeding east with its train on September 21, 1971. The large A. J. Mowerson and Company building in the background was a railroad customer for many years. (Photograph by Donald P. Wallworth; author's collection.)

Five

Franklin Lakes to Butler

Heading west from Wyckoff, the NYS&W passes through the Campgaw and Crystal Lake sections of Franklin Lakes. The NYS&W begins to drop downhill as it approaches Oakland and as the descent averages .090 percent. Oakland, for many years, was a stop for vacationers, tourists, fishermen, and hunters. There has never been an abundance of industry in Oakland, and the NYS&W has had only had a handful of shippers use the railroad. The NYS&W once again crosses back into Passaic County upon entering Pompton Lakes. The NYS&W experiences a minimal .019 percent westbound descent through the borough.

Continuing westward, the NYS&W makes its first appearance in Morris County upon entering Riverdale. An important connection was once found within the borough at Pompton Junction where the Erie Railroad's New York & Greenwood Lake Division crossed the NYS&W at grade. The crossing was once controlled by a tower, and an interchange between the two railroads was conducted there. Just west of Pompton Junction, the NYS&W begins a climb of .086 percent heading west into Bloomingdale, where several industries have been located, including the A. H. Matheiu plant that is still in operation under new owners. The NYS&W faces a 1.09 percent westbound ruling grade through Bloomingdale. West of Bloomingdale is Butler and what was the western terminus for the NYS&W's commuter operations. A small yard, locomotive servicing tracks, and a turntable were once found there. The NYS&W's westbound ruling grade through Butler increases to 1.28 percent, and it is not uncommon for heavy trains today to stall on this section of the railroad.

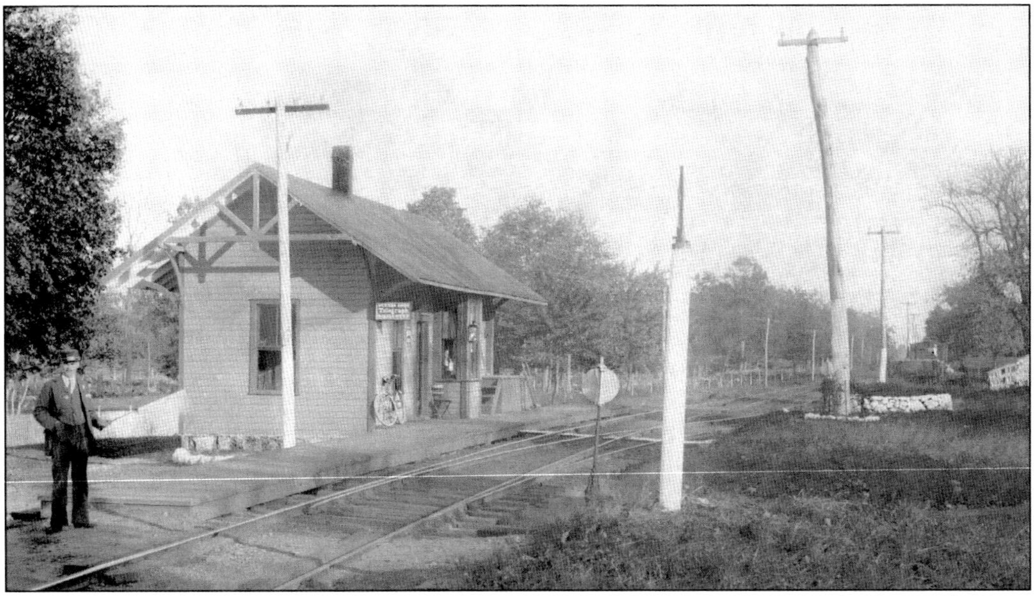

Campgaw, in the borough of Franklin Lakes, has long had a passing siding, which is still in use today. Helper locomotives, which were employed to assist trains up the grades, once used the track. Charles M. Berdan, the station agent at the time, is seen in the left of this photograph that was taken in the summer of 1895. (Courtesy of Mary Gardiner and the Maywood Station Museum Collection.)

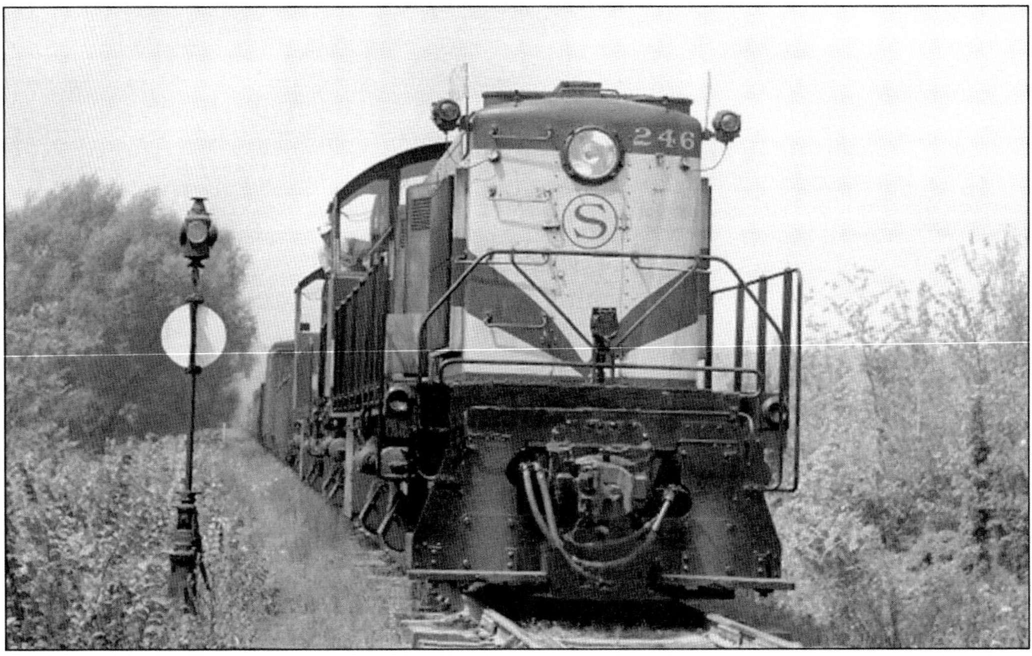

NYS&W RS-1 No. 246 and a sister RS-1 are in charge of a freight train as they approach the switch for the passing siding Campgaw in this view taken in September 1946. No. 246 has white flags above its marker lights, signifying that this is a special freight. Note the high switch stand and switch lantern—all reminders of railroading's past. (Photograph by John L. Treen; author's collection.)

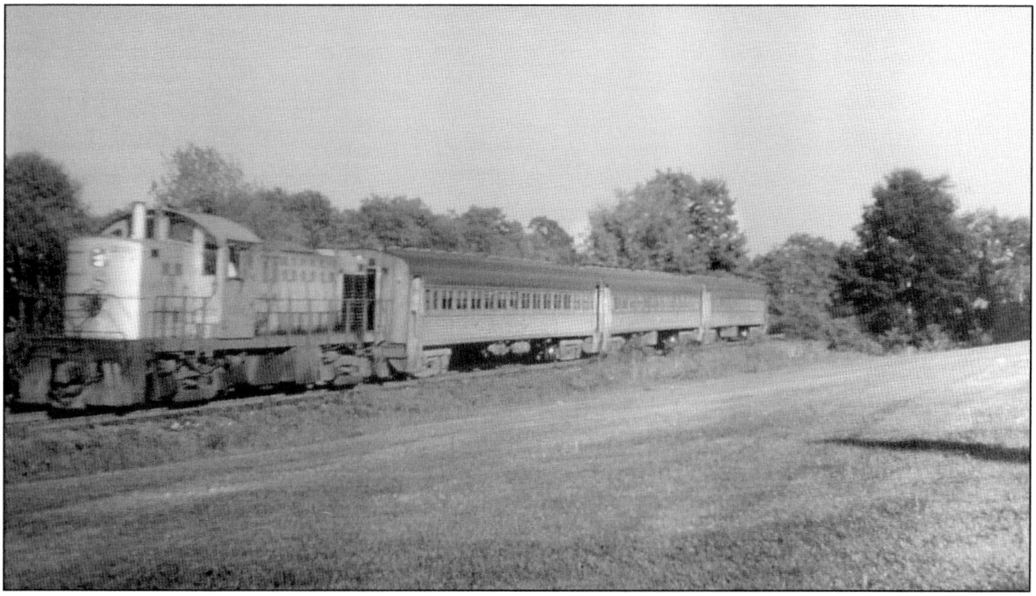

In July 1957, NYS&W RS-1 No. 232 is shown rolling through Campgaw with its three-car passenger train. The NYS&W's fleet of RS-1s were highly versatile and could be found in any work assignment ranging from powering passenger, to road, to local freight trains to yard switching service. (Author's collection.)

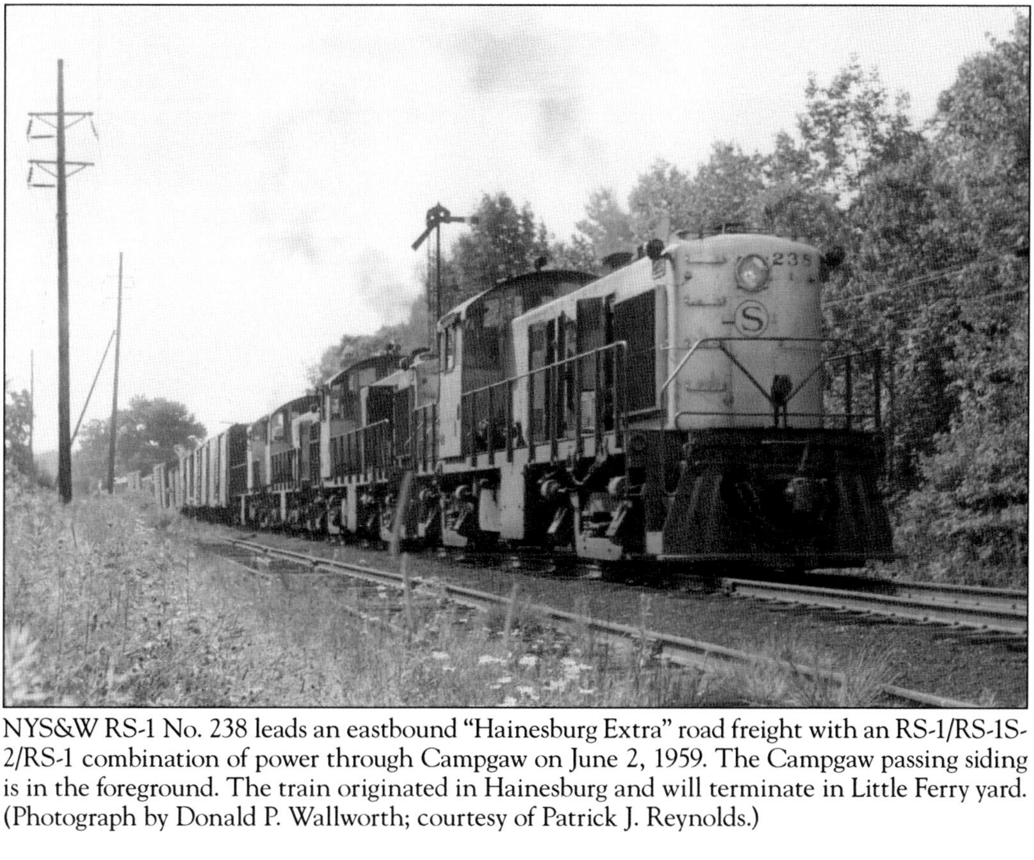

NYS&W RS-1 No. 238 leads an eastbound "Hainesburg Extra" road freight with an RS-1/RS-1S-2/RS-1 combination of power through Campgaw on June 2, 1959. The Campgaw passing siding is in the foreground. The train originated in Hainesburg and will terminate in Little Ferry yard. (Photograph by Donald P. Wallworth; courtesy of Patrick J. Reynolds.)

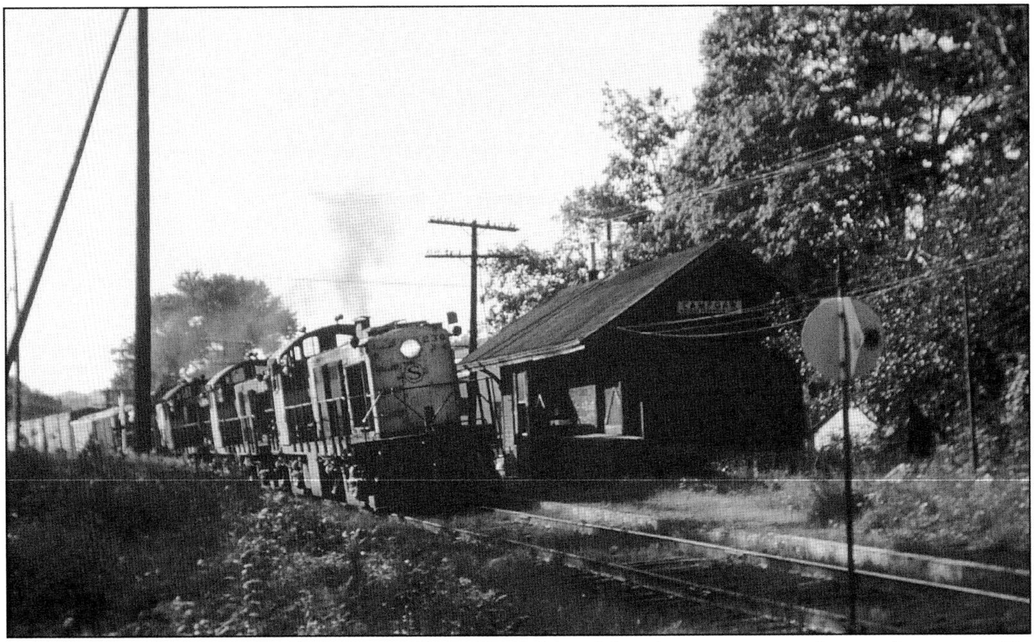

NYS&W RS-1 No. 230, with a "Hainesburg Extra" road freight consisting of interchange traffic from the Lehigh & New England Railway, leads three sister units eastbound past Campgaw station during a late afternoon in September 1959. (Photograph by Donald P. Wallworth; courtesy of Patrick J. Reynolds.)

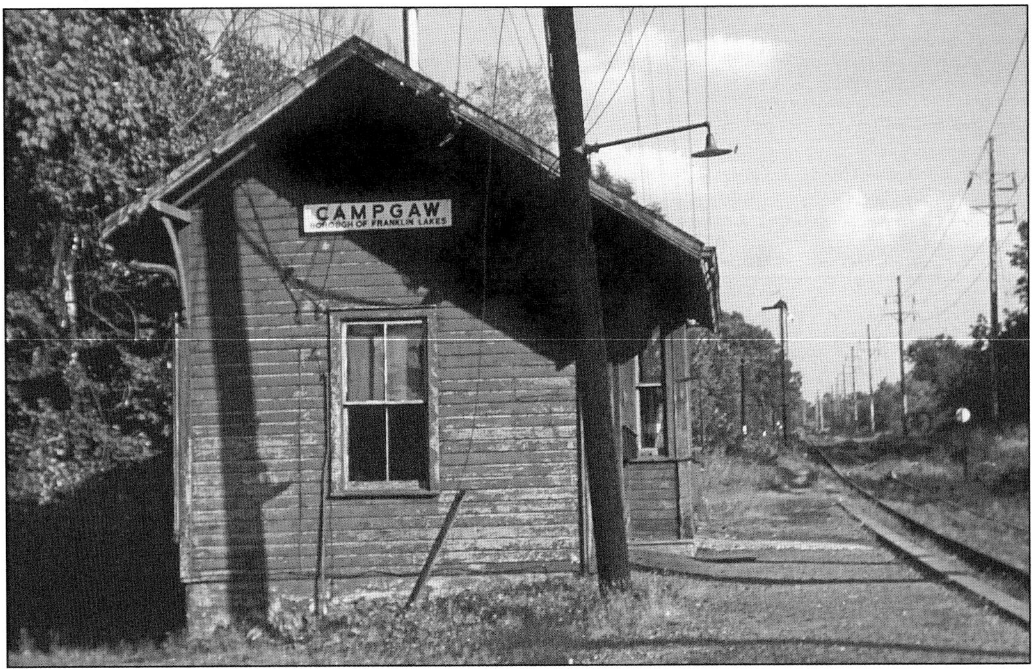

In this vantage point looking east in September 1959, Campgaw station is looking a bit worse for wear. The passing siding begins on the right, just beyond the station, and in the distance a semaphore signal can be seen. (Photograph by Donald P. Wallworth; courtesy of Patrick J. Reynolds.)

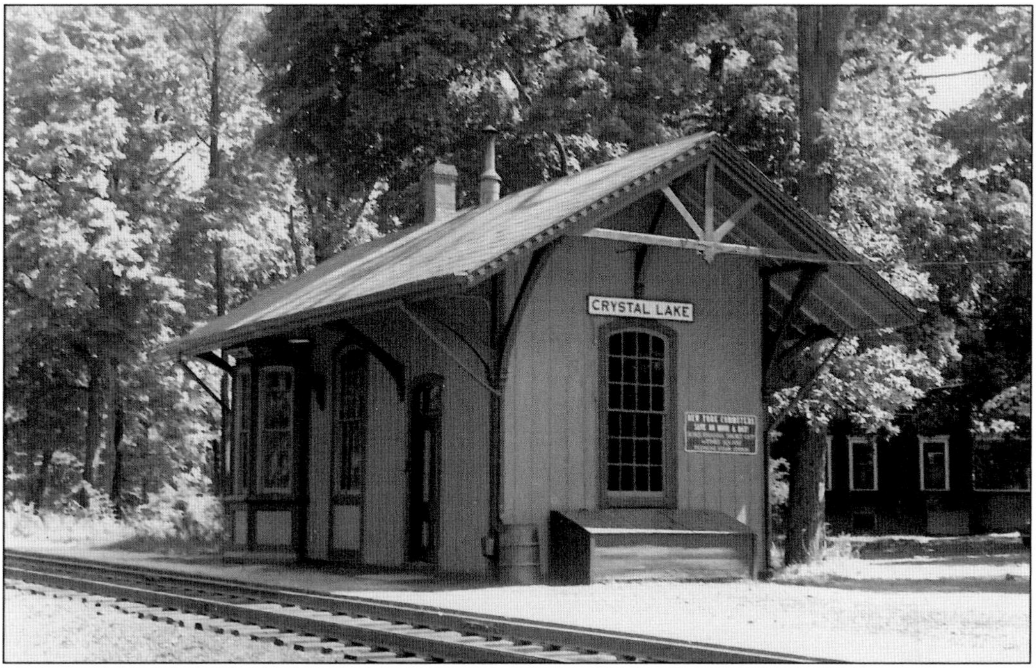

Crystal Lake station in the borough of Franklin Lakes served primarily as a stop for the nearby lake, which was frequented by vacationers during the first half of the 1900s. Crystal Lake station exhibited a typical design used for many of the NYS&W's suburban stations utilizing board and batten exteriors. This view was taken in September 1939. (Courtesy Railroad Avenue Enterprises; author's collection.)

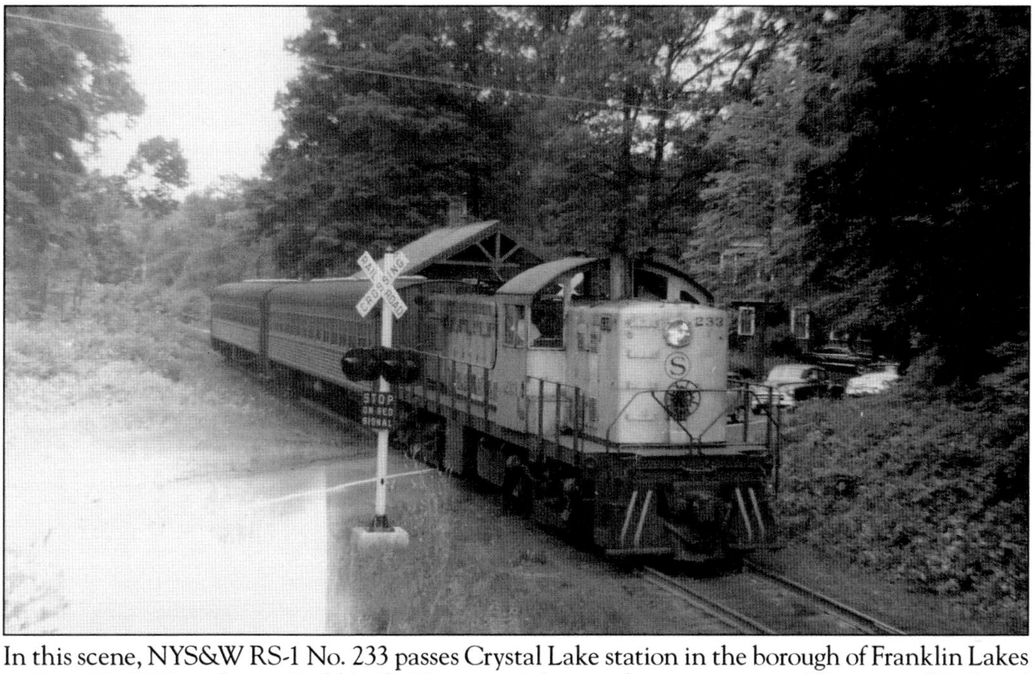

In this scene, NYS&W RS-1 No. 233 passes Crystal Lake station in the borough of Franklin Lakes on June 19, 1959, with two Budd-built 85-seat stainless steel passenger cars. (Courtesy of Railroad Avenue Enterprises; author's collection.)

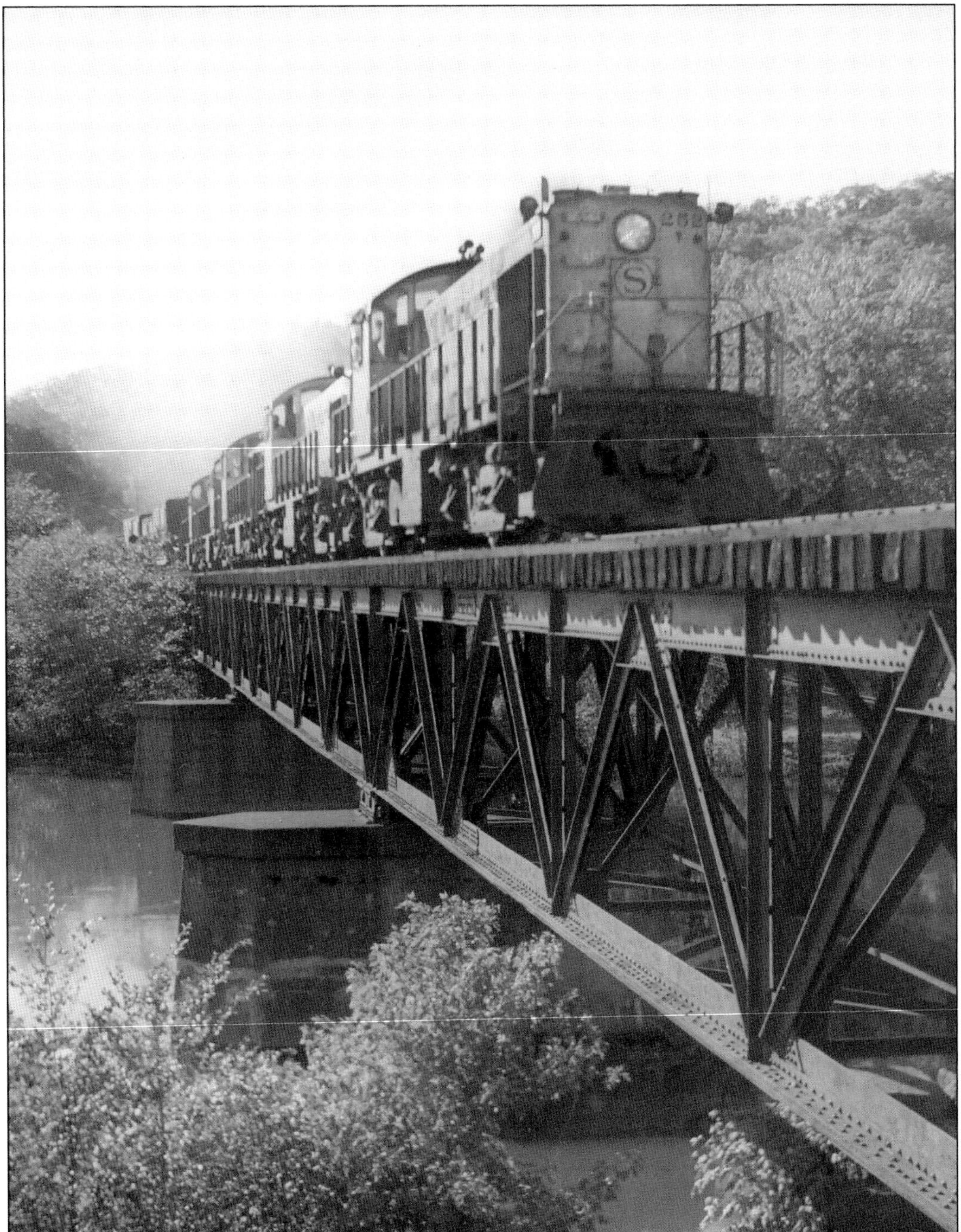

Noted railroad photographer Donald P. Wallworth took this dramatic view on September 14, 1960, of NYS&W RS-1 No. 252 leading four sister RS-1s and its freight train eastbound across the bridge over the Ramapo River in Oakland. (Photograph by Donald P. Wallworth; courtesy of Patrick J. Reynolds and the Maywood Station Museum Collection.)

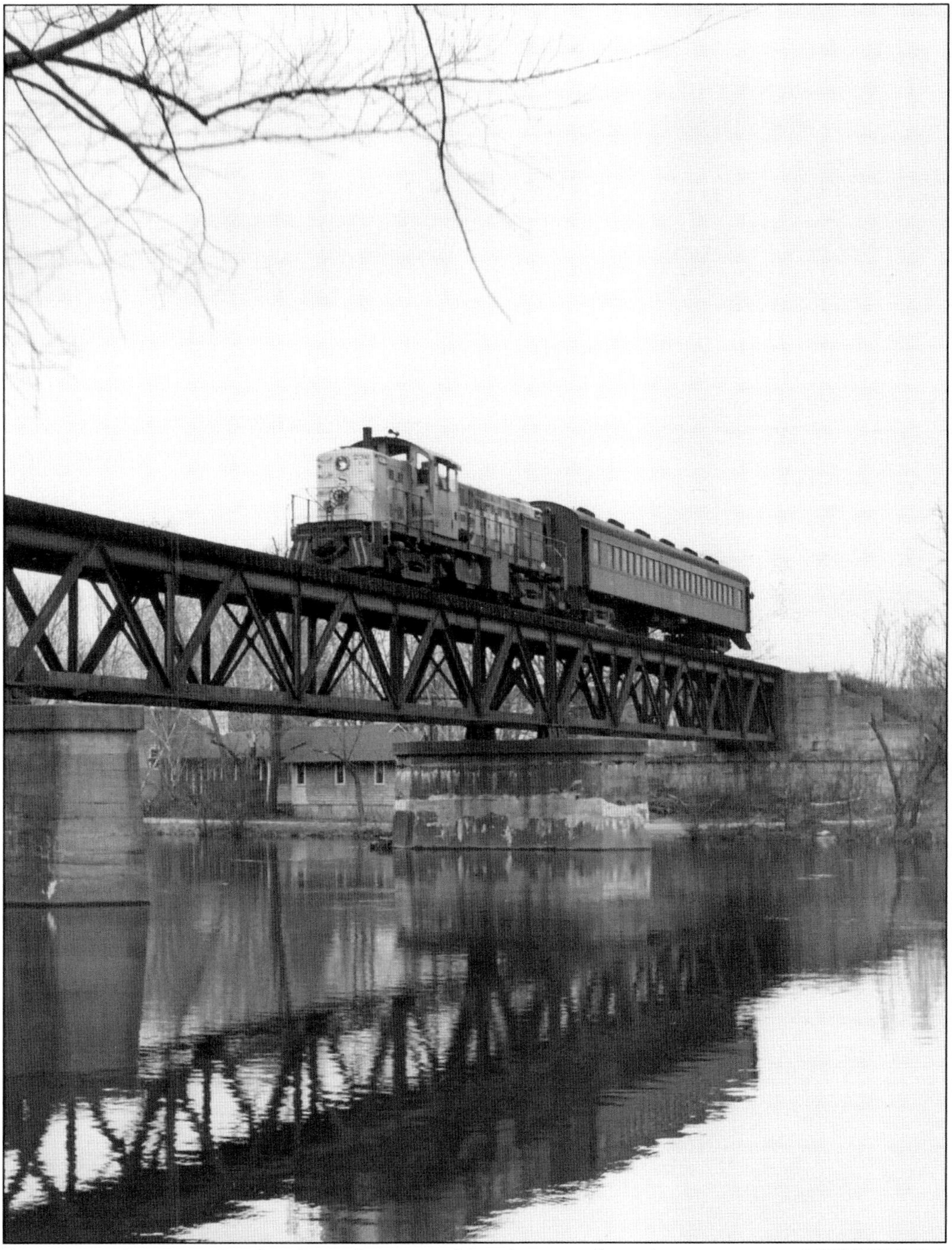

At a scenic location that has been frequented by photographers for many years, NYS&W RS-1 No. 236 heads westbound with one passenger car as it crosses the bridge over the Ramapo River in Oakland in December 1961. The Ramapo River is a favorite of trout fishermen and recreation enthusiasts. (Photograph by Donald P. Wallworth; courtesy of Patrick J. Reynolds and the Maywood Station Museum Collection.)

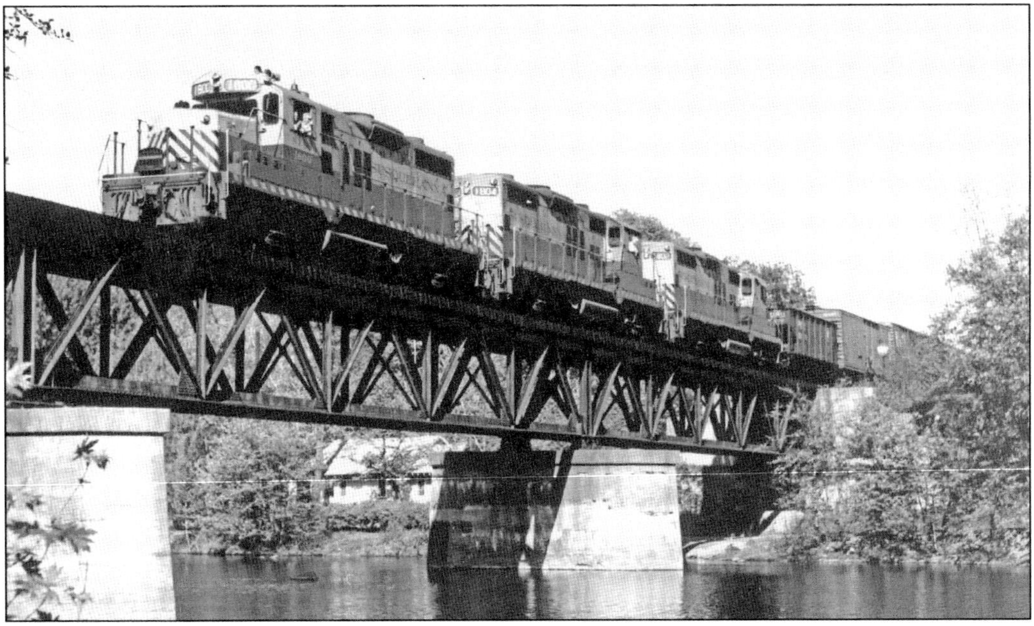

In another beautiful view of the bridge over the Ramapo River in Oakland, all three of the NYS&W GP18s led by No. 1800 and its train are visible in September 1966. It must be very large freight since the entire roster of GP18s are being utilized on this day. (Photograph by Donald P. Wallworth; author's collection.)

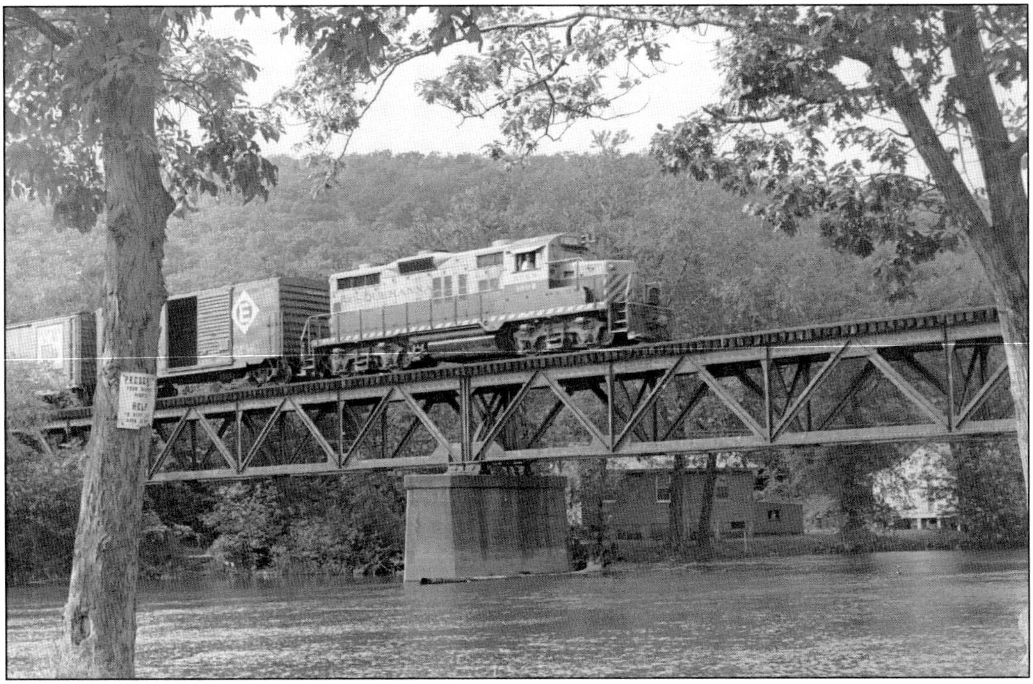

In this nicely composed scene between two trees, NYS&W GP18 No. 1804 is shown crossing the bridge over the Ramapo River in Oakland with an eastbound freight on September 21, 1972. There must have been recent heavy rains in the area since the river is swelled to the banks. (Photograph by Donald P. Wallworth; author's collection.)

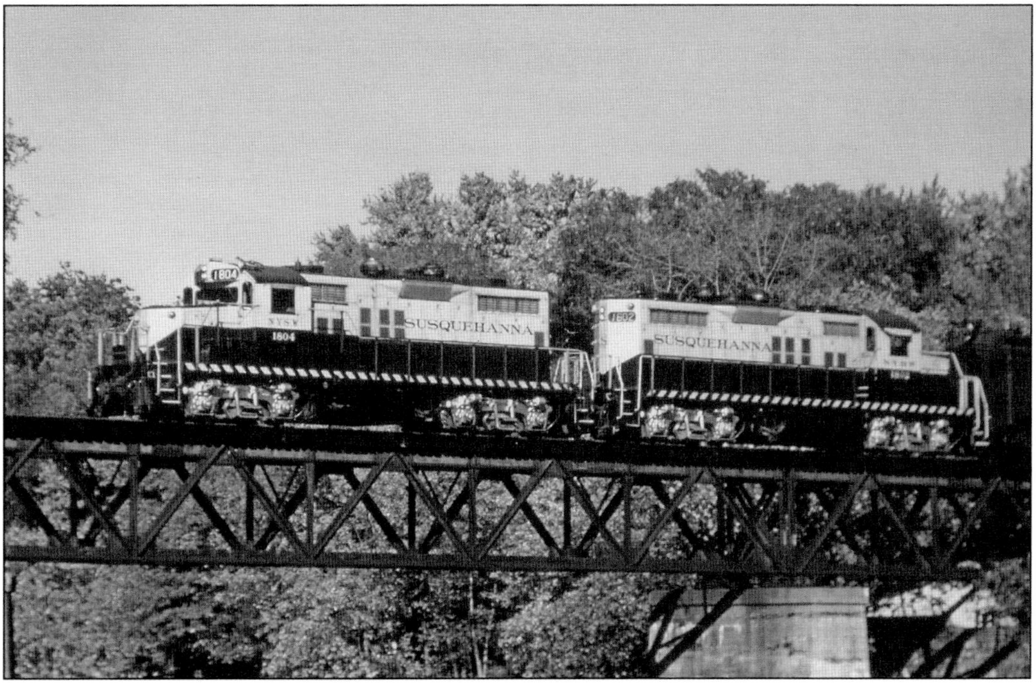

NYS&W GP18 Nos. 1804 and 1802 are high above the Ramapo River in Oakland in this scene taken in October 1981. Both locomotives have been recently repainted in a new, modified scheme for the GP18s. The chevron stripes on the ends are gone but the S-ball logo has been applied in their place, the truck side frames are now silver instead of black, and the top of the hoods and cab roofs are now black instead of yellow. (Author's collection.)

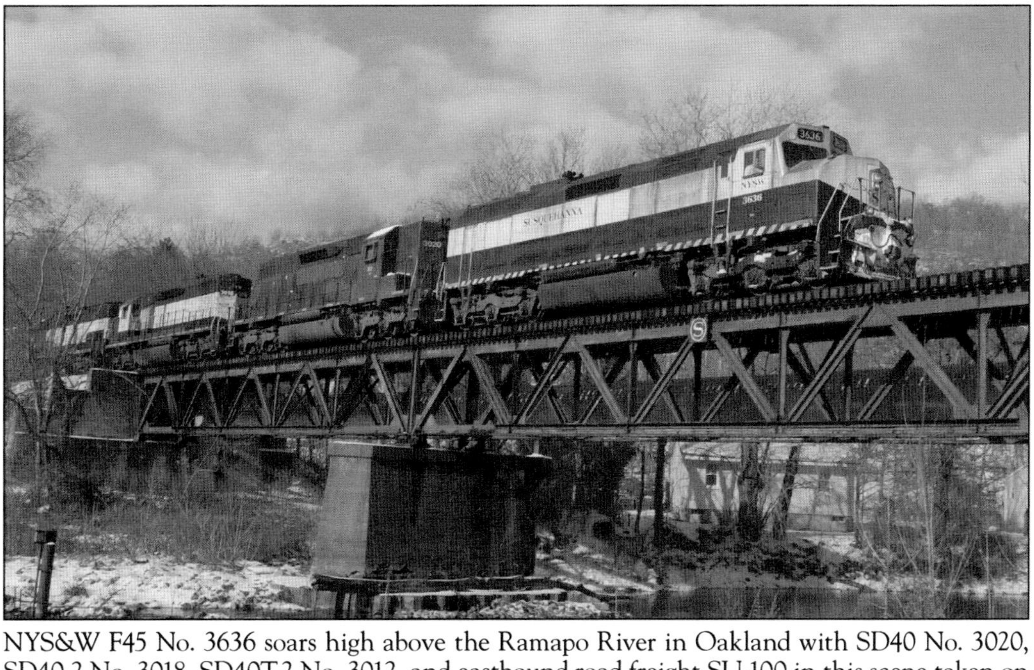

NYS&W F45 No. 3636 soars high above the Ramapo River in Oakland with SD40 No. 3020, SD40-2 No. 3018, SD40T-2 No. 3012, and eastbound road freight SU-100 in this scene taken on a sunny but frigid December 14, 2007. (Photograph by the author.)

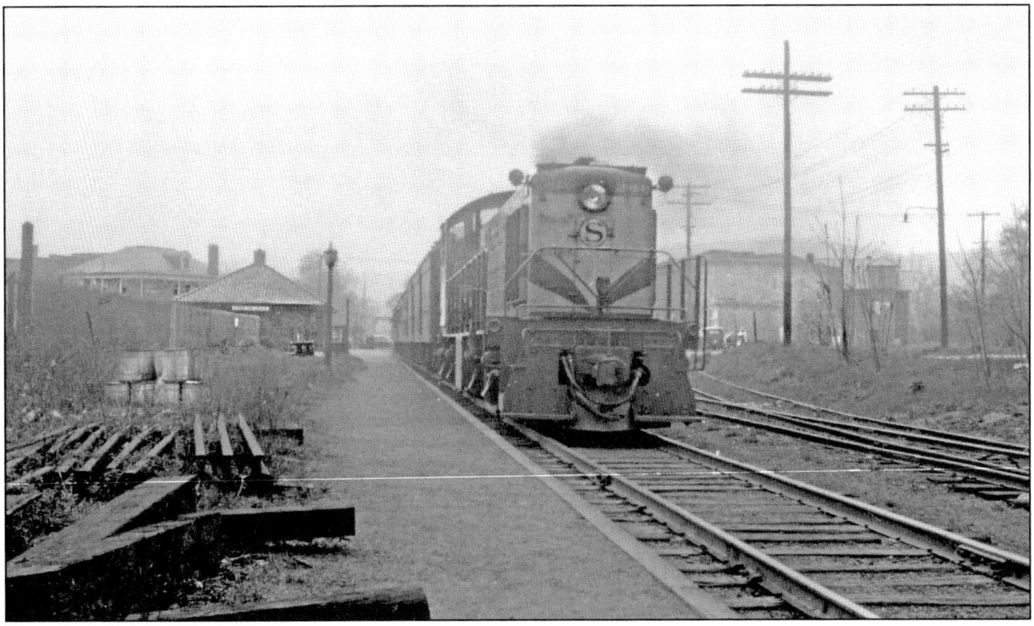

Through the years, numerous industries in Pompton Lakes have provided the NYS&W with carloads of traffic. In this view, NYS&W RS-1 No. 240 is shown leaving the Pompton Lakes station with eastbound passenger train No. 950 on May 17, 1947. The station still exists today and is privately owned. (Photograph by John L. Treen; courtesy of Thomas J. Callan and the Maywood Station Museum Collection.)

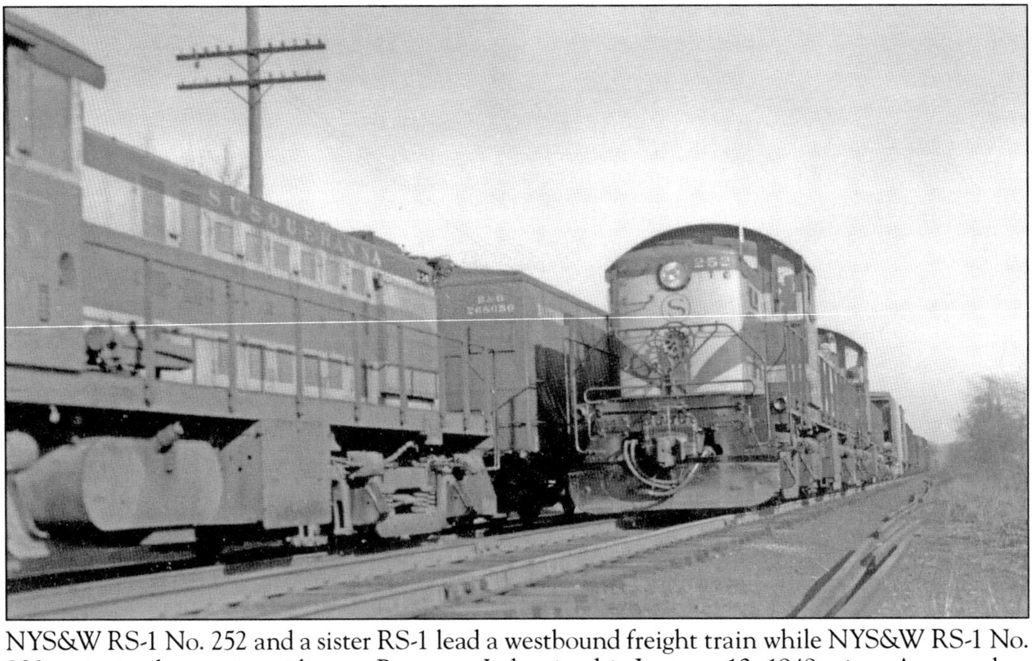

NYS&W RS-1 No. 252 and a sister RS-1 lead a westbound freight train while NYS&W RS-1 No. 230 waits in the passing siding at Pompton Lakes in this January 13, 1949, view. A snowplow appears on the front pilot of No. 252, which was not a common feature on the NYS&W fleet of RS-1 diesel locomotives. (Photograph by John L. Treen; courtesy of Thomas J. Callan and the Maywood Station Museum Collection.)

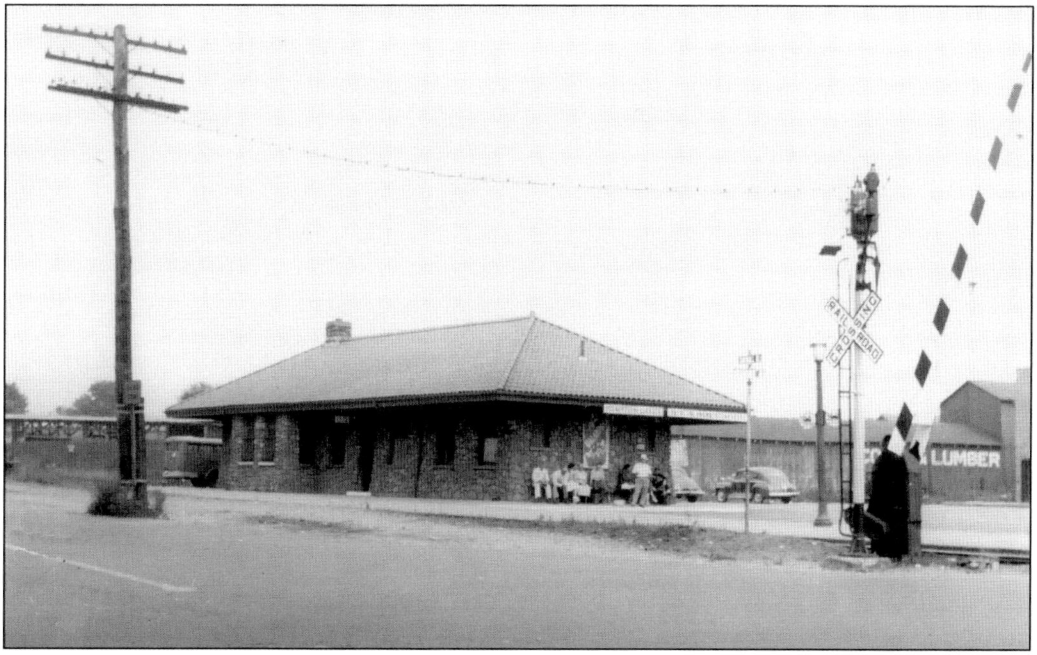

Pompton Lakes station was different than all the other NYS&W stations. Under Erie Railroad control in the 1920s, the original wood-designed station was replaced with a concrete and stone station during a period of modernization on the railroad, as shown in this view taken in July 1955. (Courtesy of Railroad Avenue Enterprises; author's collection.)

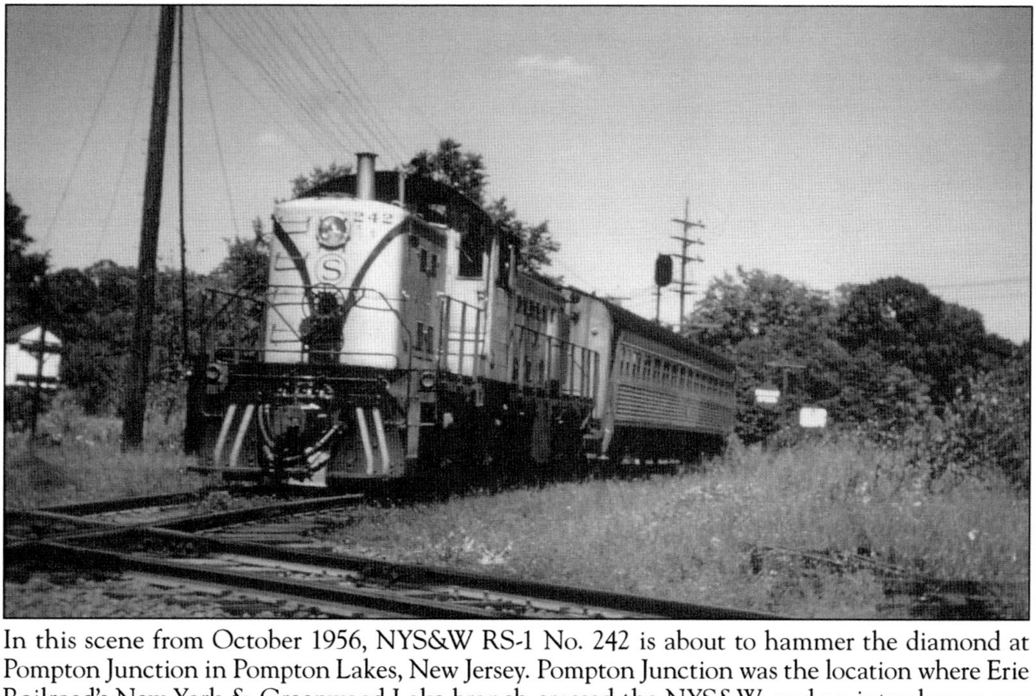
In this scene from October 1956, NYS&W RS-1 No. 242 is about to hammer the diamond at Pompton Junction in Pompton Lakes, New Jersey. Pompton Junction was the location where Erie Railroad's New York & Greenwood Lake branch crossed the NYS&W, and an interchange was conducted at this location. Today a small portion of the NY&GL branch is owned and operated by the NYS&W between Pompton Junction and Riverdale. (Author's collection.)

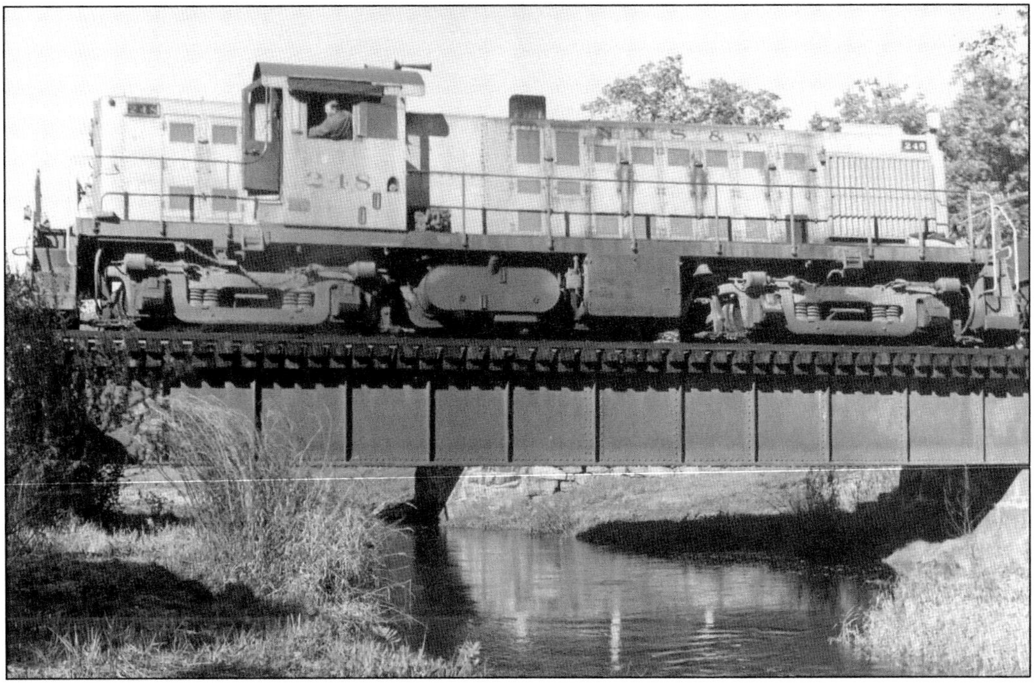

The photographer has elected to take a broadside angle of NYS&W RS-1 No. 248 crossing a small bridge in Pompton Lakes in this scene recorded on September 29, 1961. The side lit view accentuates the many details found on the locomotive. (Photograph by Donald P. Wallworth; courtesy of Patrick J. Reynolds and the Maywood Station Museum Collection.)

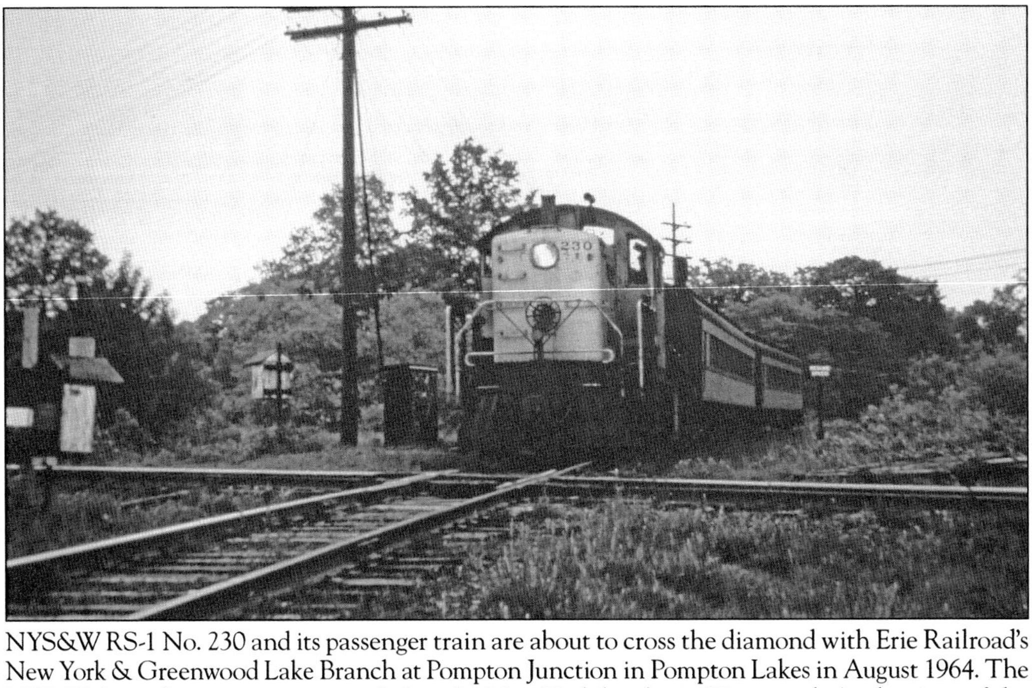

NYS&W RS-1 No. 230 and its passenger train are about to cross the diamond with Erie Railroad's New York & Greenwood Lake Branch at Pompton Junction in Pompton Lakes in August 1964. The NY&GL branch at one time extended to the New York border in Ringwood. At the time of the photograph, it ran only as far was Wanaque-Midvale. (Courtesy of Pat Reynolds collection.)

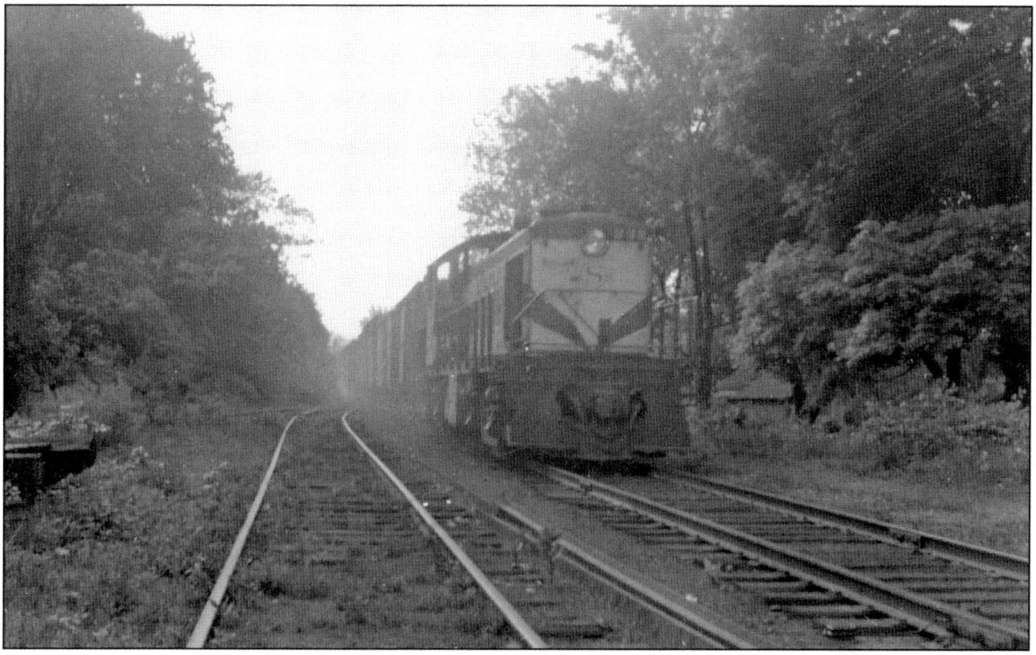

NYS&W RS-1 No. 232 is in charge of a long local freight as it drifts through Bloomingdale in this rural-looking scene taken on June 3, 1947. Bloomingdale is just east of Butler and has been the site of several smaller industries, which have been customers of the railroad through the years. (Photograph by John L. Treen; courtesy of Thomas J. Callan and the Maywood Station Museum Collection.)

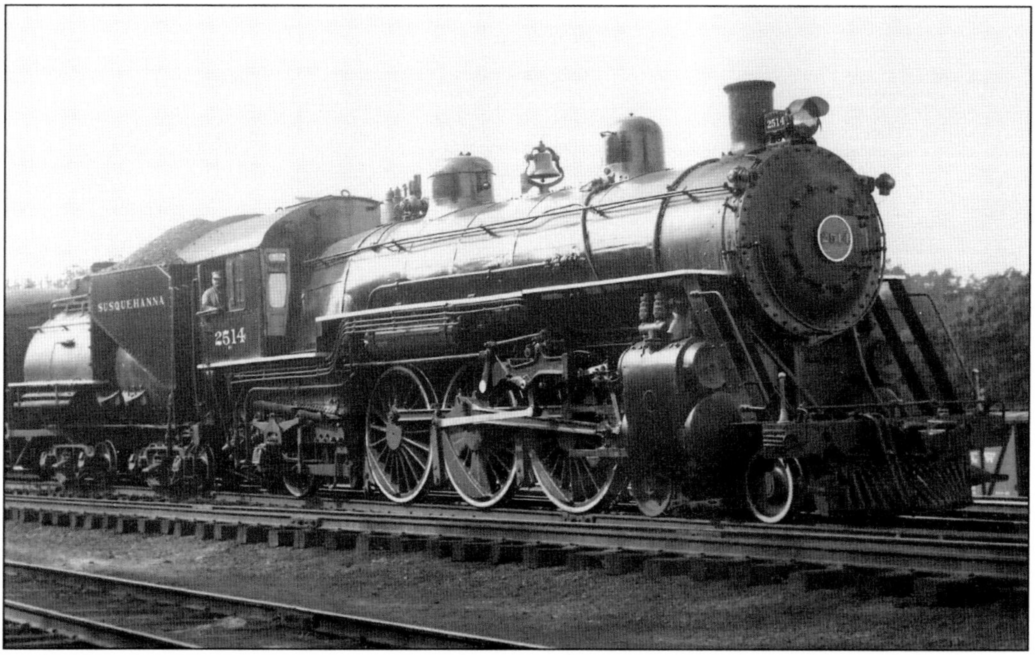

NYS&W 4-6-2 No. 2514 prepares to get underway with an eastbound passenger run in this image taken in August 1940 at Butler yard. After the 1930s, Butler was the western terminus of the NYS&W's passenger train operations. (Author's collection.)

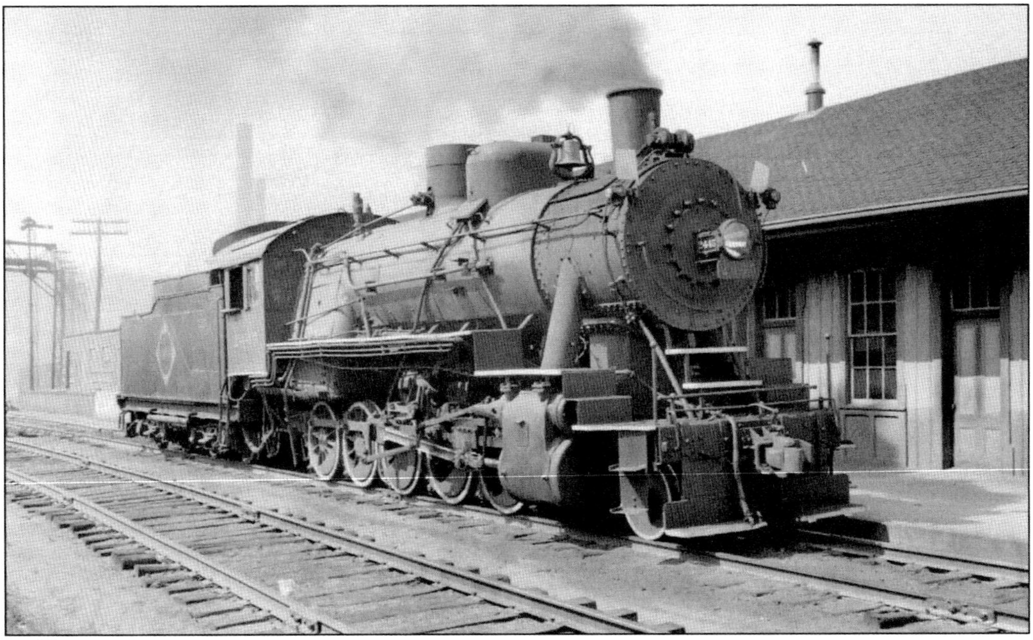

Erie Railroad 2-10-0 No. 2445 rests at the Butler station in this view taken in late 1940. In 1868, the Newbrough Hard Rubber Company built a factory in Butler. In 1898, it merged with other companies to form the American Hard Rubber Company. For the next 60 years, Butler and rubber were nearly synonymous and provided a vast amount of carload freight traffic for the NYS&W. (Courtesy of the Maywood Station Museum Collection.)

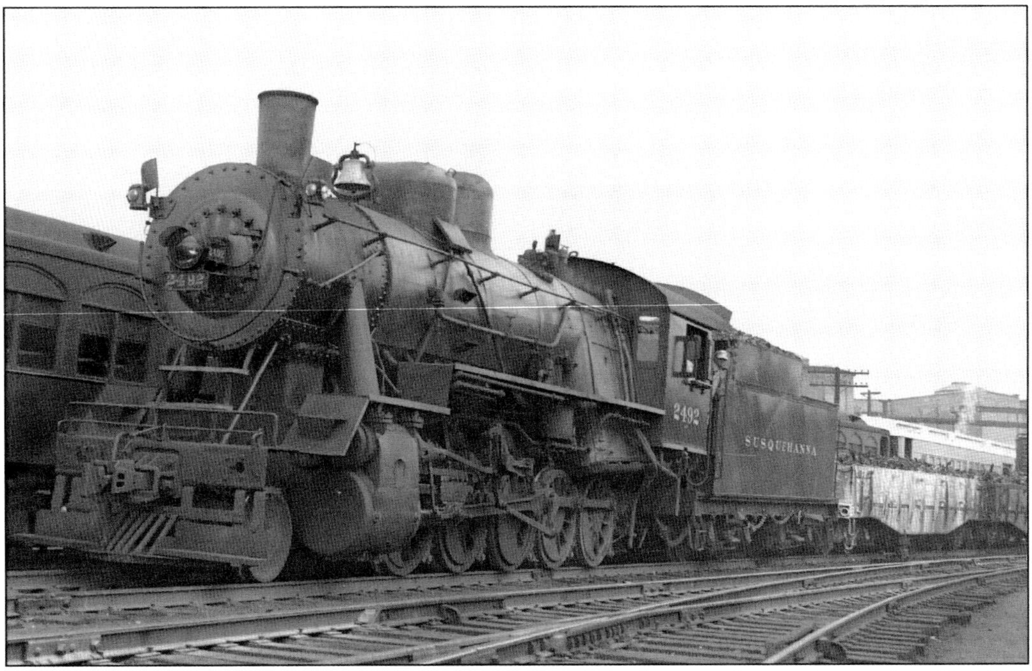

NYS&W 2-10-0 No. 2492 drifts through Butler yard in this scene taken on November 10, 1940. Leased Erie Railroad and former Erie Railroad Stillwell coaches are evident behind of the train. (Author's collection.)

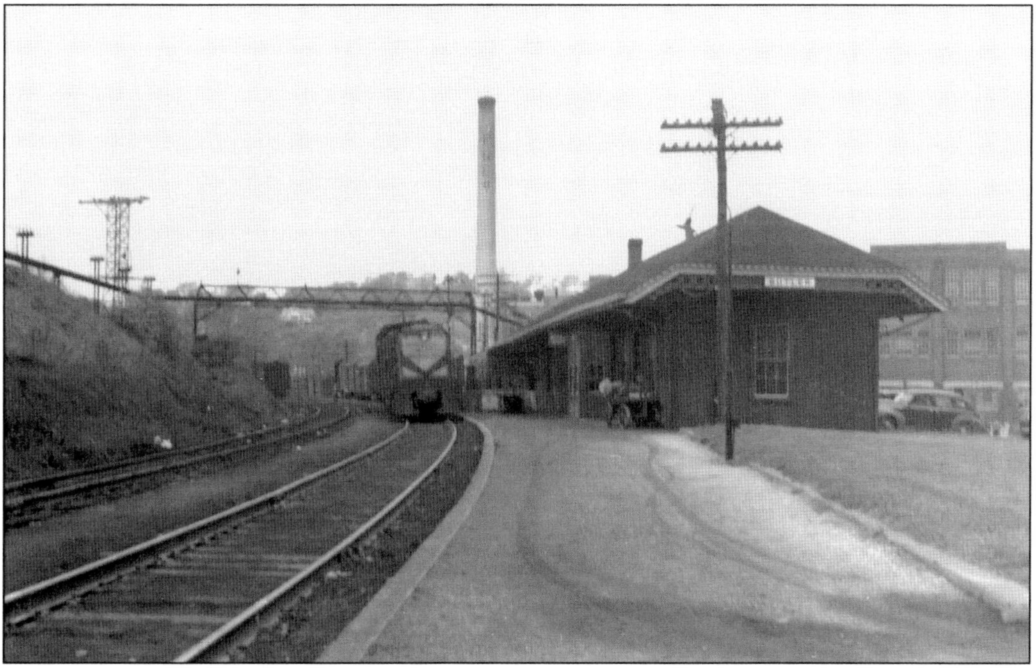

Butler station looms prominently while NYS&W S-2 No. 206 switches the yard in this view taken on May 7, 1946. Today the station contains the Butler Historical Society collection and is open to the public periodically. (Photograph by John L. Treen; courtesy of Thomas J. Callan and the Maywood Station Museum Collection.)

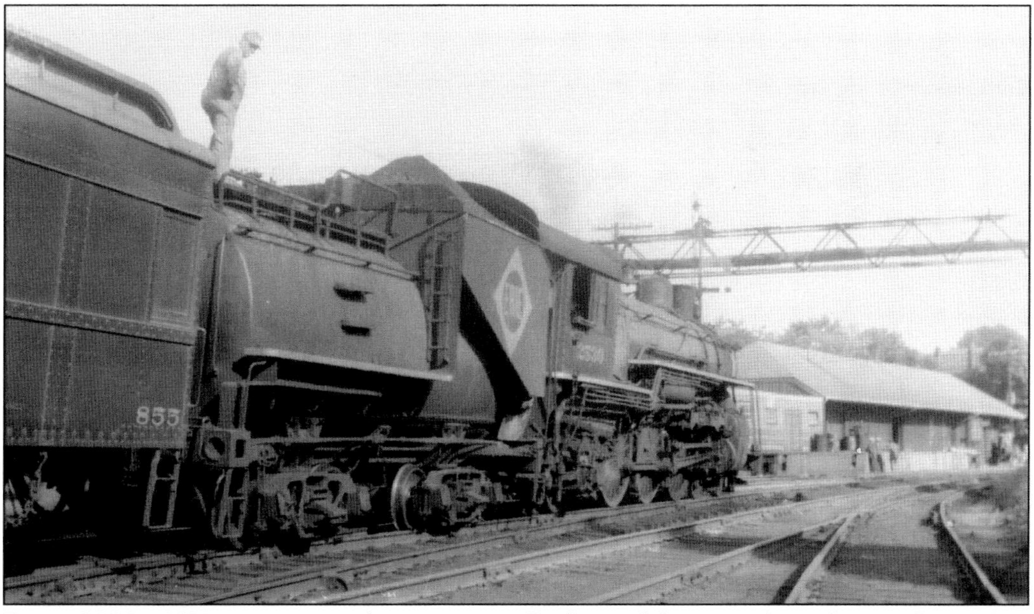

Erie 4-6-2 No. 2530 prepares to take on water in Butler yard for its eastbound trip to Jersey City with train No. 924 in this view taken on October 24, 1947. In the fall of 1947, the NYS&W briefly leased two steam locomotives from the Erie Railroad due to a shortage of diesel power. These two locomotives were the last of steam to operate on the NYS&W. (Photograph by John L. Treen; courtesy of Thomas J. Callan and the Maywood Station Museum Collection.)

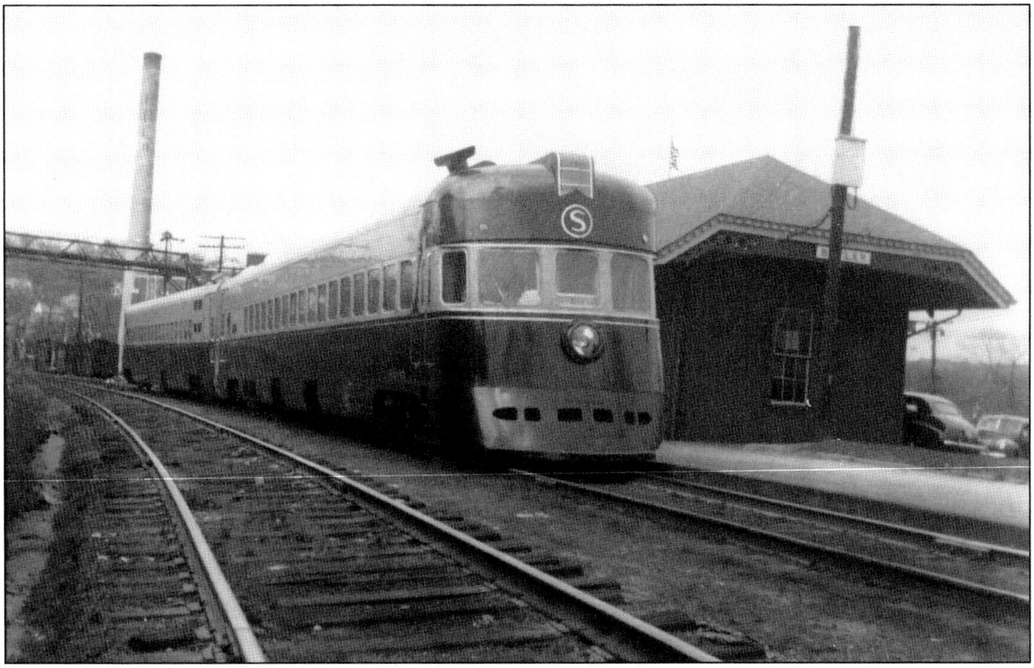

American Car & Foundry–built Motorailer NYS&W No. 1005 and a sister Motorailer are seen in this view at Butler station on November 17, 1947. The Motorailers primarily operated between the Paterson City branch and Susquehanna Transfer in North Bergen but were occasionally assigned to special trains on the railroad and made appearances in different locations. (Photograph by John L. Treen; courtesy of Thomas J. Callan and the Maywood Station Museum Collection.)

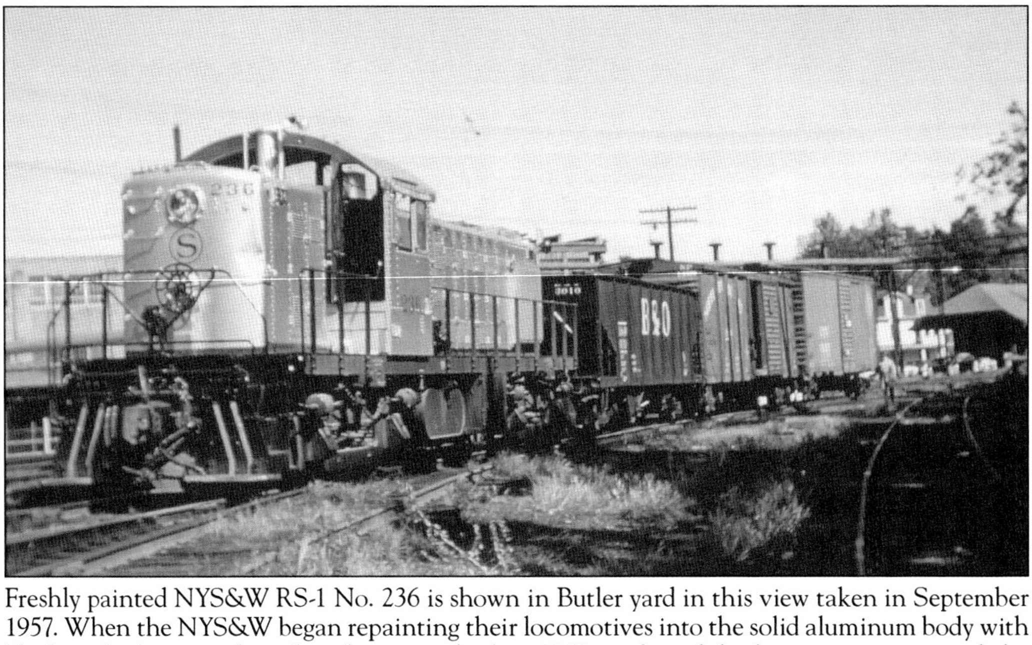

Freshly painted NYS&W RS-1 No. 236 is shown in Butler yard in this view taken in September 1957. When the NYS&W began repainting their locomotives into the solid aluminum body with black underframe and trucks scheme in the late 1950s, a few of the locomotives received the addition of dark green paint on their side sills. RS-1 Nos. 234, 236, and 244 have been documented as wearing this short-lived scheme. (Author's collection.)

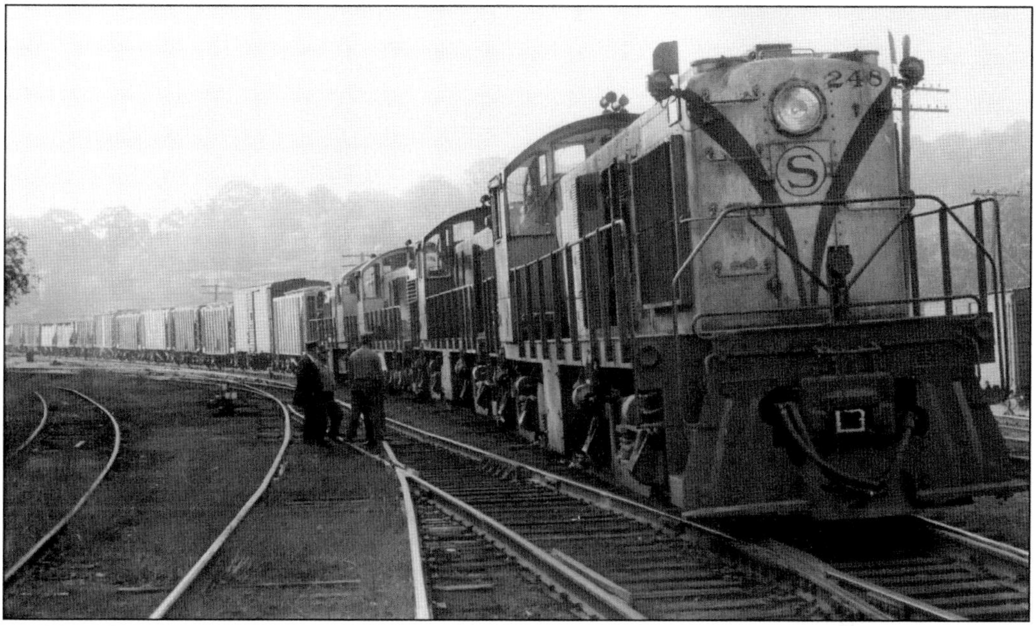

NYS&W RS-1 No. 248 is in charge of two sister RS-1s and one S-2 as they pause with their "Hainesburg Extra" freight train in this scene taken in Butler yard in September 1958. The train originated in Hainesburg with a destination of Little Ferry. (Photograph by Donald P. Wallworth; courtesy of Patrick J. Reynolds and the Maywood Station Museum Collection.)

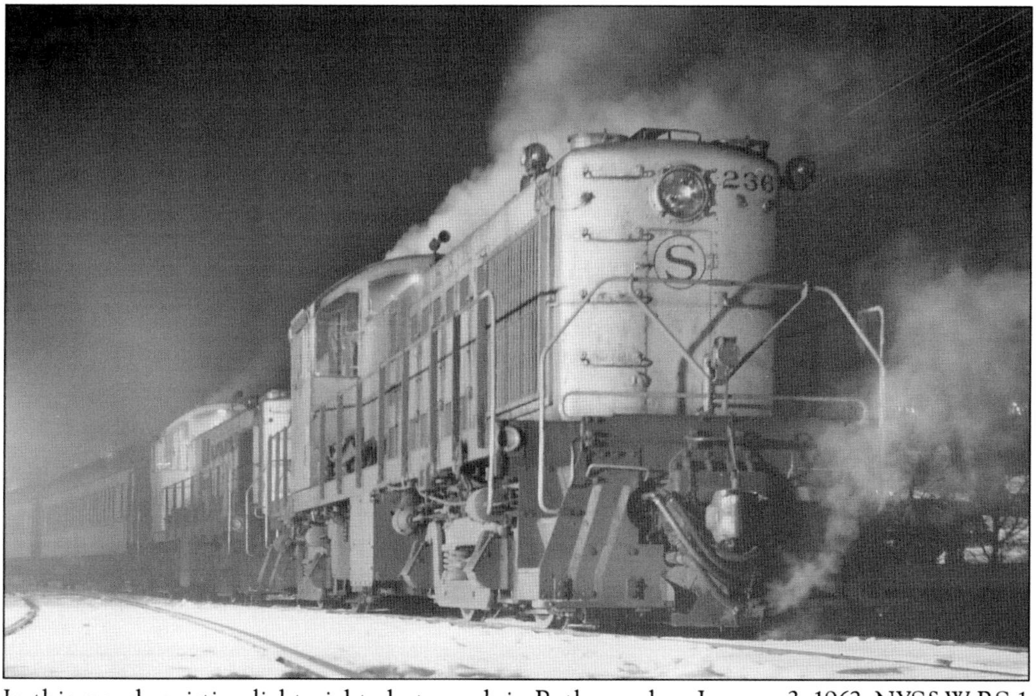

In this moody existing light night photograph in Butler yard on January 3, 1962, NYS&W RS-1 Nos. 236 and 230 pose as they await their next eastbound passenger run. It must be a very cold night, judging by the amount of steam emanating from the locomotives. (Photograph by Donald P. Wallworth; courtesy of Patrick J. Reynolds and the Maywood Station Museum Collection.)

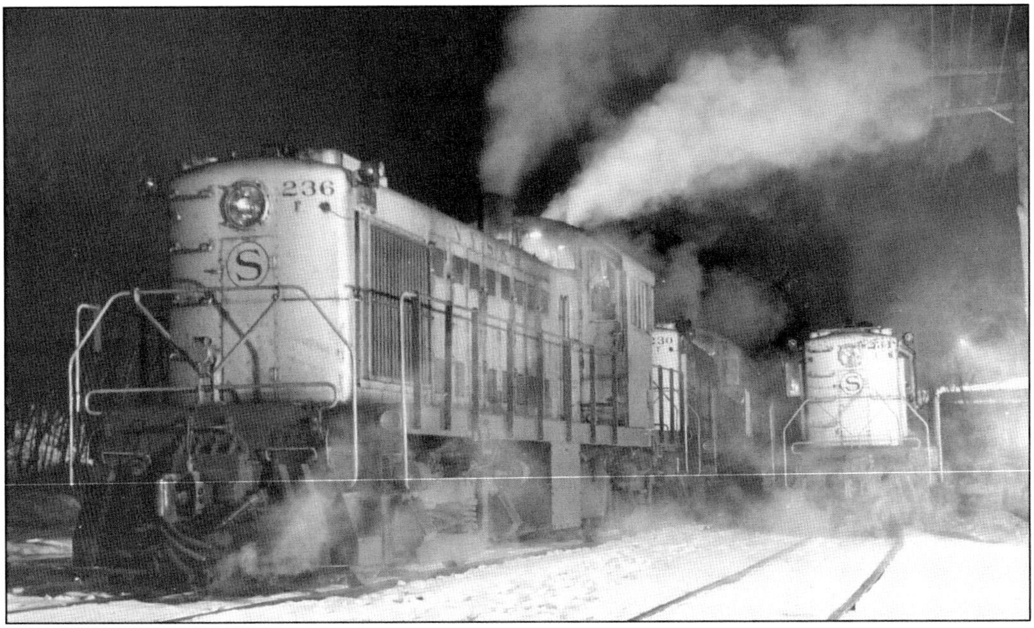

This companion view of the previous photograph is taken from a different angle in Butler Yard, where NYS&W RS-1 Nos. 236 and 230 are seen on one track and NYS&W RS-1 No. 234 on an adjacent track as they wait for their next eastbound passenger train assignments on January 3, 1962. (Photograph by Donald P. Wallworth; courtesy of Patrick J. Reynolds and the Maywood Station Museum Collection.)

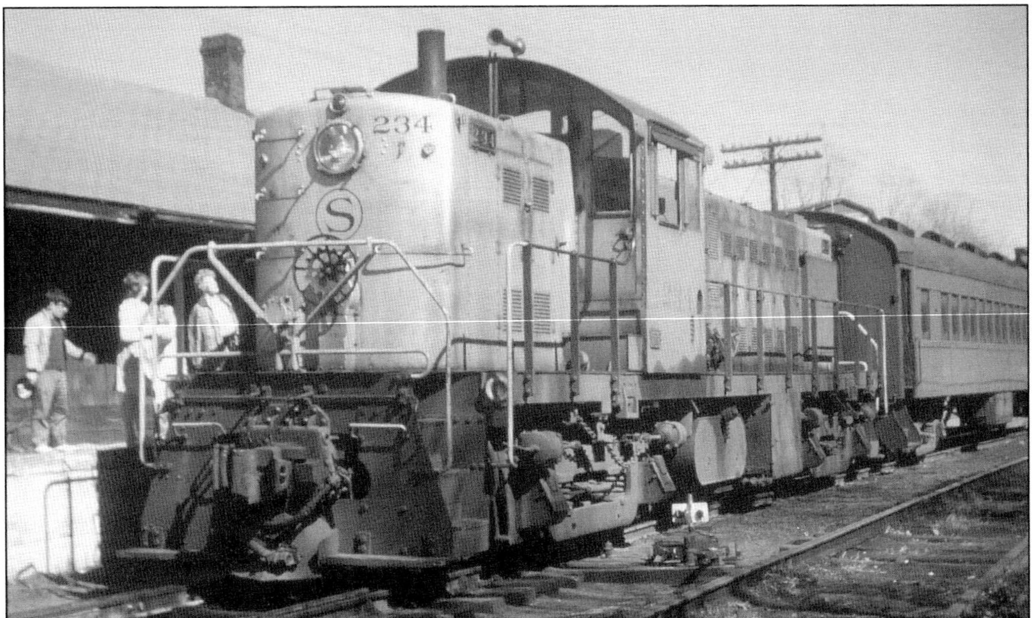

NYS&W RS-1 No. 234 has arrived at Butler station with its passengers train in this view taken in April 1965 as commuters gaze up at the locomotive. The 1,000-horsepower American Locomotive Company RS-1s served the NYS&W well for many years in any type of service they were called upon. (Author's collection.)

Six

West of Butler

Continuing west from Butler, the NYS&W traverses some of its most operationally challenging terrain. A 1.36 percent westbound ruling grade, the biggest on the railroad, is encountered in Stockholm between mileposts 50 and 51. The railroad also is nearly 1,000 feet above sea level at this location—the highest of any railroad in the state of New Jersey. Beaver Lake, just west of Stockholm, once was the site of a medium-sized yard and locomotive servicing facility complete with a turntable and a water tower. It was also the site where the Hanford branch once went north to Middletown, New York.

The railroad between Butler, New Jersey, and Stroudsburg, Pennsylvania, never had a dense freight traffic base except for the mines near Franklin. Much of the region was undeveloped, and the only significant online business came from a few creameries, like the one in Stillwater, and local consignees on team tracks located on sidings near stations.

Passenger service was eliminated west of Butler during World War II. However, important freight interchanges existed for many years with the Wharton & Northern Railroad (Central Railroad Company of New Jersey) at Green Pond Junction near Charlotteburg; the Lehigh & Hudson River Railway at Sparta; the Lehigh & New England Railway at Hainesburg; the Middletown & Unionville Railroad at Hanford; and the Delaware, Lackawanna & Western Railroad at Stroudsburg.

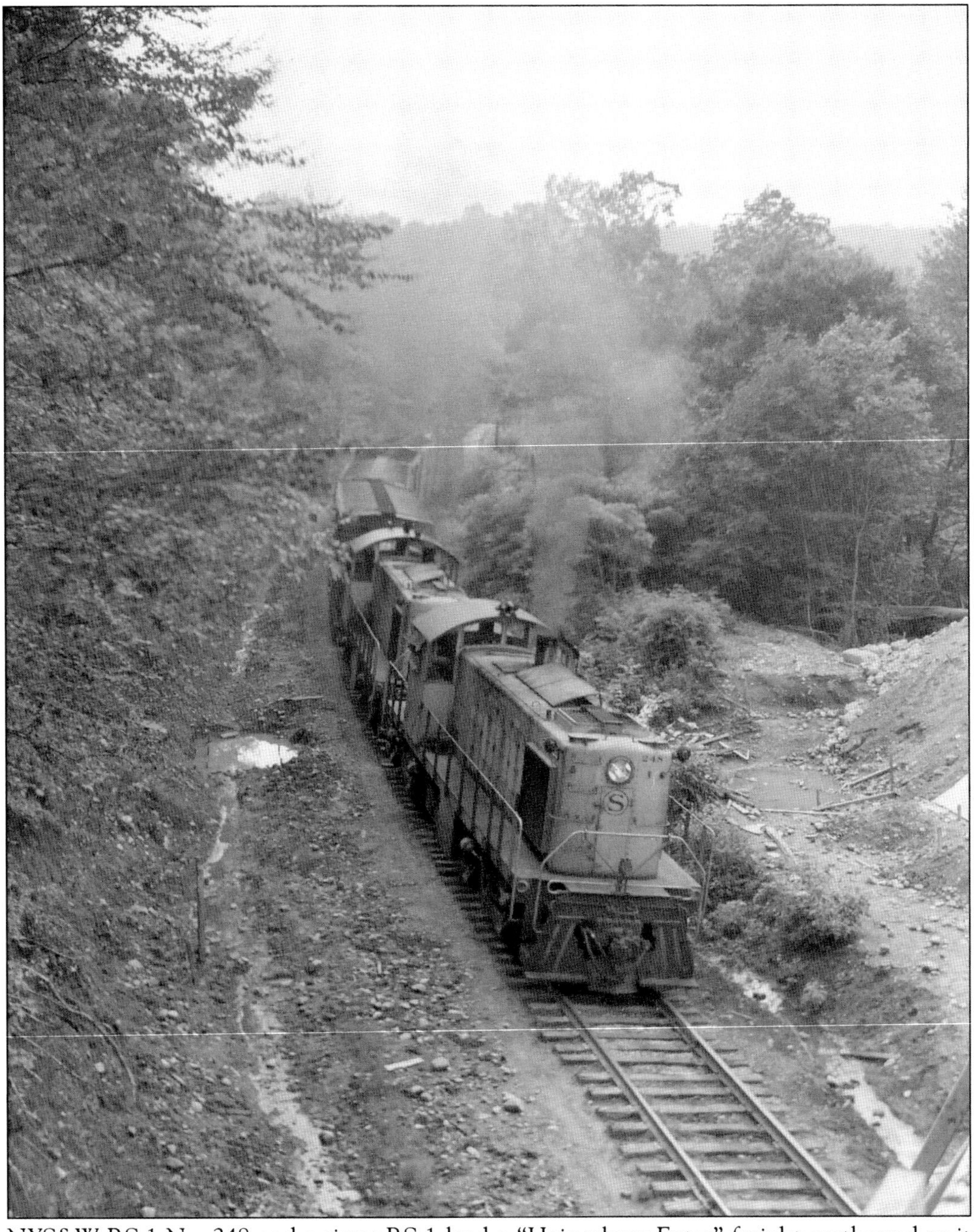

NYS&W RS-1 No. 248 and a sister RS-1 lead a "Hainesburg Extra" freight eastbound as it works downgrade and is about to go under the Route 23 overpass in Smith Mills in July 1961. (Photograph by Donald P. Wallworth; courtesy of Patrick J. Reynolds and the Maywood Station Museum Collection.)

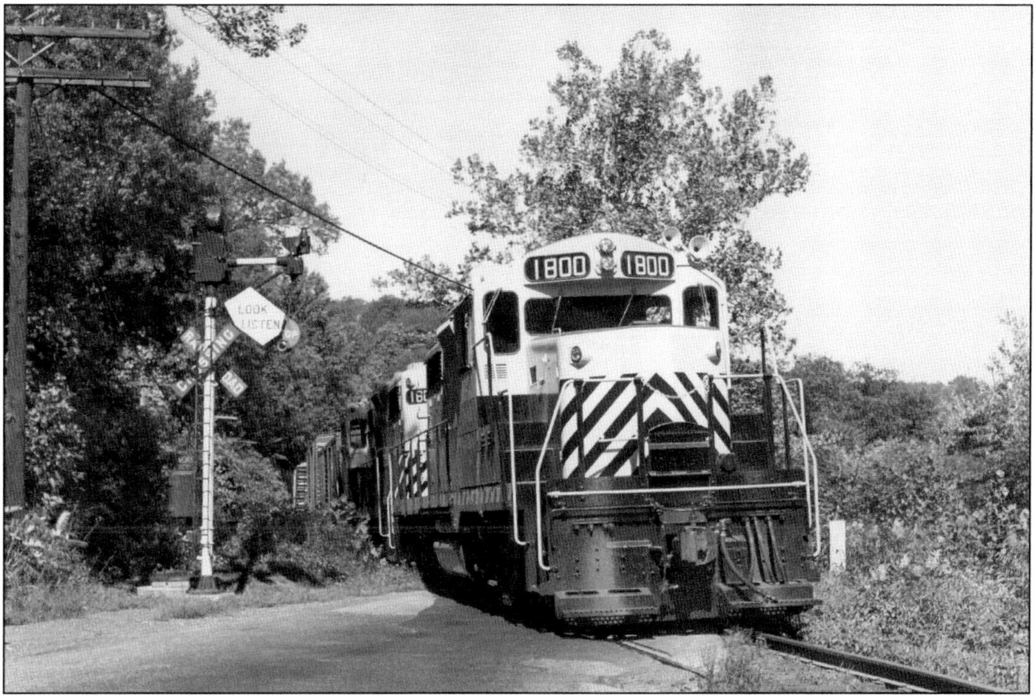

NYS&W GP18 No. 1800 is trailed by another GP18 and its freight as it crosses the Hamburg Turnpike in Smith Mills in this view on September 15, 1962. Smith Mills is located just west of Butler, and the remoteness of this area is obvious in the photograph. Note the wigwag warning device on the grade crossing protection. (Photograph by Donald P. Wallworth; courtesy of Patrick J. Reynolds and the Maywood Station Museum Collection.)

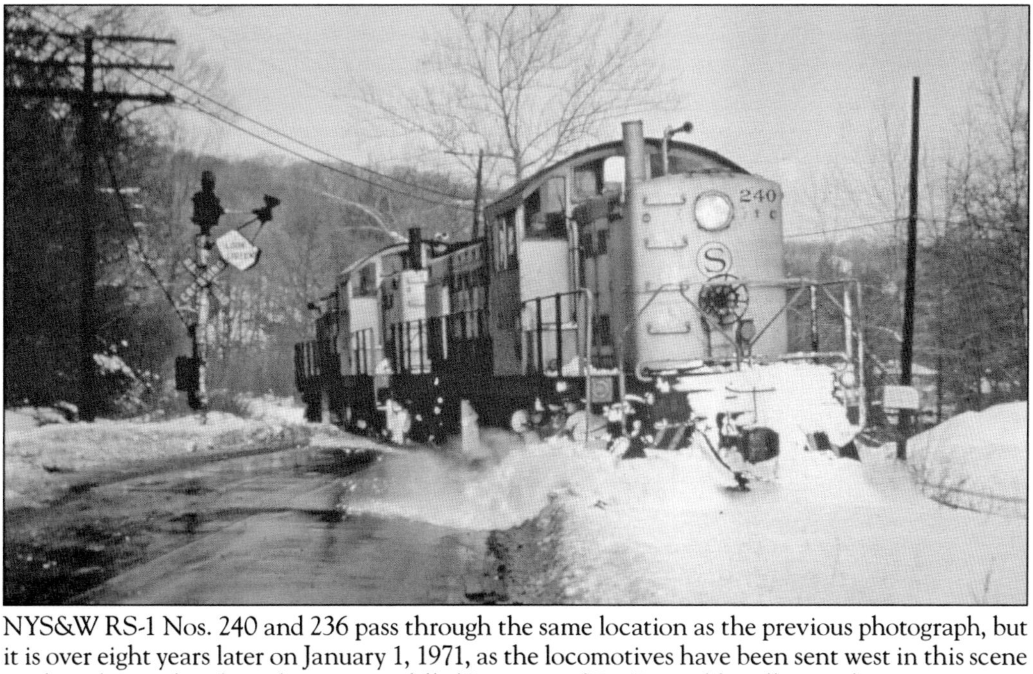

NYS&W RS-1 Nos. 240 and 236 pass through the same location as the previous photograph, but it is over eight years later on January 1, 1971, as the locomotives have been sent west in this scene to clear the tracks after a heavy snowfall. (Courtesy of Pat Reynolds collection.)

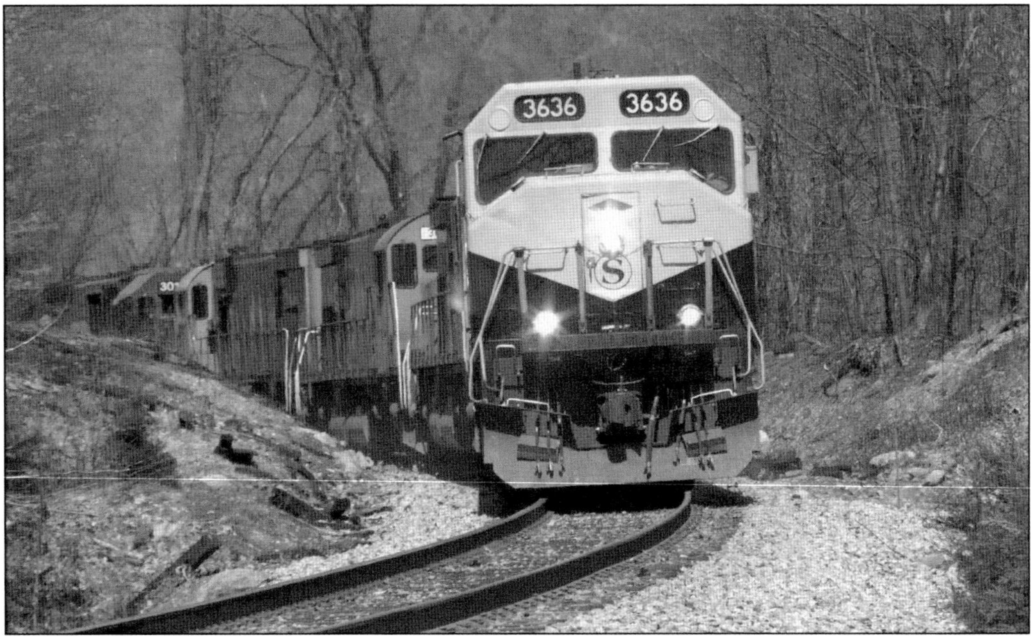

NYS&W F45 No. 3636 climbs the grade in Smoke Rise with three additional units pulling eastbound road freight SU-100 in this view taken on April 27, 2006. The location is not far from the scene of the washout that occurred in April 1971 that cut the NYS&W back to a Jersey City to Butler operation before being rebuilt and reopened from Butler to Sparta in 1986. (Photograph by the author.)

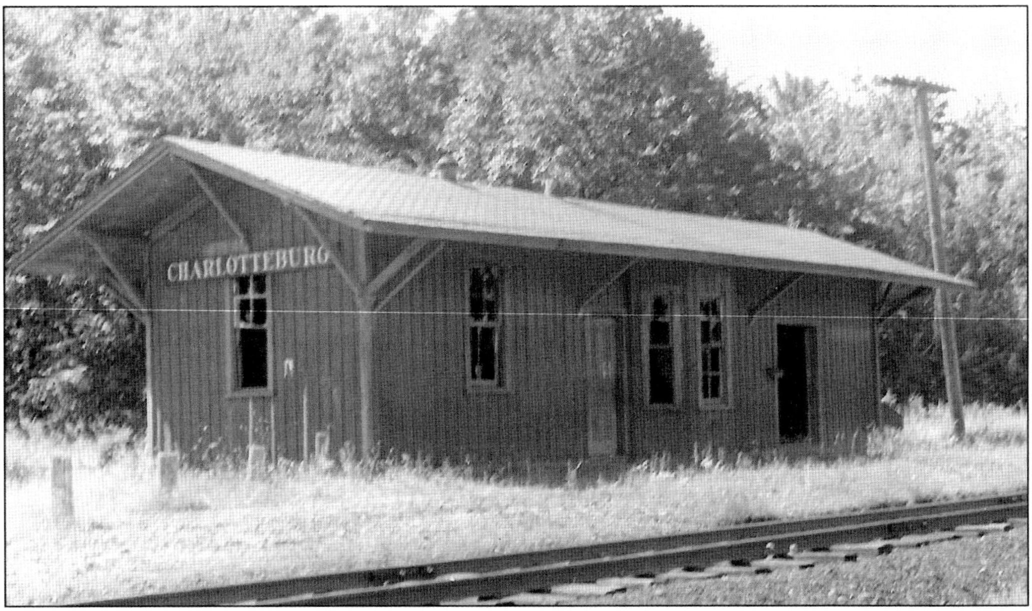

This image of Charlottesburg station was captured in September 1939. When the photograph was taken, the station was no longer being used by the NYS&W, and visible evidence of vandalism was occurring, as seen in the broken windows and open doors. Also note that the letter "S" is missing in "Charlottesburg" on the station sign. (Courtesy of Railroad Avenue Enterprises; author's collection.)

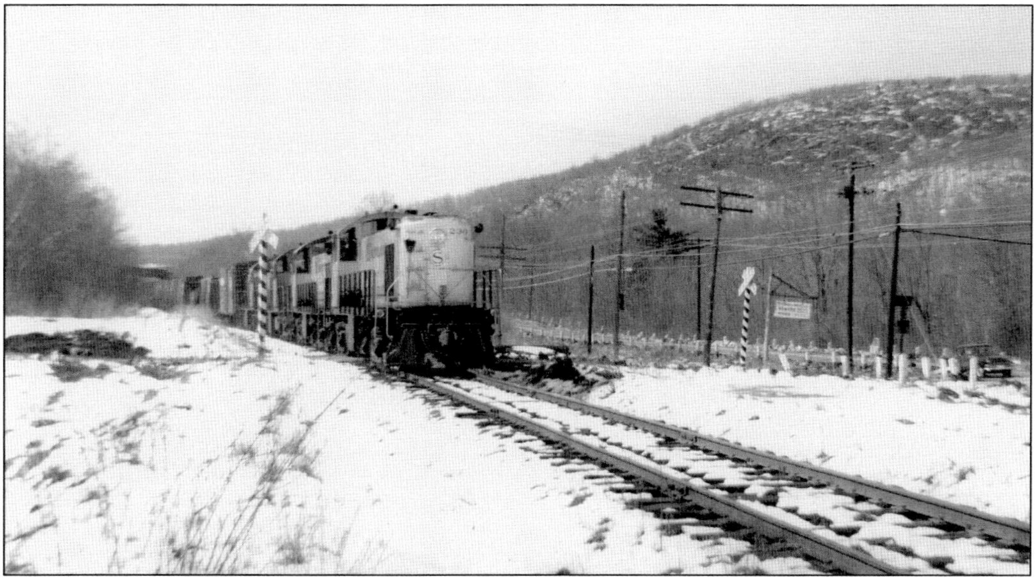

NYS&W RS-1 No. 230 leads three sister units and a long "Hainesburg Extra" freight that originated in Hainesburg eastbound through Charlottesburg in this image taken on March 25, 1961. Route 23 can be seen to the right of the train, and the hilly northern New Jersey landscape and typical winter weather of this area are all evident in this view. (Courtesy Railroad Avenue Enterprises; author's collection.)

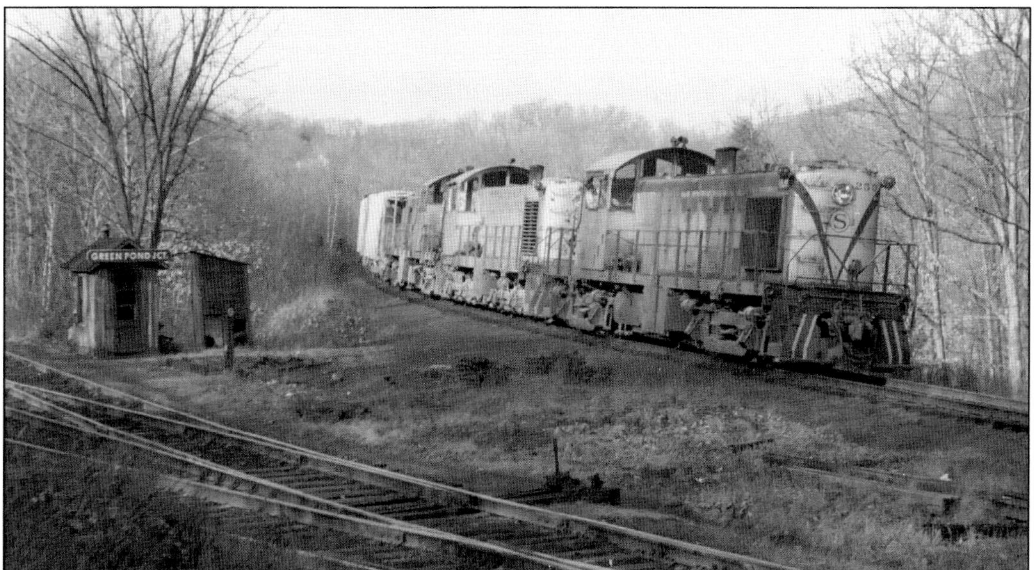

An RS-1/S-2/RS-1 combination led by NYS&W RS-1 No. 250 is in charge of an eastbound "Hainesburg Extra" freight as it passes the site of the old Green Pond Junction connection with the Central Railroad Company of New Jersey's Wharton & Northern line in Charlottesburg. In 1958, the connection was severed when the Charlottesburg Reservoir was built and the W&N was relocated to the west side of the reservoir. A new Green Pond Junction connection was then built about a mile west, just east of New Foundland. (Photograph by Donald P. Wallworth; courtesy of Patrick J. Reynolds and the Maywood Station Museum Collection.)

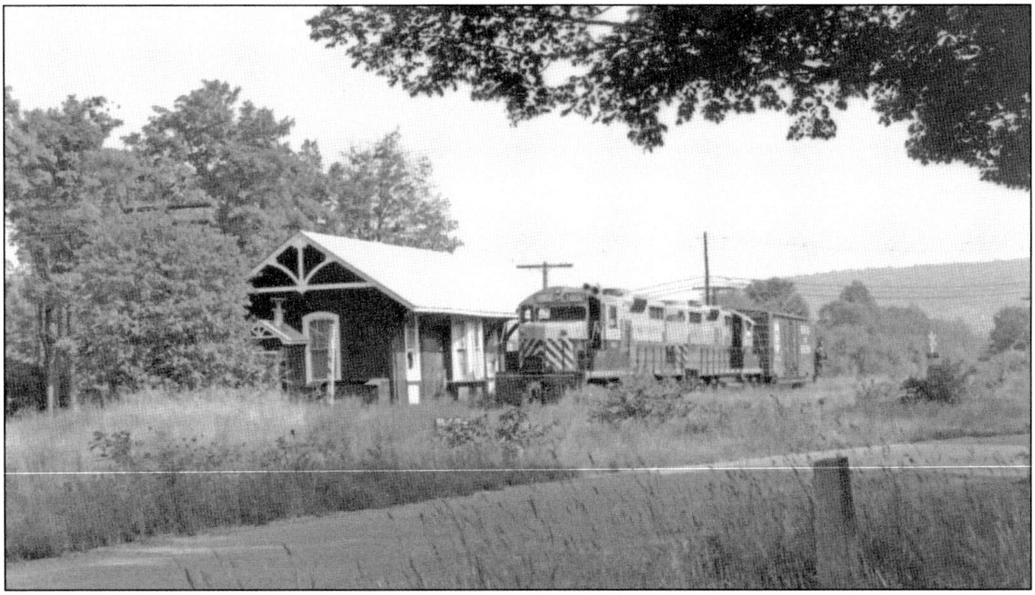

NYS&W GP18 Nos. 1802 and 1804 lead one boxcar west past New Foundland station in this view taken in April 1971. This train was the last one to operate west off Butler until late 1986. A washout near Smoke Rise a few days later embargoed the line, as it did not merit repairing the damage since there were very little active customers west of Butler. From 1974 to 1980, a portion of the line was reopened when the Morris County Central Railroad tourist operation was relocated to New Foundland from Whippany, New Jersey. (Photograph by George Berisso; author's collection.)

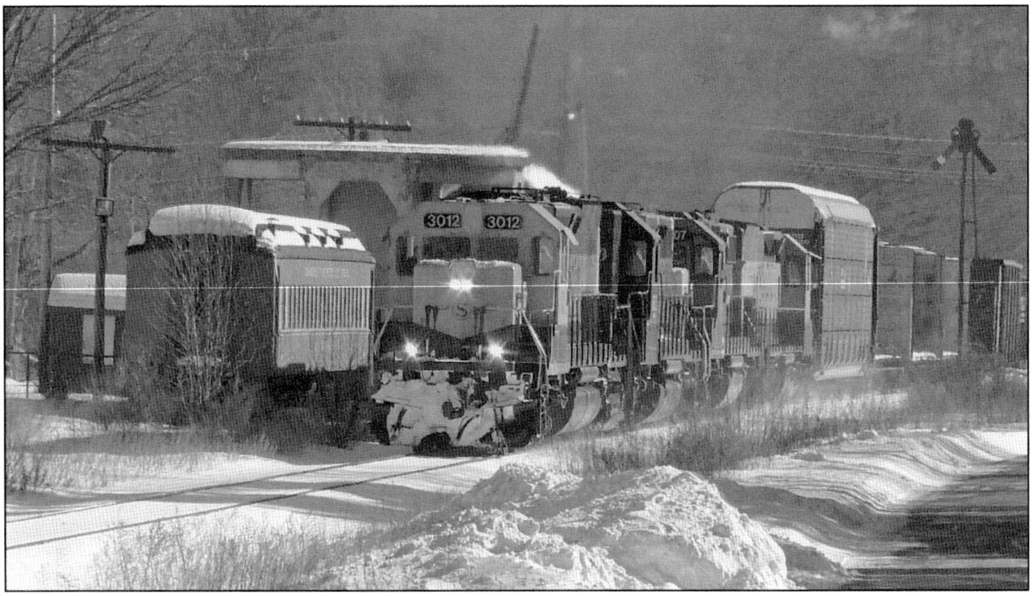

NYS&W SD40T-2 No. 3012 rolls westbound with road freight SU-99 in this view captured on January 30, 2004, at New Foundland. To the left of No. 3012 is a passenger car that once belonged to the Morris County Central tourist train operation and is now privately owned. Also visible is the concrete foundation for what was once part of the water tower at the New Foundland station. (Photograph by the author.)

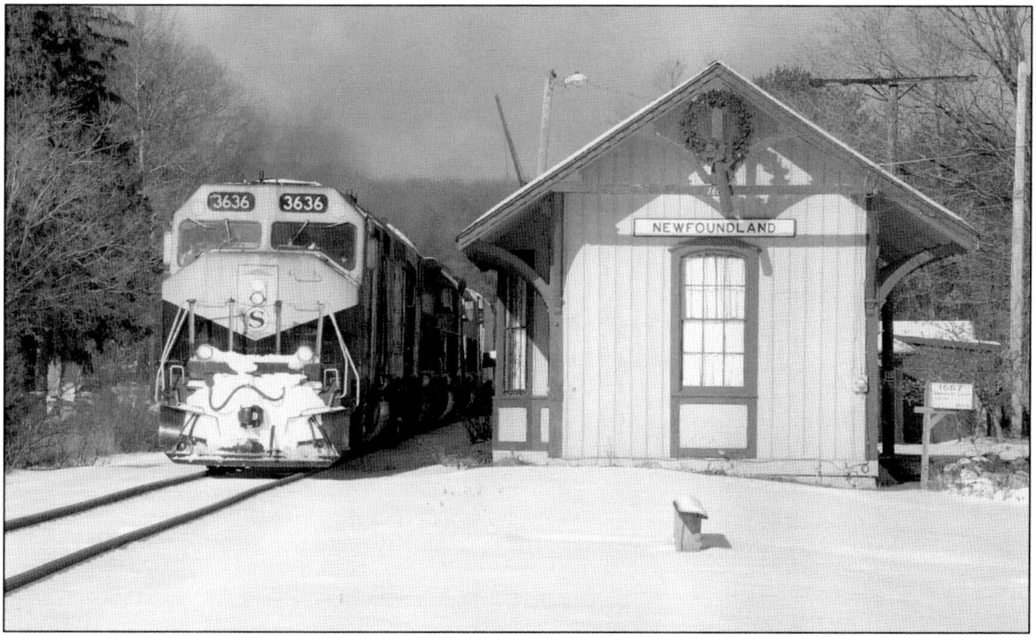

NYS&W F45 No. 3636 leads eastbound road freight SU-100 past New Foundland Station in this photograph taken on a cold, snowy but sunny December 14, 2007. New Foundland station dates to about 1880 and is neatly maintained by its current private owners. (Photograph by the author.)

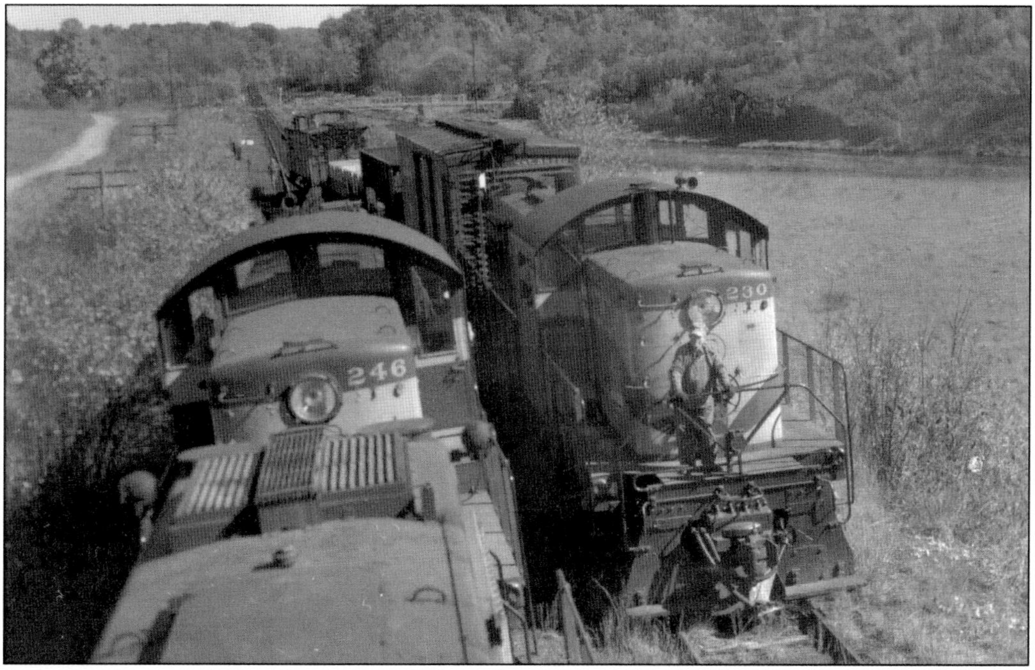

NYS&W RS-1 No. 230 and its short westbound local freight take the passing siding in Oak Ridge while the photographer is atop the trailing locomotive behind NYS&W RS-1 No. 246 and its freight train, which originated in Hainesburg and is destined to Little Ferry, waits on the main. This unique perspective was captured on October 13, 1949. (Photograph by John L. Treen; courtesy of Thomas J. Callan and the Maywood Station Museum Collection.)

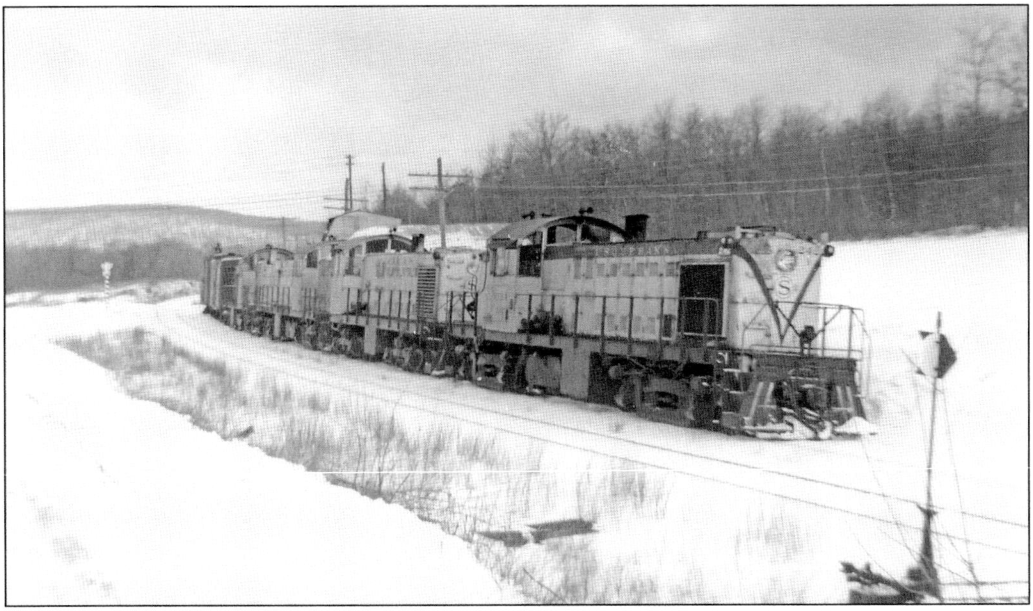

NYS&W RS-1 No. 242 leads an S-2 and two RS-1s on this "Hainesburg Extra" freight as it passes through Oak Ridge on a cold and snowy March 21, 1959. The multiple-unit equipped ALCO S-2s (Nos. 202, 204, 206, and 208) occasionally could be found assisting in road freight service. (Author's collection.)

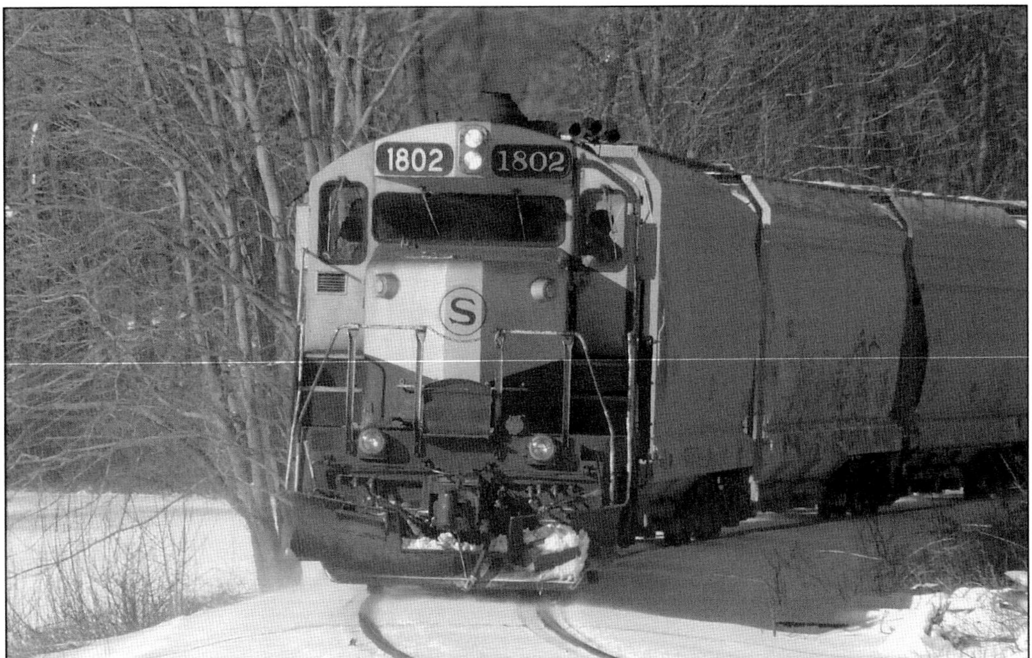

The 42-year-old NYS&W GP18 No. 1802 is actually moving away from the photographer and is pushing hard on the end of heavy westbound road freight SU-99 in this scene rounding the curve in Stockholm on January 30, 2004. The three 1962-built GP18s were still active in everyday service on this date. (Photograph by the author.)

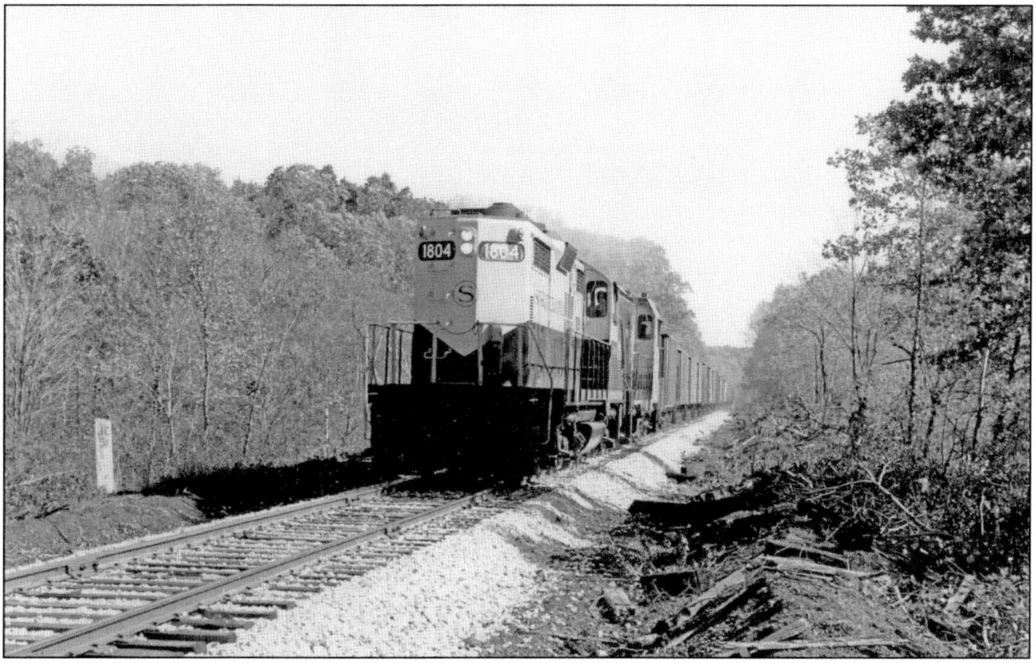

NYS&W GP18 No. 1804 leads a leased ex-Atchison, Topeka & Santa Fe Railway CF7 and a long string of ballast hoppers through Stockholm in this view taken on October 7, 1986. The train was dropping ballast between Butler and Sparta, which had been dormant since 1971 and was in the process of being rehabilitated and reopened. (Courtesy of Railroad Avenue Enterprises; author's collection.)

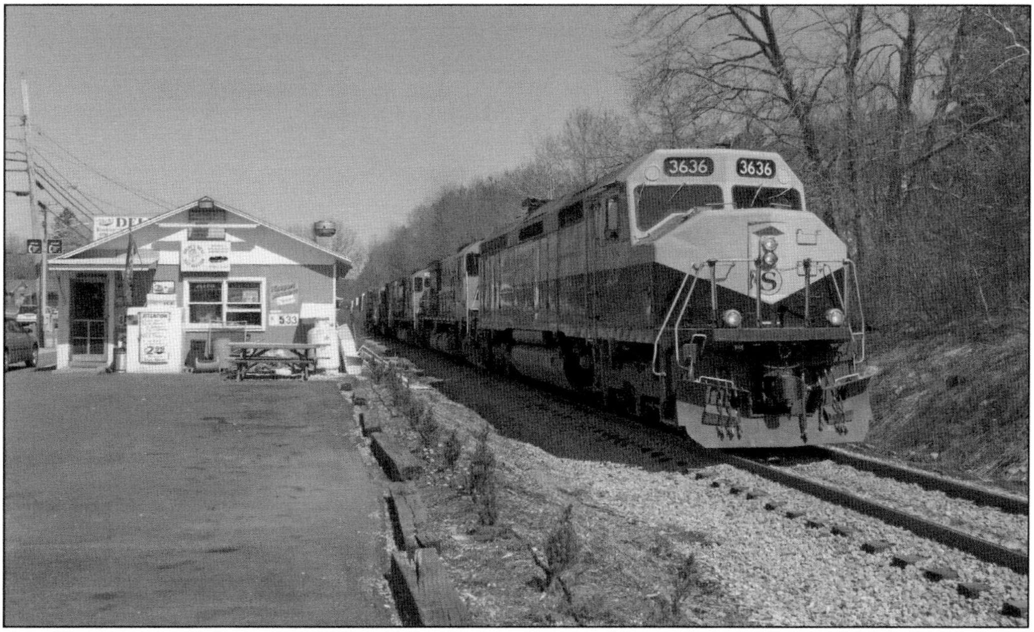

NYS&W F45 No. 3636 is shown with eastbound road freight SU-99 in Stockholm in this scene taken on April 27, 2006. Next to the train is the popular Rich's Deli, a fixture along Route 23 and a popular spot for NYS&W train crew changes. (Photograph by the author.)

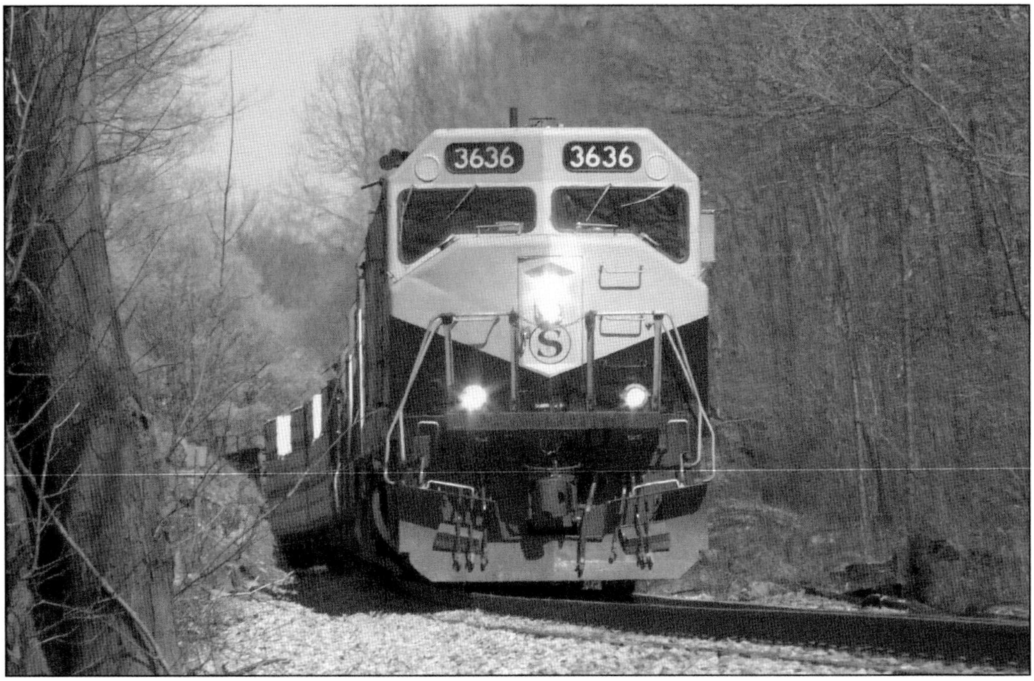

In this image, the same train as seen in the previous photograph is now moving eastbound through a curve in Stockholm on April 27, 2006. NYS&W No. 3636 was one of two F45s purchased secondhand from Burlington Northern in 1986. The other unit, No. 3638, was sold to the Montana Rail Link in 1993. (Photograph by the author.)

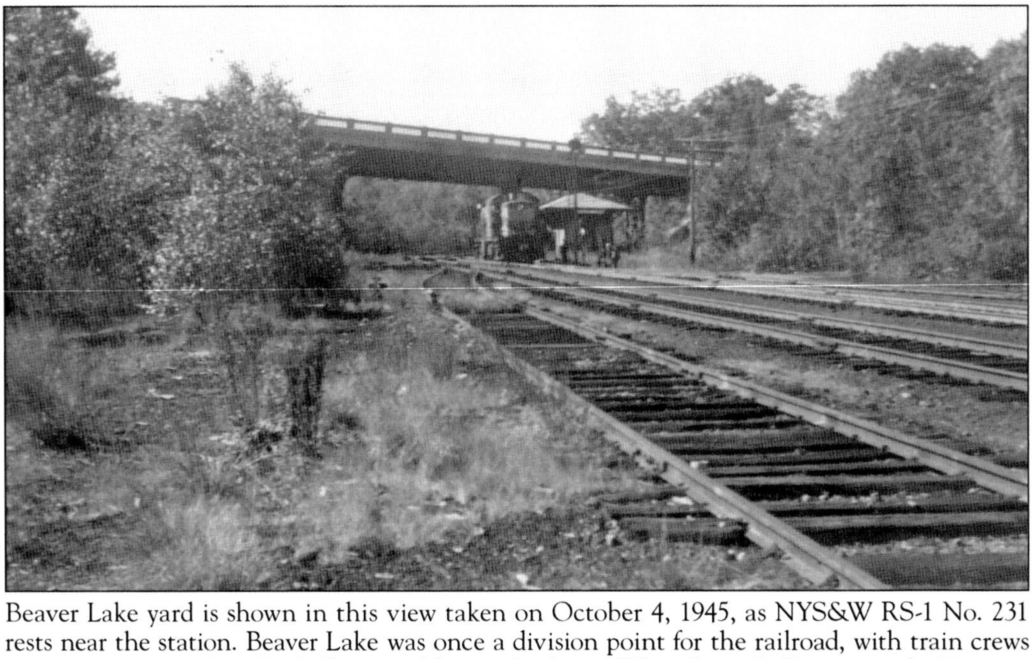

Beaver Lake yard is shown in this view taken on October 4, 1945, as NYS&W RS-1 No. 231 rests near the station. Beaver Lake was once a division point for the railroad, with train crews operating to there from Little Ferry and from subsidiary Wilkes-Barre & Eastern in the Poconos of Pennsylvania. The Hanford branch diverged north from this location. (Photograph by John L. Treen; courtesy of Thomas J. Callan and the Maywood Station Museum Collection.)

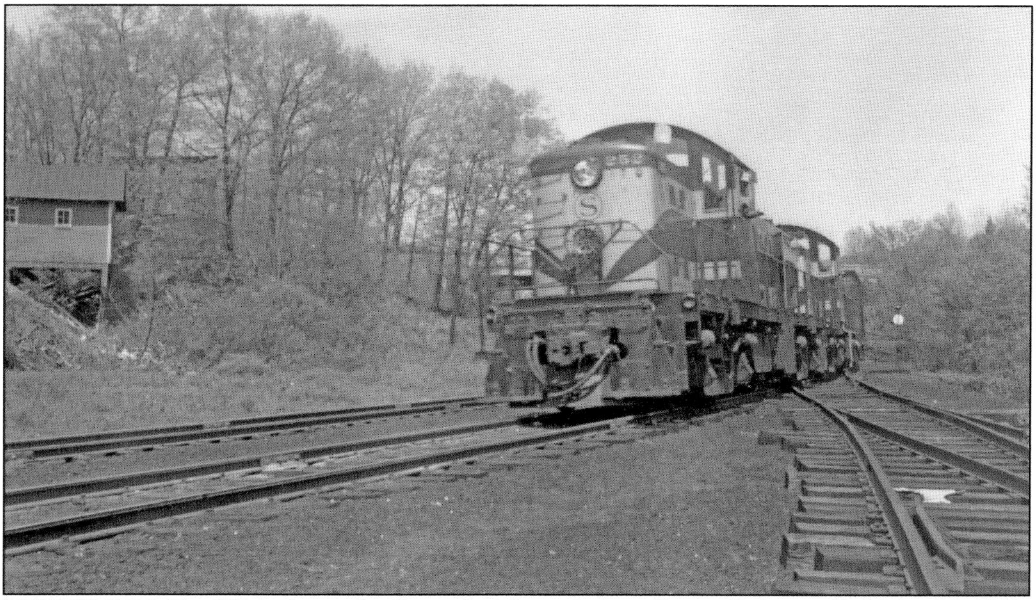

NYS&W RS-1 No. 252 is shown leading a freight train into Beaver Lake yard on May 20, 1948. At this date, Beaver Lake yard was still an active location on the railroad and contained several long yard tracks. No. 252 was the longest surviving of the NYS&W RS-1s and was in active service into the late 1980s. (Photograph by John L. Treen; courtesy of Thomas J. Callan and the Maywood Station Museum Collection.)

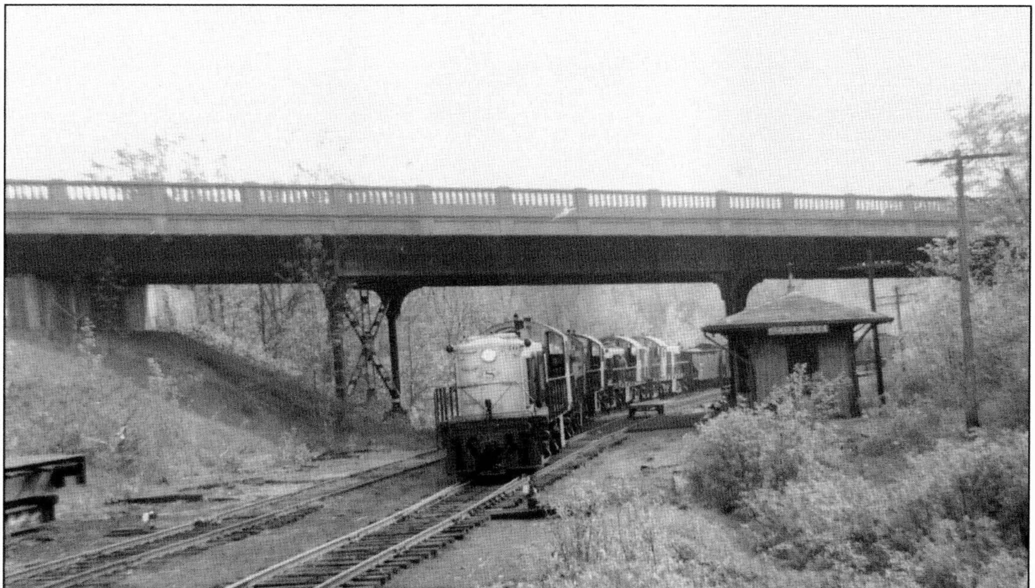

NYS&W RS-1 No. 240 leads and S-2 and three additional units with an eastbound "Hainesburg Extra" freight as it enters Beaver Lake yard in this scene taken on May 14, 1960. The small station underneath Route 23 was used at this time for storage by the NYS&W maintenance-of-way crews. Today pieces of the station partially exist in severely deteriorated condition. (Courtesy of Railroad Avenue Enterprises; author's collection.)

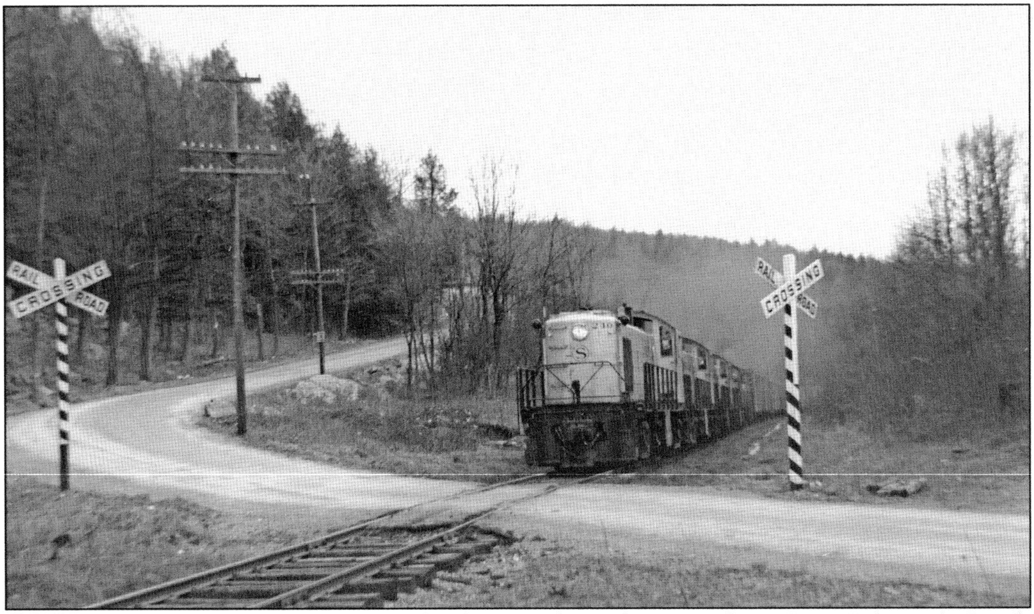

Five NYS&W RS-1s behind No. 240 lead an eastbound "Hainesburg Extra" through South Ogdensburg at Edison Road in this view taken on April 9, 1960. In the early 1900s, a small passenger shelter was on the south side of the tracks and a coal company had a siding on the north side of the tracks. When this photograph was taken, barely any evidence of these structures remained. (Courtesy of Railroad Avenue Enterprises; author's collection.)

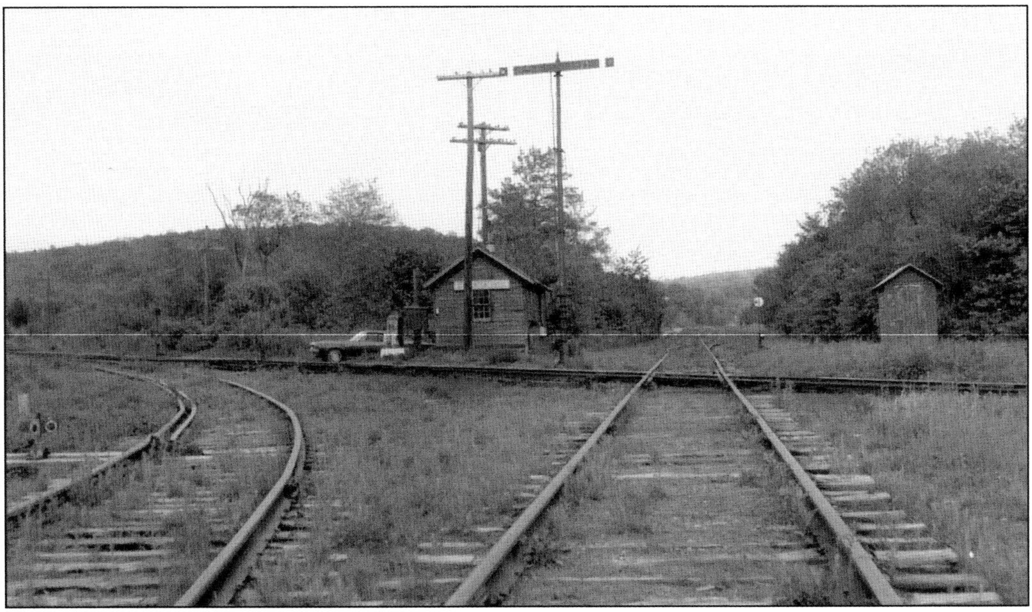

This view looking east on the NYS&W at Sparta Junction was taken on May 30, 1966. The NYS&W and Lehigh & Hudson River Railway conducted an interchange at this location until 1968, when a bridge on the NYS&W in Sparta was embargoed and service was then cut back to Oak Ridge. Previously, in 1962, after the Lehigh & New England Railway was abandoned, this location became the western end of the NYS&W. (Courtesy of Railroad Avenue Enterprises; author's collection.)

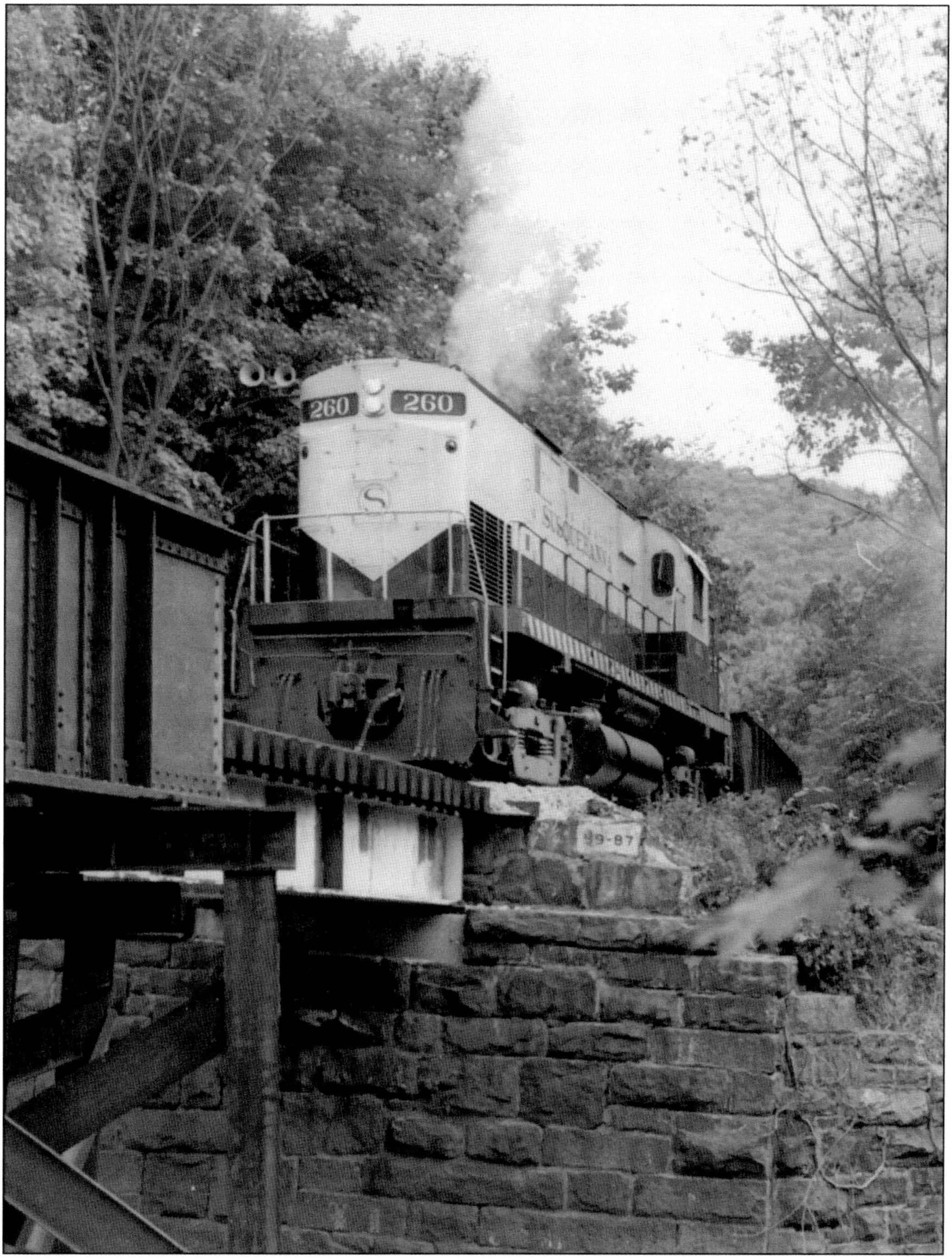

NYS&W C-420 No. 260 is in charge of a work train as it crosses a bridge in Sparta in this scene taken on August 29, 1986. The train was being employed in the rebuilding of the original NYS&W mainline between Butler and Sparta Junction. The rebuilt bridge the train is about to cross is the same one that was embargoed in 1968, which severed the NYS&W's connection with the Lehigh & Hudson River Railway. (Courtesy of Railroad Avenue Enterprises; author's collection.)

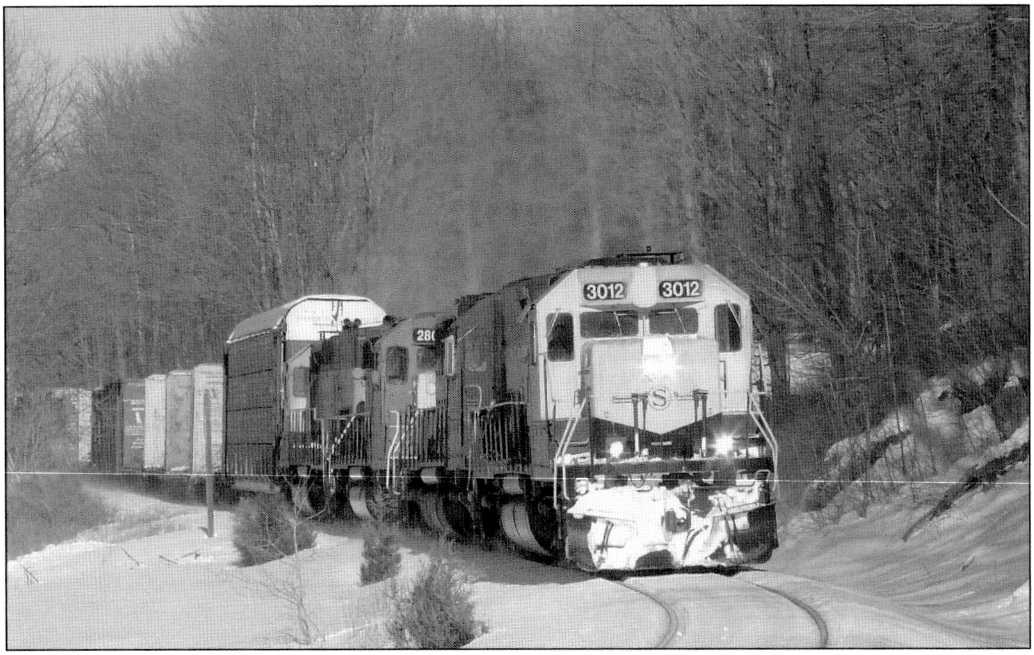

NYS&W SD40T-2 No. 3012 is shown here, winding its way through Sparta with westbound road freight SU-99 on January 30, 2004. In 2003, the NYS&W acquired four secondhand SD40T-2s, three former Southern Pacific units and one former Denver & Rio Grande Western unit, to supplement its fleet of road power. (Photograph by the author.)

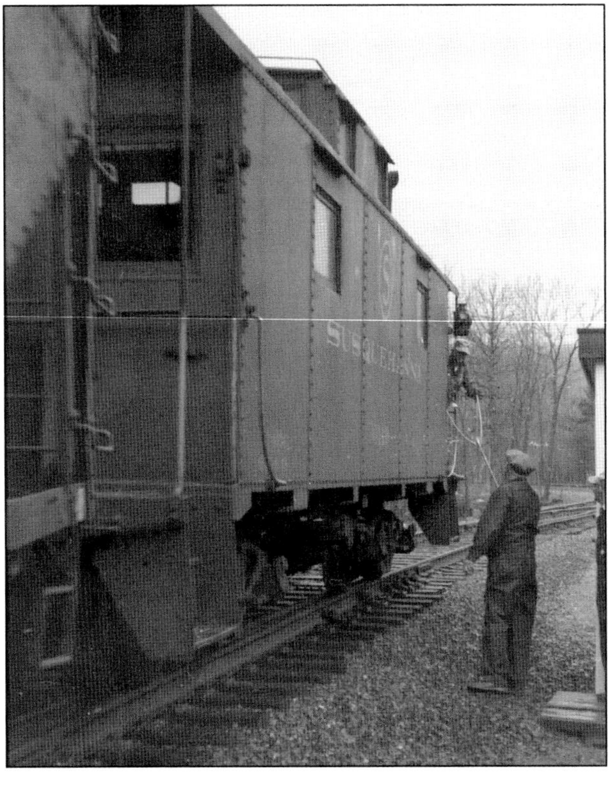

In this scene taken in December 1960, the operator at Swartswood Junction is shown hooping up train order instructions to conductor John L. Treen in NYS&W caboose No. 0116. The Lehigh & New England had trackage rights on an 18-mile section of track from Hainesburg Junction to Swartswood Junction until October 31, 1961, when the L&NE was abandoned. (Photograph by Donald P. Wallworth; courtesy of Patrick J. Reynolds and the Maywood Station Museum Collection.)

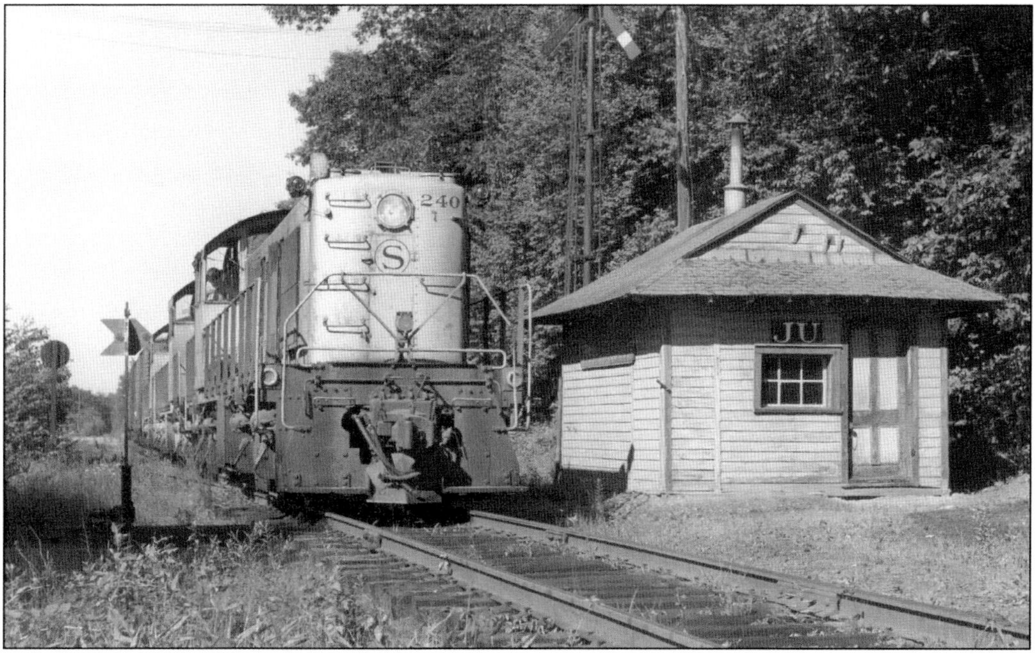

NYS&W RS-1 No. 240 is in charge of two sister RS-1s and its "Hainesburg Extra" freight as it passes Swartswood Junction on June 27, 1962. The Lehigh & New England Railway connection has been abandoned, but the switch is still in place, and the operator's office at "JU" is no longer needed. (Photograph by Donald P. Wallworth; courtesy of Patrick J. Reynolds and the Maywood Station Museum Collection.)

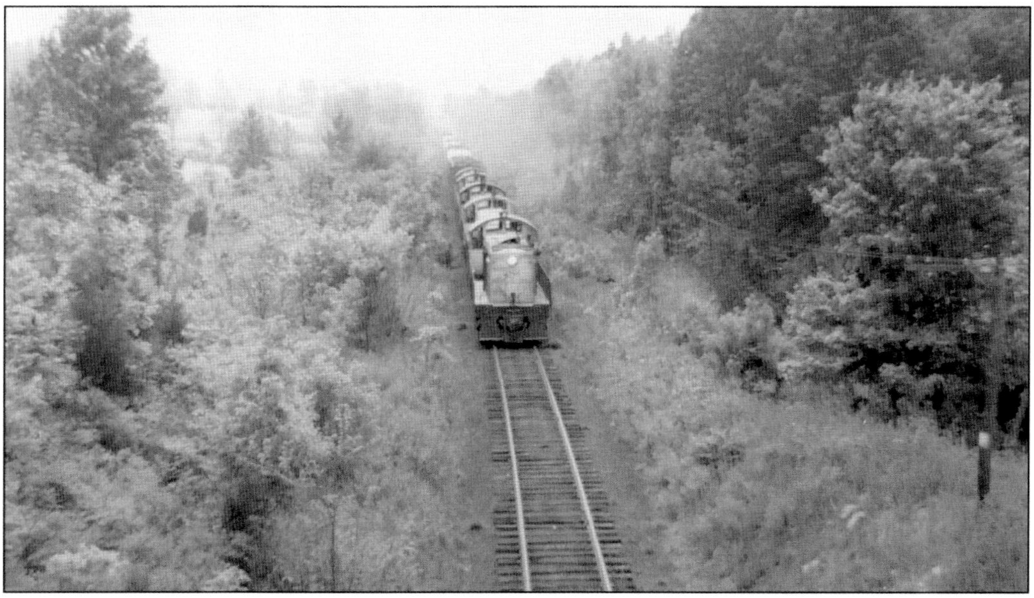

NYS&W RS-1 No. 250 leads four sister RS-1s with an eastbound "Hainesburg Extra" freight just east of Stillwater in this image captured on May 28, 1960. As seen by the scenery in this photograph, this area on the NYS&W was quite rural, but a creamery in Stillwater generated traffic right up to the end of service west of Sparta Junction in 1962. (Courtesy of Railroad Avenue Enterprises; author's collection.)

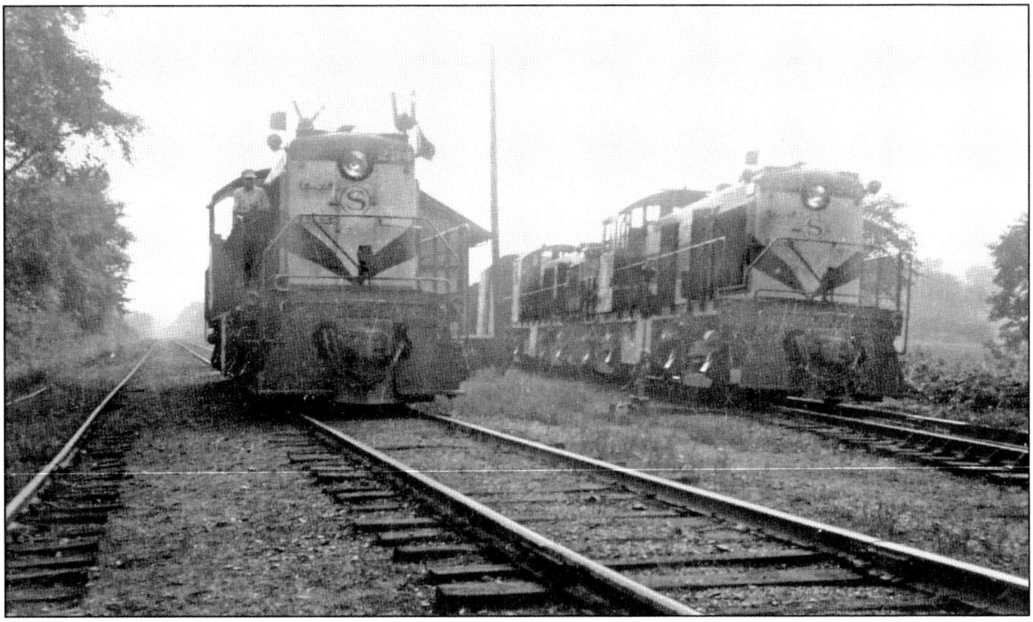

In this image taken at Hainesburg Junction in Hainesburg on September 8, 1948, NYS&W RS-1 No. 234 is on the NYS&W mainline while NYS&W No. 238 and a sister RS-1 are on Lehigh & New England track. Before 1940, the NYS&W ran into Stroudsburg, Pennsylvania, where it connected with subsidiary Wilkes-Barre & Eastern. (Photograph by John L. Treen; courtesy of Thomas J. Callan and the Maywood Station Museum Collection.)

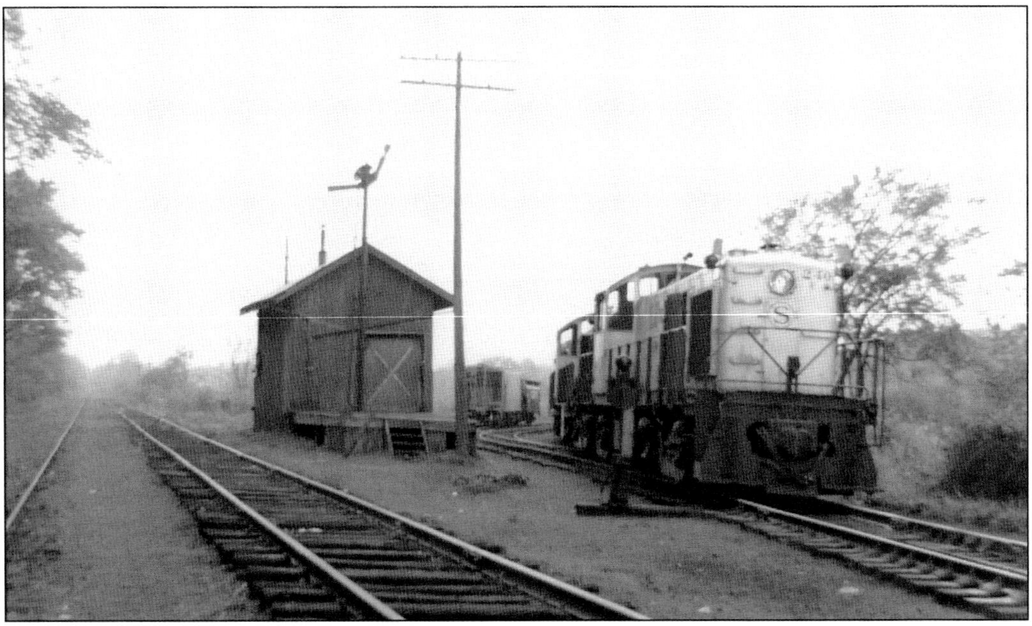

An eastbound "Hainesburg Extra" freight led by NYS&W RS-1 No. 240 prepares to get underway at Hainesburg Junction in this image taken on May 14, 1960. The train is coming off the interchange tracks with the Lehigh & New England Railway and is about to enter the NYS&W mainline. The tracks to the left are a remnant of the original NYS&W line to Stroudsburg, Pennsylvania. (Courtesy of Railroad Avenue Enterprises; author's collection.)

Seven

The Branches of Edgewater, Lodi, Passaic, and Hanford

The coming of the NYS&W Railroad in the 1890s transformed the waterfront in Edgewater into a heavily industrialized area. The NYS&W pierced the rock formation of the Palisades along the Hudson River by way of a mile-long tunnel from Little Ferry yard. The NYS&W constructed a large terminal that originally was used as a coal yard for oceangoing ships. By the early 1980s, much of Edgewater's industrial base had either moved or closed.

The Lodi Railroad was built in the 1860s to service a sprawling dye works and connect with the New Jersey & New York Railroad in the vicinity of Green Street in Teterboro/South Hackensack. In the 1880s, the NYS&W assumed control of this railroad, though it was not physically connected to it. This line was abandoned in 1898 in favor of the NYS&W's Lodi branch, which was built in 1894 and swung off the mainline at the Hackensack/Maywood border in a southerly direction for about 3 miles into Lodi. Online business for the NYS&W began to decline in the 1980s, and today the branch is used very sporadically.

The NYS&W gained access to the Passaic by way of their Passaic branch, which was built in 1898. The branch swung off the mainline at Saddle Brook near Passaic Junction in a southerly direction, then across a bridge over the Passaic River for a distance of about 3 miles. In 1968, the bridge over the Passaic River was in need of heavy repairs or replacement. Since online business in Passaic had been on the decline, the bridge and the portion of the branch were abandoned into Passaic.

The Hanford branch left the NYS&W in a northerly direction at Beaver Lake and originally terminated at Middletown, New York. The track was part of the original through route of the New York, Oswego & Midland via the New Jersey Midland to New York harbor. In 1913, the trackage in New York State was sold to the Middletown & Unionville, and an interchange was established at the New Jersey/New York state line until 1958 when the branch was abandoned.

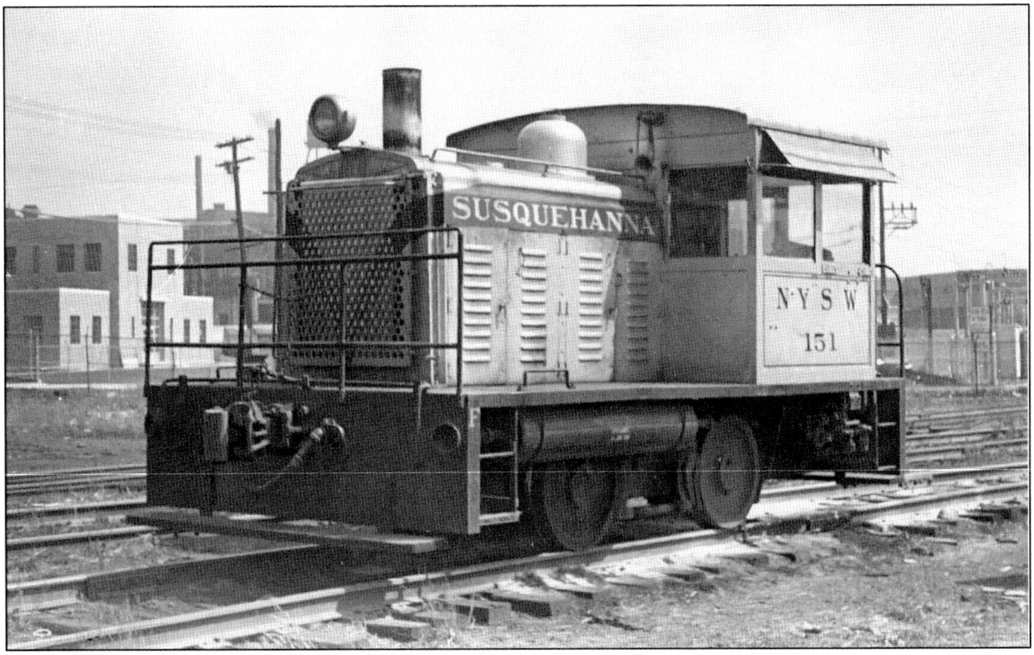

NYS&W Whitcomb switcher No. 151 is shown in Edgewater yard in this view taken in February 1954. The Susquehanna train crews dubbed this unit and sister unit No. 150 "Dinkies" in regard to their small, compact appearance. The Dinkies spent their careers shuffling freight cars onto ships at the dock in Edgewater. With the decline of anthracite coal in the 1940s, the yard found a new use for Sea Train, which loaded oceangoing railcars on its vessels. (Photograph by Sy Reich; author's collection.)

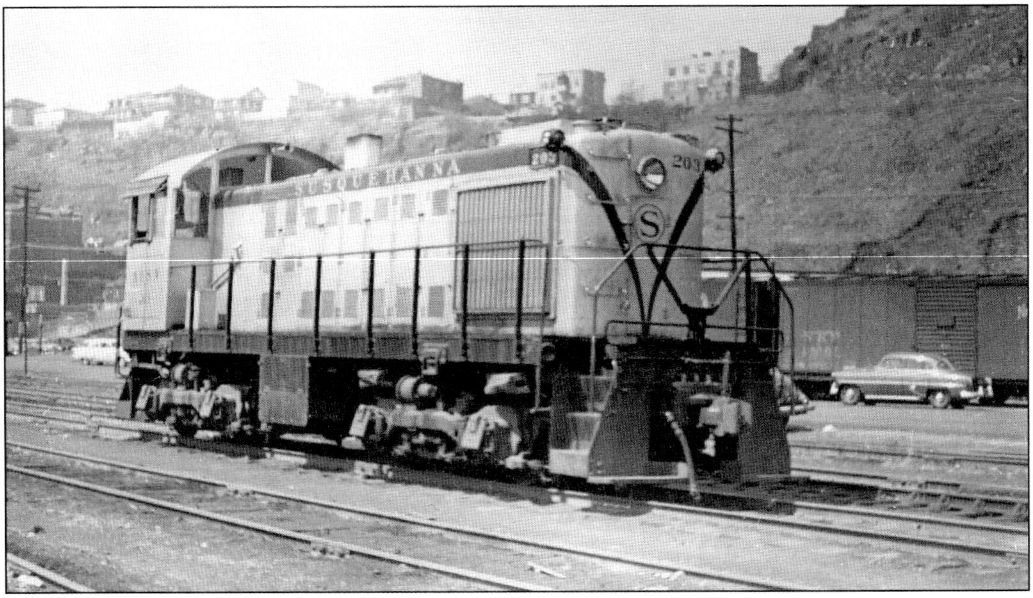

The NYS&W's fleet of six 1,000-horsepower ALCO S-2s numbered 202, 203, 204, 205, 206, and 208 were frequently found working local freights and in the yards on the eastern end of the railroad between Jersey City and Butler. In this view, NYS&W S-2 No. 203 works Edgewater yard in February 1954. (Photograph by Sy Reich; author's collection.)

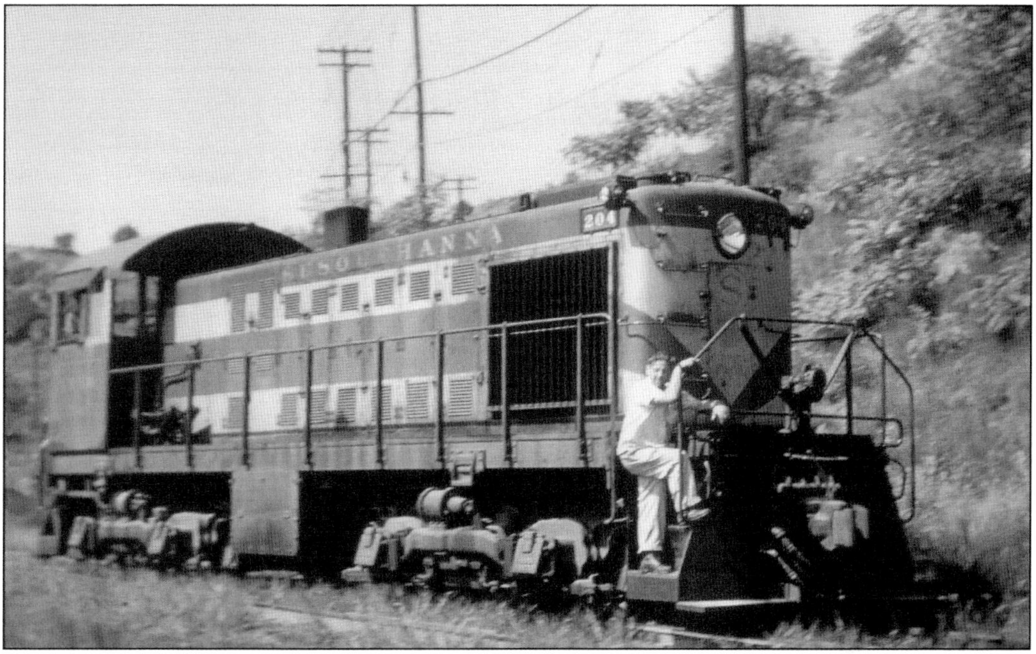

In this October 1954 view, a train crew member rides on the steps of NYS&W S-2 No. 204 during a switching move in Edgewater yard. Locomotive No. 204 still wears its 1942 as-delivered paint scheme of maroon and gray with black underframe and trucks. During this time, most of the NYS&W locomotive fleet was being repainted into the more simplistic aluminum with maroon stripes scheme. (Author's collection.)

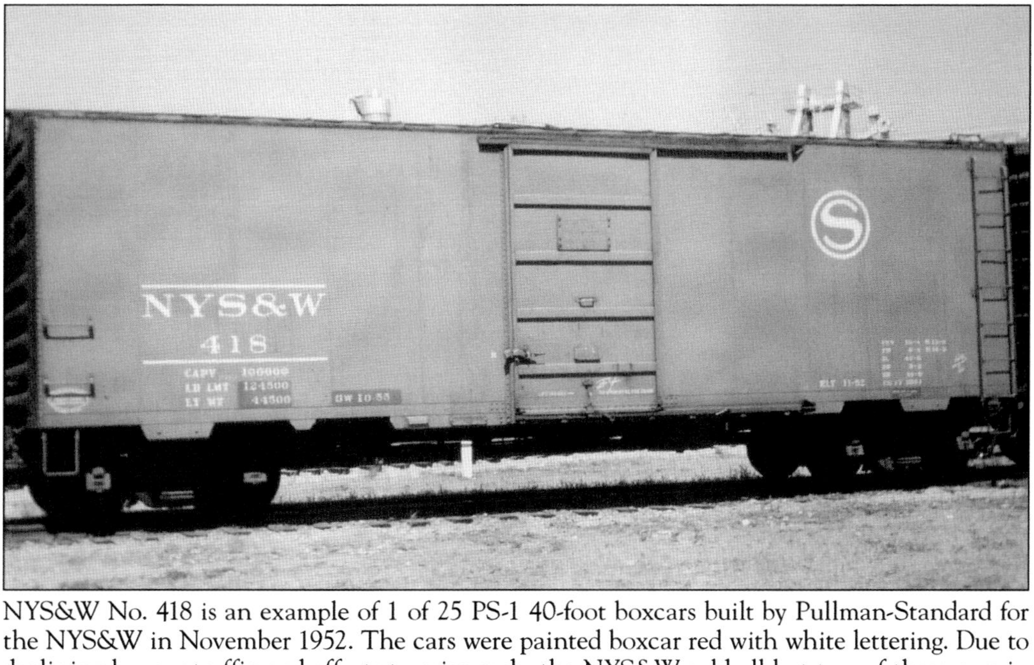

NYS&W No. 418 is an example of 1 of 25 PS-1 40-foot boxcars built by Pullman-Standard for the NYS&W in November 1952. The cars were painted boxcar red with white lettering. Due to declining boxcar traffic and efforts to raise cash, the NYS&W sold all but two of these cars in the late 1950s to the Chicago, Indianapolis & Louisville Railway (MONON). NYS&W No. 418 is shown in this view in Edgewater yard in March 1957. (Author's collection.)

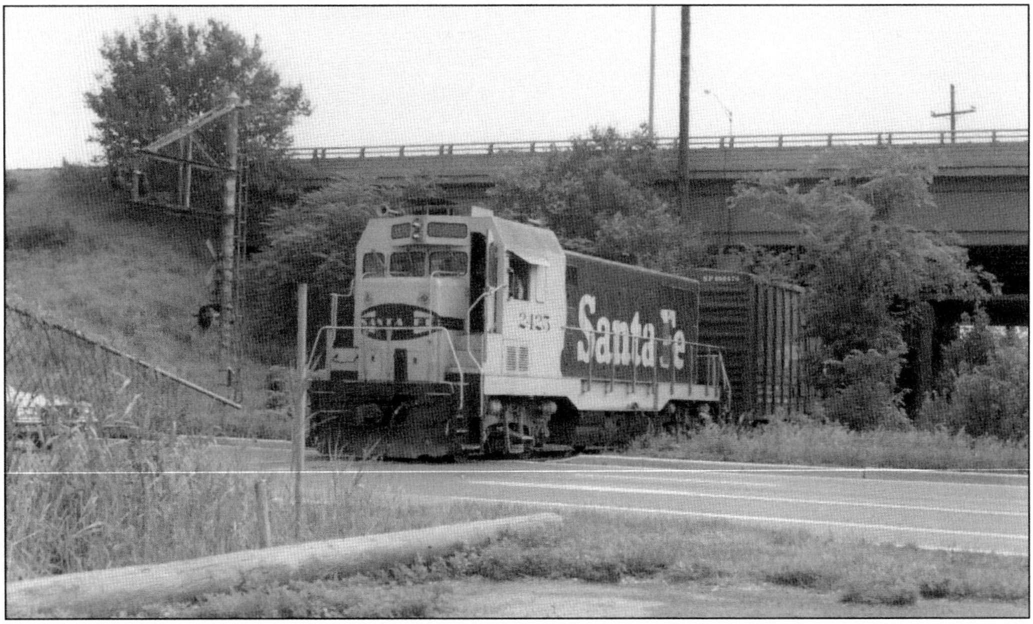

Leased ex-Atchison, Topeka & Santa Fe CF-7 No. 2425 gingerly works north across Route 17 in Lodi on the Lodi branch with one boxcar in August 1985. The Route 17 grade crossing historically presented a challenge for train crews trying to cross even though there were warning devices for motorist. (Photograph by Patrick J. Reynolds.)

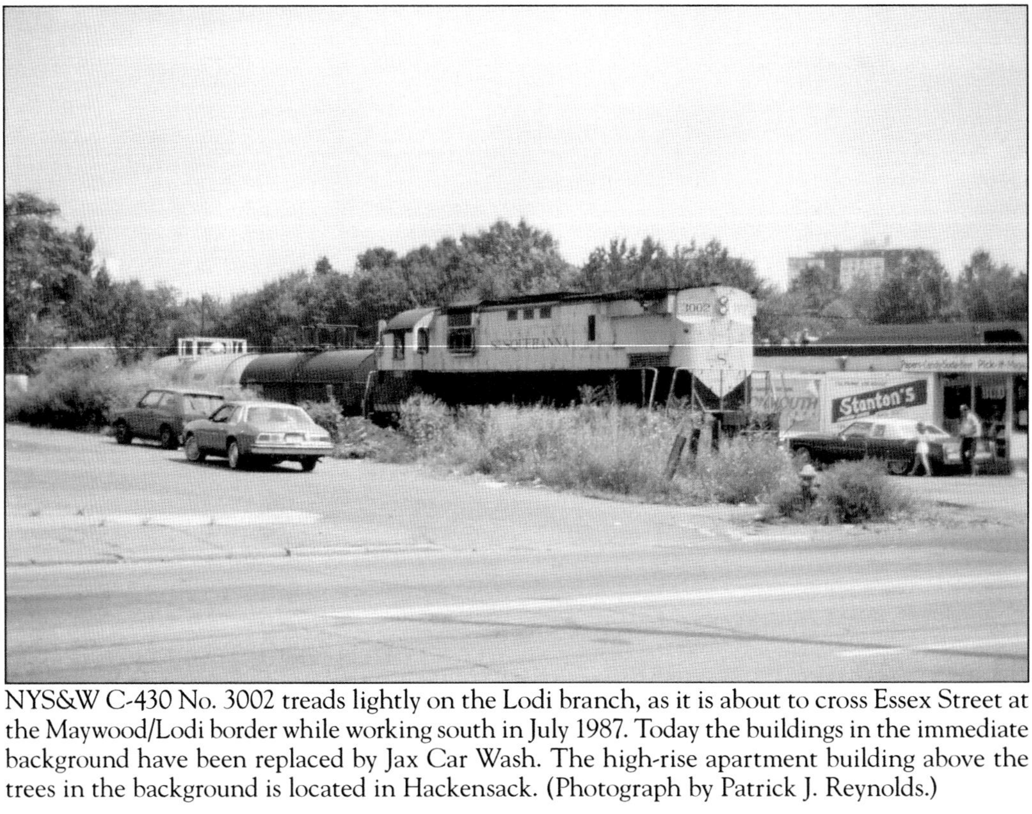

NYS&W C-430 No. 3002 treads lightly on the Lodi branch, as it is about to cross Essex Street at the Maywood/Lodi border while working south in July 1987. Today the buildings in the immediate background have been replaced by Jax Car Wash. The high-rise apartment building above the trees in the background is located in Hackensack. (Photograph by Patrick J. Reynolds.)

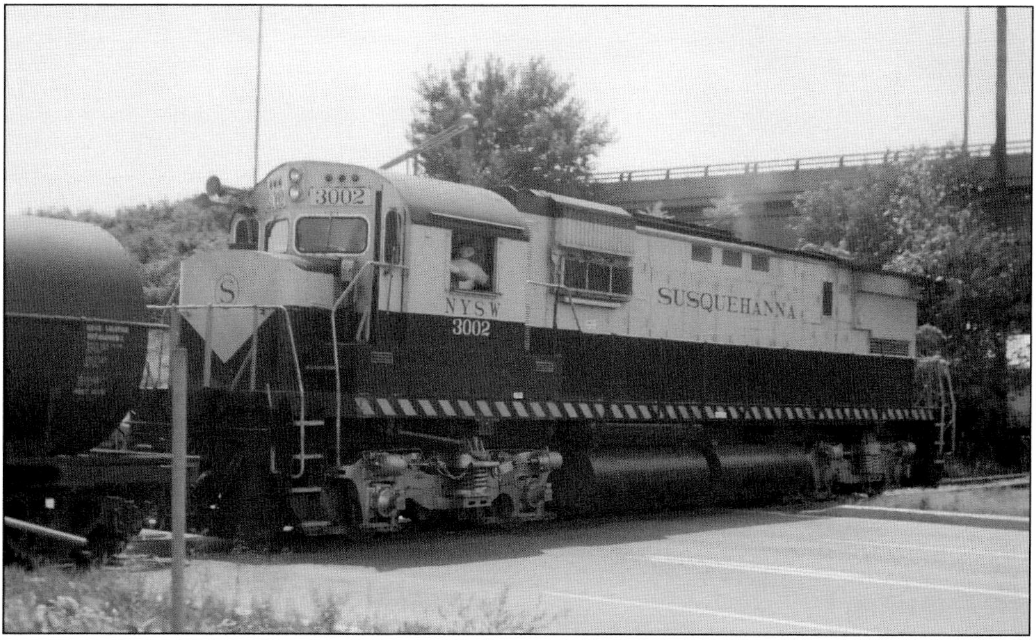

NYS&W C-430 No. 3002 is shown in this image, taken in July 1987, running long hood forward in a southerly direction in Lodi on the Lodi branch with its local freight while crossing the busy northbound lanes of Route 17. At the time of this photograph, the NYS&W's five ALCO C-430s had been replaced in road freight service by newly acquired former Burlington Northern SD45s and F-45s and were assigned to local service. (Photograph by Patrick J. Reynolds.)

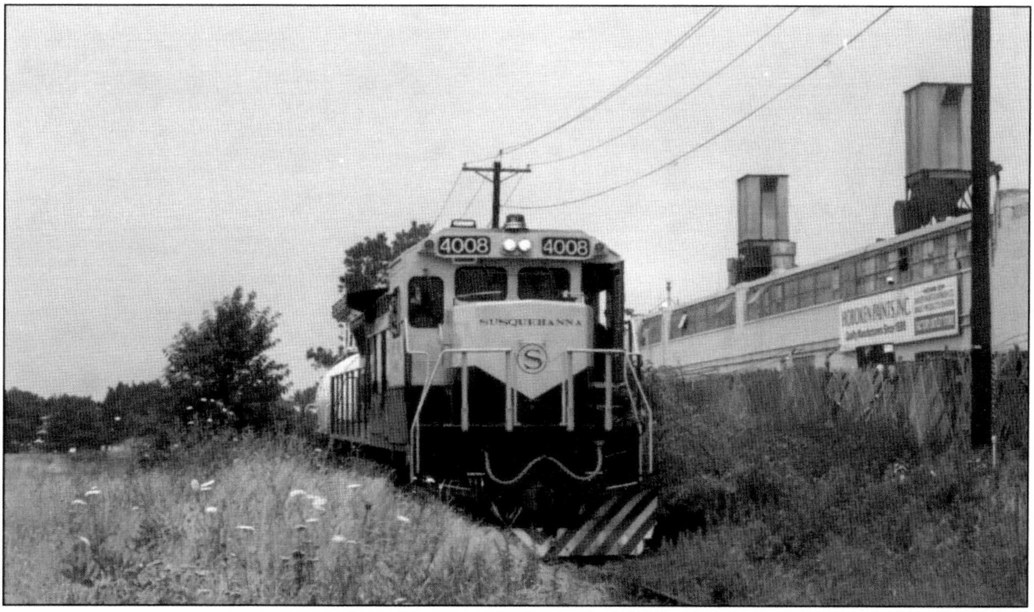

NYS&W B40-8 No. 4008 is shown pulling a tank car from the Hoboken Paints siding on the Lodi branch in October 1988. From 1911 through 1935, the Gregg Company, Ltd., had a manufacturing plant at this location that built railroad freight and passenger cars for the export market before relocating their plant operations to Belgium. Today this siding is inactive, and Hoboken Paints no longer occupies the building. (Photograph by Patrick J. Reynolds.)

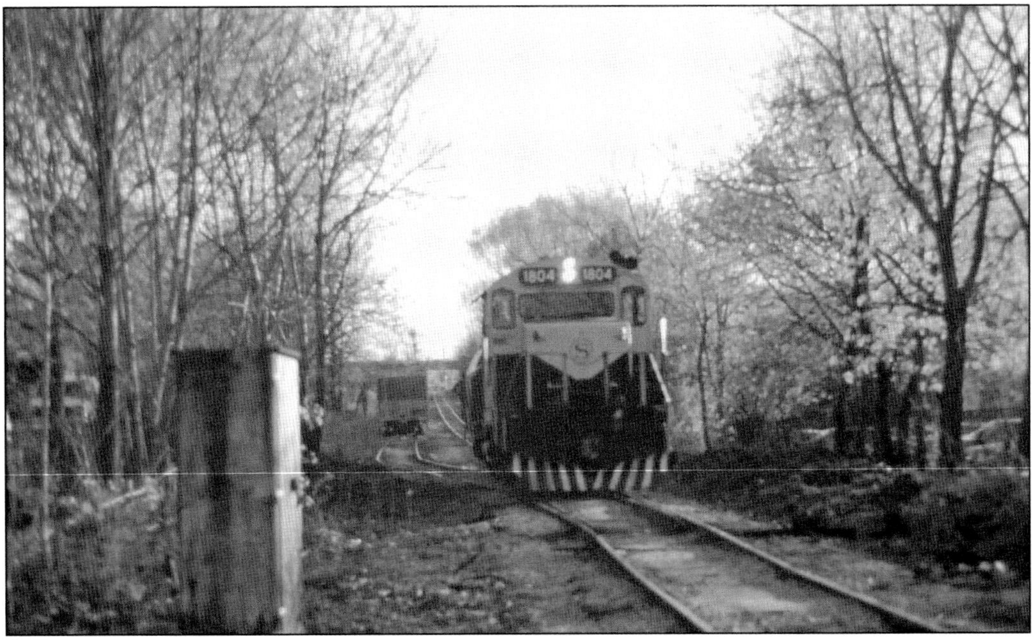

In this scene looking south on the Lodi branch in Maywood in November 1989, NYS&W GP18 No. 1804 is working north, with a tank car, toward Lodi Junction, where it will connect back with the mainline in approximately 300 yards. A covered hopper is visible in the distance on the runaround track. (Photograph by Patrick J. Reynolds.)

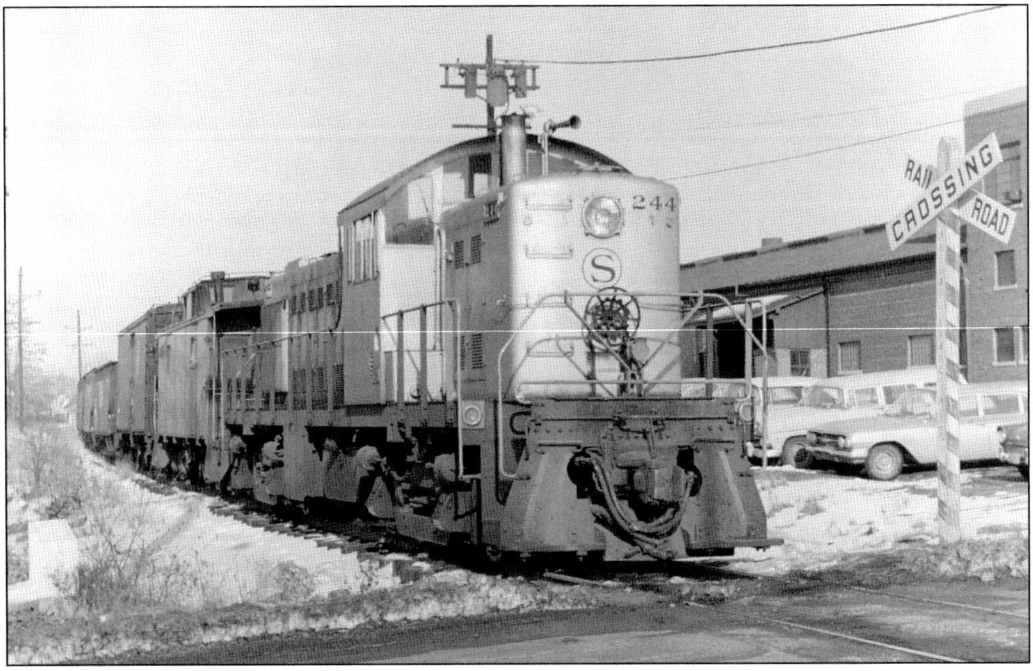

NYS&W RS-1 No. 244 is on the Passaic branch with its train and is about to cross Market Street in Garfield in this view taken on December 31, 1961. Careful inspection of the lettering on the wooden crossbuck post reveals "Passaic Branch NYS&W." (Photograph by Donald P. Wallworth; courtesy of Patrick J. Reynolds and the Maywood Station Museum Collection.)

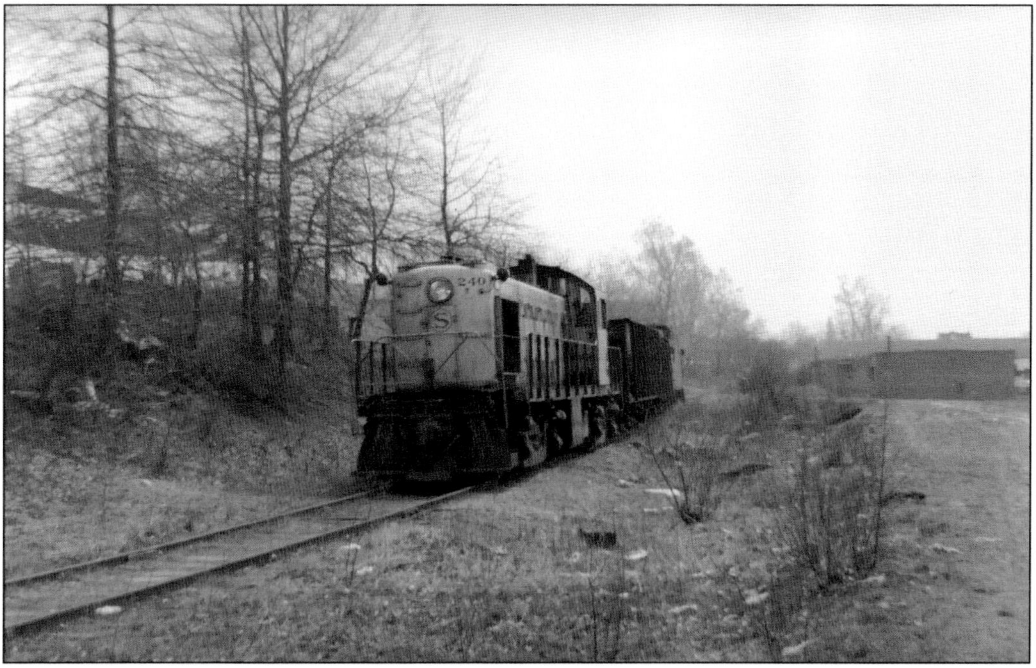

NYS&W RS-1 No. 240 leads two empty coal hoppers and a caboose through Garfield on the Passaic branch in this scene taken on April 13, 1963. Beginning in the 1970s, Garden State Paper in Garfield became a major shipper on the railroad. The plant recently closed and was the last shipper in the branch. Today the branch is lightly used, mainly to store freight cars. (Courtesy of Railroad Avenue Enterprises; author's collection.)

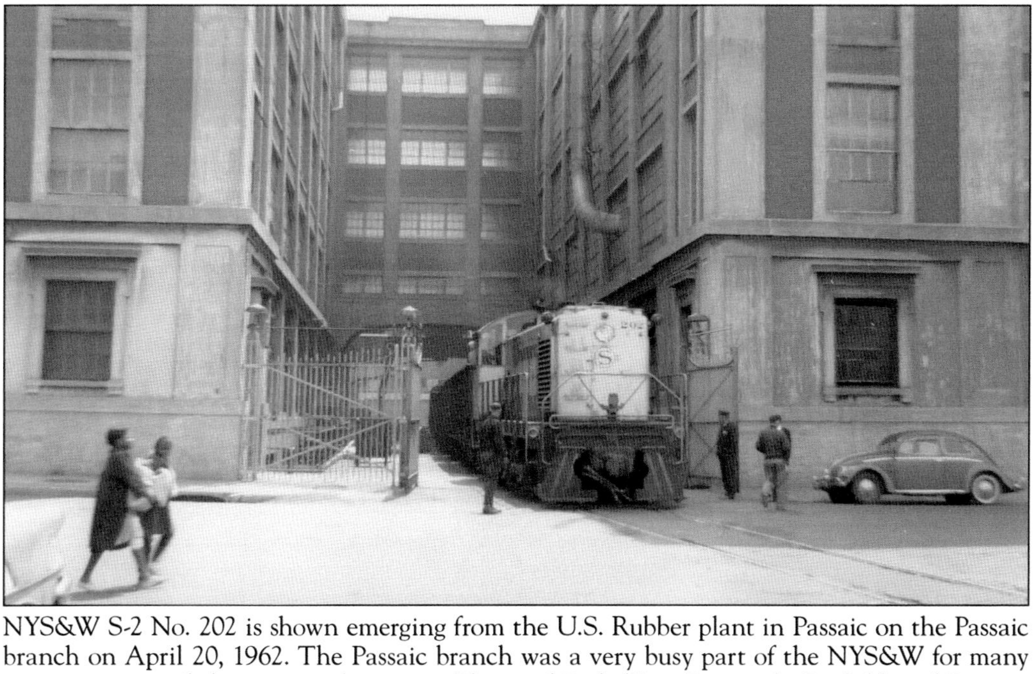

NYS&W S-2 No. 202 is shown emerging from the U.S. Rubber plant in Passaic on the Passaic branch on April 20, 1962. The Passaic branch was a very busy part of the NYS&W for many years, as it served the many industries in Elmwood Park (East Paterson), Garfield, and Passaic. (Courtesy of Railroad Avenue Enterprises; author's collection.)

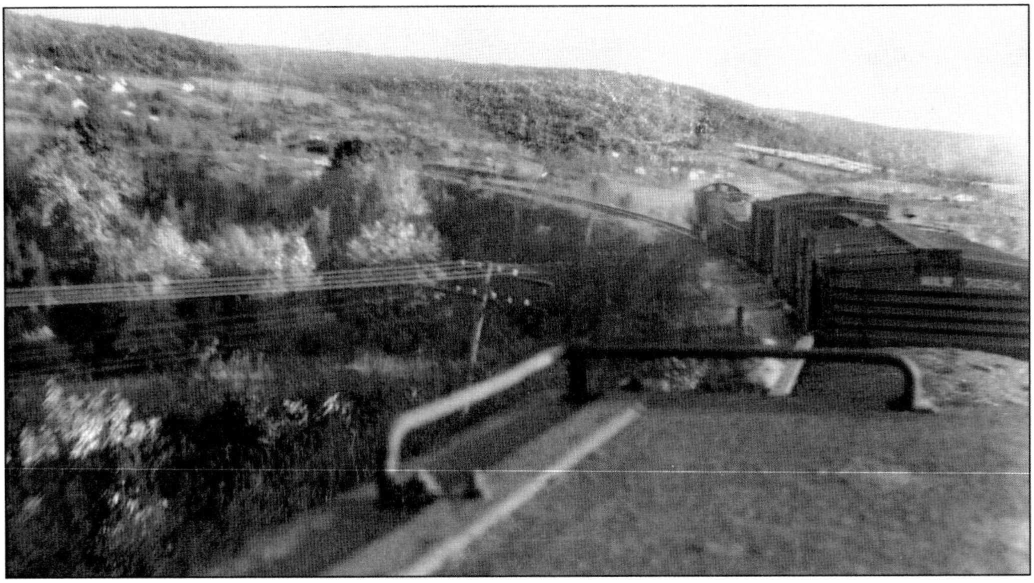

NYS&W RS-1 No. 231 and its local freight are shown rounding the high-fill curve in Ogdensburg on the Hanford branch in this view taken from the top of the caboose on October 11, 1945. Milk traffic was an important source of revenue for the NYS&W on the Hanford branch, but by the 1950s, much of this traffic had either dried up or had been lost to trucks. (Photograph by John L. Treen; courtesy of Thomas J. Callan and the Maywood Station Museum Collection.)

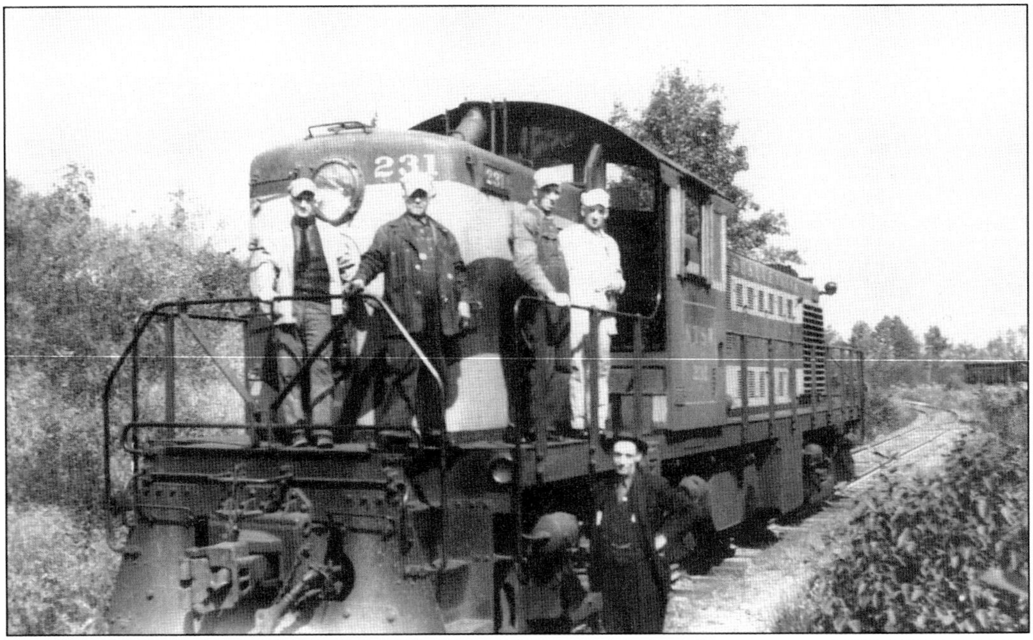

The crew of a local freight on the Hanford branch pose with their locomotive, NYS&W RS-1 No. 231, at Ogdensburg on October 11, 1945. The crew is the same one responsible for the train in the above photograph on this page. From left to right, standing on No. 231 are C. G. Thompson, flagman; Clark Day, brakeman; Wes Hoag, fireman; and A. C. Oakley, engineer. Standing on the ground is E. W. Flynn, conductor. (Photograph by John L. Treen; courtesy of Thomas J. Callan and the Maywood Station Museum Collection.)

About the Author

Edward S. Kaminski is a widely known historian who has held a lifelong interest in railroads and their histories. He is an avid photographer, and many of his images have appeared in books, newspapers, prototype railroad magazines, model railroad magazines, annual reports, brochures, travel guides, Web sites, and calendars. In addition, he has had numerous articles published in magazines and occasionally lectures on history-related topics at seminars and for historical societies. He is employed as East Coast district sales manager by American Railcar Leasing (formerly ACF Industries), a lessor of railroad freight cars, and also serves as a consultant for a leading model railroad manufacturer. He is a graduate of Rutgers University with a bachelor's degree in history.

On May 29, 2002, Kaminski formed the Maywood Station Historical Committee—a division of the New York, Susquehanna & Western Technical & Historical Society—in an effort to save the historic New York, Susquehanna & Western railroad station in Maywood, New Jersey from impending demolition. He has served as chairman of the organization since its inception and has helped guide the restoration of the station, formation of its museum, and its associated restoration projects, including New York, Susquehanna & Western ALCO S-2 locomotive No. 206 and caboose No. 24542. Maywood Station and New York Susquehanna & Western ALCO S-2 locomotive No. 206 are now listed on the National and New Jersey Registers of Historic Landmarks. Additional information about the Maywood Station Historical Committee can be found on the Web site at www.maywoodstation.com and on the New York, Susquehanna & Western Technical & Historical Society Web site at www.nyswths.org .

This is the author's eighth book. He authored *Maywood: The Borough, the Railroad, and the Station*, the most recent published in 2010 by Arcadia Publishing. He has written five books published by Signature Press entitled *American Car & Foundry Company, A Centennial History 1899–1999*; *Magor Car Corporation; American Car & Foundry Tank Cars, 1865–1955; Pullman-Standard Freight Cars, 1900–1960*; and *Billboard Refrigerator Cars*; as well as a self-published book, *The Gregg Company LTD., A Centennial History 1903–2003*.

The author is a lifelong resident of northern New Jersey, where he resides with his wife, Rosemarie, and their three daughters, Kristen, Kaitlyn, and Kayleigh.